The Collected Courses of the Academy of European Law

Series Editors: Professor Marise Cremona,
Professor Bruno de Witte,
Professor Francesco Francioni

European University Institute, Florence

Assistant Editor: Anny Bremner

European University Institute, Florence

VOLUME XX/2
Compliance and the Enforcement of EU Law

The Collected Courses of the Academy of European Law
Edited by Professor Marise Cremona,
Professor Bruno de Witte, and Professor Francesco Francioni
Assistant Editor: Anny Bremner

Each year the Academy of European Law in Florence, Italy, invites a group of outstanding lecturers to teach at its summer courses on Human Rights law and European Union law.
A 'general course' is given in each of the two fields by a distinguished scholar or practitioner, who examines the field as a whole through a particular thematic, conceptual, or philosophical lens, or looks at a theme in the context of the overall body of law.
In addition, a series of 'specialized courses' brings together a group of highly qualified scholars to explore and analyse a specific theme in relation to Human Rights law and EU law.
The Academy's mission, to produce scholarly analyses which are at the cutting edge of these two fields, is achieved through the publication of this series, the Collected Courses of the Academy of European Law.

Compliance and the Enforcement of EU Law

Edited by

MARISE CREMONA

OXFORD
UNIVERSITY PRESS

OXFORD
UNIVERSITY PRESS

Great Clarendon Street, Oxford OX2 6DP
United Kingdom

Oxford University Press is a department of the University of Oxford.
It furthers the University's objective of excellence in research, scholarship,
and education by publishing worldwide. Oxford is a registered trade mark of
Oxford University Press in the UK and in certain other countries

First published 2012
Reprinted 2013

Published in the United States of America by Oxford University Press
198 Madison Avenue, New York, NY 10016, United States of America

British Library Cataloguing in Publication Data
Data available

Library of Congress Cataloging in Publication Data
Library of Congress Control Number 2012931698

ISBN 978-0-19-964473-5

Cover illustration: *La Gerbe*, 1953, by Henri Matisse. Ceramic tile embedded in plaster, 108 x 156" (274 x 396.24 cm); weight: 2000 lbs. Los Angeles County Museum of Art (LACMA). Gift of Frances L. Brody, in honour of the Museum's twenty-fifth anniversary (m.2010.1). © Succession H. Matisse/DACS 2012. Digital Image © Museum Associates/LACMA/ Art Resource NY/Scala, Florence.

Contents

List of Contributors

Edoardo Chiti is Professor of Administrative Law at the University of La Tuscia, Italy. His principal research interests cover administrative law beyond the state, both EU and global, as well as comparative administrative law. Edoardo's principal publications include *Le agenzie europee. Unità e decentramento nelle amministrazioni comunitarie* (2002); *L'integrazione amministrativa europea*, with C. Franchini (2003); and *L'amministrazione militare* (2007) as well as a number of edited volumes, including *Global Administrative Law and EU Administrative Law. Relationships, Legal Issues and Comparison*, with Bernardo Giorgio Mattarella (2011).

Lisa Conant is an Associate Professor of Political Science at the University of Denver. She specializes in the comparative study of law and society. Her book, *Justice Contained: Law and Politics in the European Union* (2002), examines the impact of European Court of Justice decisions on politics in the European Union (EU) and its member states. Her current research focuses on how European litigation frames citizenship rights and also on variations in human rights protections in the EU and a broader set of states within the Council of Europe.

Marise Cremona is Professor of European Law at the European University Institute, Florence, a Director of the Academy of European Law, and currently Head of the Department of Law. Until December 2005 she was Professor of European Commercial Law at the Centre for Commercial Law Studies, Queen Mary, University of London. Marise's research interest is in the external relations law of the European Union, including its foreign policy, trade, and development policies. From this perspective she is interested in the interaction between national, regional, and international legal and policy regimes. Her current research projects include the constitutional basis for EU foreign relations law, the legal and institutional dimensions of the EU's external commercial policy, and the export of values and norms in EU external policy.

Michael Dougan is Professor of European Law, and Dean of the Liverpool Law School, University of Liverpool. He also holds a Jean Monnet Chair in European Union Law. As well as publishing regularly in journals and edited collections, Michael is the author of *National Remedies before the Court of Justice* (2004); co-author of *Wyatt and Dashwood's European Union Law* (6th edn., 2011); and co-editor of *A Constitutional Order of States? Essays in EU law in Honour of Alan Dashwood* (2011), *50 Years of the European Treaties: Looking Back and Thinking Forward* (2009), *and Social Welfare and EU Law* (2005). Michael is one of the joint editors of the *Common Market Law Review*.

Sibylle Grohs is a Commission official working as a lawyer in the Compliance Promotion, Governance and Legal Issues unit in the Environment Directorate General of the European Commission in Brussels. Before joining the Commission as an official in 1999, she worked in the then Waste unit of the Environment Directorate General. Prior to this she qualified as a barrister in London, specializing in planning and environmental law. She also worked as a legal adviser and researcher for the environmental organization Friends of the Earth in London.

André Nollkaemper is Professor of Public International Law, Vice-Dean for Research at the Faculty of Law of the University of Amsterdam, and (external) adviser to the Minister of Foreign Affairs of the Netherlands. He is a Member of the Board of the European Society of International Law, Chair of the Study Group of the International Law Association on the Principles on the Application of International Law by Domestic Courts. Since 2010 he has directed the project on Shared Responsibility in International Law (SHARES). He is also editor in chief of the *International Law in Domestic Courts (ILDC)* module of the Oxford Reports on International Law and author of *National Courts and the International Rule of Law* (2011).

Darinka Piqani is a Lecturer in EU Law at the Europa Institute of Leiden University. Her research interests include the interaction between the EU and national legal orders and the role of courts in that context, constitutional law of the EU, and EU integration in the Western Balkans. Darinka has published on issues related to her core research interests and has presented (invited) papers at several academic conferences.

Table of Cases

CASES OF THE EUROPEAN COURT

ALPHABETICAL TABLE OF CASES OF THE EUROPEAN COURT

EFTA CASES

EUROPEAN COMMISSION OF HUMAN RIGHTS CASES

EUROPEAN COURT OF HUMAN RIGHTS CASES

EUROPEAN OMBUDSMAN

INTERNATIONAL CENTRE FOR SETTLEMENT OF INVESTMENT DISPUTES

INTERNATIONAL COURT OF JUSTICE

PERMANENT COURT OF INTERNATIONAL JUSTICE

UN HUMAN RIGHTS COMMITTEE

NATIONAL CASES

Argentina

Australia

Bangladesh

Belgium

Bulgaria

Poland

Portugal

Romania

Serbia

South Africa

Switzerland

Turkey

Uganda

Table of Legislation

EU TREATIES

Europe Agreements and Stabilization and Association Agreements

INTERNATIONAL TREATIES

UN GENERAL ASSEMBLY RESOLUTIONS

EU LEGISLATION

Regulations

Directives

Decisions

NATIONAL LEGISLATION

List of Abbreviations

AFSJ	Area of Freedom, Security and Justice
BCBS	Basel Committee on Banking Supervision
CAC	Codex Alimentarius Commission
CAP	Common Agricultural Policy
CEE	Central and Eastern Europe
CHAP	Secretariat General of the European Commission's central registry for complaints
EAW	European Arrest Warrant
ECHR	European Convention on Human Rights
ECtHR	European Court of Human Rights
ECJ	European Court of Justice
EEAA	European Economic Area Agreement
EFTA	European Free Trade Association
EU	European Union
FCC	[German] Federal Constitutional Court
GATT	General Agreement on Tariffs and Trade
GDP	Gross Domestic Product
GMOs	genetically modified organisms
IAIS	International Association of Insurance Supervisors
ICCPR	International Covenant on Civil and Political Rights
ICESCR	International Covenant on Economic, Social and Cultural Rights
IDI	Institut de Droit International
IFAC	International Federation of Accountants
ILC	International Law Commission
IOSCO	International Organization of Securities Commissioners
IR	international relations
MARPOL	International Convention for the Prevention of Pollution from Ships
MEPS	members of the European Parliament
NGOs	non-governmental organizations
OMC	open method of coordination
ILDC	[Oxford Reports on] International Law in Domestic Courts
P-A	principal-agent
PCIJ	Permanent Court of International Justice
PIOB	Public Interest Oversight Board
SAA	Stabilization and Association Agreements
SEA	Single European Act
SPS Agreement	the WTO Agreement on the Application of Sanitary and Phytosanitary Measures
TFEU	Treaty on the Functioning of the European Union
TEU	Treaty on the European Union
VCLT	Vienna Convention on the Law of Treaties
WADA	World Anti-Doping Agency
WTO	World Trade Organization
YB ILC	Yearbook of the International Law Commission

Introduction

Marise Cremona

This collection of essays derives from the course of specialized lectures given at the Academy of European Law in July 2009. The aim of the lectures was to examine different aspects of EU law enforcement, including court-based enforcement procedures at Union and national level but also looking at the broader non-court-based mechanisms and processes designed to promote compliance. This immediately raises the question of the relationship between, and the meaning given to, the concepts of 'compliance' and 'enforcement', both used in the title of this work. It will be helpful, in approaching the legally-oriented discussion in the remainder of the book, to bear in mind the contrasting approaches of scholars from the disciplines of political science and international relations explored by Lisa Conant in Chapter 1.

In the literature on compliance in the context of international legal regimes in general and the EU in particular, compliance is the more generic term, whereas enforcement has a more specific coercive meaning. A distinction is made between the two alternative compliance strategies of enforcement and management.[1] An enforcement strategy is based on the theory that states will sometimes have an interest in non-compliance and will tend to comply when the incentives to do so are higher than the costs of non-compliance. The enforcement strategy will therefore emphasize the need to increase non-compliance costs through coercion methodologies based on monitoring and sanctions. It might also be argued that the greater the degree of commitment and the greater the depth of cooperation required in a particular treaty system, the greater the incentive to renege on those commitments and the greater the need for enforcement.[2] Following this approach, an enforcement system which rarely has recourse to sanctions may reflect a relatively low level of commitment (less deep integration) in the specific treaty regime; conversely, a treaty regime that makes major demands on its members but rarely uses sanctions to promote enforcement is likely to be a weak or ineffective system.

A management strategy on the other hand, is based on the theory that non-compliance is not often the result of deliberate policy-choices by the state, but rather flows from failures in the system itself, such as rule ambiguity, or failures

[1] In addition to Conant in Chapter 1, for a helpful summary see J. Tallberg, 'Paths to Compliance: Enforcement, Management and the European Union', 56 *International Organisation* (2002), at 609.

[2] G.W. Downs, D.M. Rocke, and P.N. Barsoom, 'Is the Good News about Compliance Good News about Cooperation?', 50 *International Organization* (1996), at 379.

in the State's capacity to manage compliance. The management strategy will thus emphasize problem-solving, capacity building, rule interpretation, and transparency. The distinction between these two approaches to compliance is useful in helping to analyse different processes and procedures. However the essays in this book reflect the argument that these strategies need not be seen as incompatible alternatives, but that on the contrary an effective compliance regime is likely to contain elements of both. Although seen by some as alternative approaches to compliance, in practice a system which combines elements of both, of which the EU is a good example, is most effective.

> In the EU, monitoring, sanctions, capacity building, rule interpretation, and social pressure coexist as means for making states comply. In the daily practice of the EU compliance system, these instruments are mutually reinforcing, demonstrating the merits of combining coercive and problem-solving strategies.[3]

The fundamental starting point for all discussion of compliance mechanisms within the context of the European Union legal order is a pair of principles: (1) that the primary responsibility for ensuring the implementation of Union law lies with the member states,[4] and (2) that ultimately it is the role of the institutions (and in particular the Commission and the Court of Justice) to ensure that the law is observed.[5] At the basis of all compliance procedures is the principle enshrined in Article 4(3) TEU. This so-called loyalty obligation not only supports obligations found elsewhere in the Treaties, it has also formed the basis for the development by the Court of Justice of specific obligations relating to the enforcement of Union law: for example the action for damages in breaches for Union law norms and other principles relating to the enforcement of Union law-based rights at the national level. In fact it is perhaps the development of enforcement mechanisms at national level, based on enforceable rights, that is seen as typifying and exemplifying EU compliance; it is their effectiveness which is often cited as the basis for the remarkable reach and penetration of EU norms into national systems, harnessing and even extending the enforcement mechanisms available within the domestic legal order.

However the particular characteristic and strength of the EU's compliance system might be said to lie in its combination of methodologies (enforcement and management approaches) and levels of enforcement, both at Union and national levels, as well as the breadth of the scope of the compliance obligation, extending not only to member states' implementation of treaty-based and secondary norms but also affecting their exercise of domestic competences. The EU system has been driven by the strength of its autonomous institutions, especially the Commission and the Court of Justice. Indeed, Snyder argued in 1993 that the 'new challenge of compliance' for the Union arising out of the single market programme of the

[3] J. Tallberg, *supra* note 1, at 614.

[4] Art 291(1) TFEU. 'Ultimately the impact of European Union rules depends on the willingness and capacity of Member State authorities to ensure that they are transposed and enforced effectively, fully and on time. Late transposition, bad transposition and weak enforcement... The prime responsibility... lies with national administrations and courts.' EC Commission, Governance White Paper 2001, 25 July 2001, COM (2001) 428, p 25.

[5] Arts 17(1) and 19(1) TEU.

1990s required an integration of the administrative mechanisms applied by the Commission and the judicial measures administered by the Court of Justice.[6] To this one might add the effect of the recent enlargements of the EU, which has both highlighted the challenges of compliance and helped to suggest new compliance methodologies.[7]

In Chapter 2 Edoardo Chiti uses the term 'governance' to refer to the 'steering or guiding' instruments designed to complement coercive enforcement within the EU. He argues that compliance is 'not only an outcome, but also a practice': compliance 'does not refer to the simple result of obedience, but to the overall process through which obedience is gradually constructed'. This chapter examines the instruments designed to steer this compliance process, ranging from the essentially hierarchical to more horizontal methods based on learning, negotiation, and consensus-building, to assess the extent to which they represent 'new' forms of governance and some of the issues of efficacy and legitimacy that they raise. As Chiti comments, it is not yet possible to make a definitive assessment of the efficacy of these 'new' administrative compliance systems: the detailed empirical studies have not yet been done, a point made also by Conant.[8] Questions may be asked concerning the capacity of national administrations to participate fully in the emerging European administrative structures, the risks of regulatory capture, variable protection for private parties and risks of sectoral fragmentation within national administrations. Chiti ends with some reflections on the possible impact of the new Article 197 TFEU, the basis for EU action to support administrative cooperation and capacity building.

A second strand in our analysis of the EU system of compliance and enforcement is concerned with the level at which the compliance mechanism operates: the regional (EU) level or the national level, which may be referred to (as by Piqani in this collection) as centralized and decentralized models of enforcement respectively. Indeed, we can refine this distinction and distinguish between compliance systems that operate 'from above', those that operate 'from below' and those that operate at a 'horizontal' level.[9] Horizontal compliance takes the form of inter-state action at the regional or international level; this is the only mechanism available within some international systems such as the WTO, but is relatively unimportant (although available[10]) within the EU. Compliance 'from above', requires the ability

[6] F. Snyder, 'The Effectiveness of European Community Law: Institutions, Processes, Tools and Techniques', 56 *Modern Law Review* (1993), at 19.

[7] U. Sedelmeier, 'Pre-Accession Conditionality and Post-Accession Compliance in the New Member States', in W. Sadurski, J. Ziller and K. Zurek (eds), *Après Enlargement: Legal and Political Responses in Central and Eastern Europe*, RSCAS EUI 2005; J.T. Checkel, 'Compliance and Conditionality', Arena Working Paper WP 2000/18, <http://www.arena.uio.no/publications/> last accessed 12 December 2011.

[8] See also J.A.E. Vervaele, 'Transnational Cooperation of Enforcement Authorities in the Community Area', in J.A.E. Vervaele (ed), *Compliance and Enforcement of European Community Law* (1999).

[9] For this distinction, applied in the context of the WTO, see A. Tancredi, 'EC Practice in the WTO: How Wide is the 'Scope for Manoeuvre?', 15 *European Journal of International Law* 933 (2004), at 959.

[10] Art 259 TFEU.

of the system's institution(s) to instigate compliance proceedings autonomously, as for example enforcement actions instigated by the European Commission. One of the Commission's primary tasks under Article 17 TEU is to 'ensure the application of the Treaties and of measures adopted by the institutions pursuant to them'. This duty is given expression, as far as formal proceedings are concerned, in Article 258 TFEU,[11] a procedure which Harlow and Rawlings argued in 2006 'has taken on a new lease of life, partly perhaps as a consequence of EU enlargement, demonstrating a much sharper cutting edge.'[12]

Cases come to the Commission in a number of ways: individual complaints, via the European Ombudsman, petitions to the European Parliament, through the Commission's own investigations or monitoring procedures. It is not possible for the Council of Ministers, or the European Parliament, or private individuals or organizations to bring enforcement actions before the Court of Justice; they have to rely on informing the Commission of alleged infringements, and (in the case of natural and legal persons) the possibility of bringing an action in national courts, possibly with a reference to the Court of Justice under Article 267 TFEU. Such enforcement actions have two stages: an administrative stage and a judicial stage. The administrative stage (the 'infringement procedure') itself is in three parts: a letter of formal notice from the Commission to the member state setting out its view that there may be a breach of an EU obligation, the observations in answer by the member state, and then—if it so decides—the Commission's reasoned opinion. Thus the administrative stage involves discussion between the Commission and the member state in an essentially bilateral procedure. The duty of cooperation between the member states and the Community institutions enshrined in Article 4(3) TEU (which is the basis of all compliance principles) comes into play to support the process, the aim of which is to resolve the matter before it gets to the Court. The Commission has discretion within this administrative process (for example to negotiate a compliance schedule) and also as to whether or not to bring the case before the Court of Justice if the member state does not comply in time with the reasoned opinion.[13] As Sibylle Grohs points out in Chapter 3, the primary purpose of the Article 258 TFEU procedure is to induce a member state to come into line and this is reflected in the fact that wherever possible the Commission will try to negotiate compliance rather than resorting to the Court. In turn, the emphasis of the Court on the Commission's discretion[14] means that it would be

[11] Art 258 TFEU provides, 'If the Commission considers that a Member State has failed to fulfil an obligation under the Treaties, it shall deliver a reasoned opinion on the matter after giving the State concerned the opportunity to submit its observations. If the State concerned does not comply with the opinion within the period laid down by the Commission, the latter may bring the matter before the Court of Justice of the European Union.'

[12] C. Harlow and R. Rawlings, 'Accountability and Law Enforcement: The Centralised EU Infringement Procedure', 31 *European Law Rev* 447 (2006), at 448.

[13] Case C-317/92, *Commission v Germany*, [1994] ECR I-2039, para 5; Case C-422/92, *Commission v Germany*, [1995] ECR I-1097, paras 16–18.

[14] Case 416/85, *Commission v UK*, [1988] ECR 3127, paras 8–9. A. Evans, 'The Enforcement Procedure of Article 169 EEC: Commission Discretion' 4 *EL Rev* 442 (1979); F. Snyder, 'The Effectiveness of European Community Law: Institutions, Processes, Tools and Techniques', 56 *Modern Law Review* 19 (1993), at 30.

difficult to challenge a Commission decision not to bring an action in a specific case, even if that appeared to be part of a systematic policy.[15] Over the last decade the Commission, while defending its discretion at each stage of an enforcement action, has attempted to show that its exercise of that discretion is not arbitrary by publishing its priorities.[16] Following a report by the European Ombudsman the need to keep complainants informed has been recognized and the Commission is now more explicit about the administrative procedures which it will follow in relation to a complaint and in informing individual complainants of the reasons why a case might be discontinued.[17]

In Chapter 3 Sibylle Grohs provides an insight into how the procedure envisaged in the Treaty works in practice, from the perspective of a sector where enforcement against member states has been particularly important: environmental policy. Although the general procedures for handling complaints are the same across the Commission, the individual Directorates-General have different approaches, depending on the number and type of complaints they receive. In the field of environment, cases of alleged 'bad application' of Union law are relatively more frequent but are also harder to establish since, as Grohs points out, the Commission does not have inspectors that it can send to member states to verify conflicting claims *in situ*. Here again, it is negotiated compliance rather than Court action that is most important. Grohs's conclusion is that although the direct enforcement procedure led by the Commission will remain important, the Commission is also encouraging the improvement of enforcement procedures at national level, through national courts.

The infringement procedure in the Court of Justice cannot itself compensate individuals or declare national law invalid, and may be too late. For speedy action to stop an infringement and actual compensation, national remedies are more effective. The next three chapters, by Dougan, Piqani, and Nollkaemper, indeed focus on different aspects of compliance seen from a national perspective. As Piqani says, 'The mandate conferred by the Union upon national courts to fully and correctly apply EU law and set aside national law when it conflicts with EU law is one of the many pre-emptive tools for avoiding non-compliance by Member States'.

Michael Dougan offers a rich analysis of both bases for the use of criminal sanctions to enforce EU law: first the ability of member states to choose to include in their national systems criminal penalties for the enforcement of EU law rules, and second the possibility of 'own sanctions', the possibility of criminal sanctions

[15] Actions bought by private litigants against the Commission for failure to act under former Art 232 EC, or for an annulment of the Commission's alleged decision not to proceed with a case against a member state have been rejected by the Court on the ground of the Commission's discretion: Case 247/87 *Star Fruit v Commission* [1989] ECR 291; Case C-87/89, *Sonito v Commission*, [1990] ECR I-1981.

[16] EC Commission, Governance White Paper 2001, 25 July 2001, COM (2001) 428, p 26; Commission Communication on the Better Monitoring of the Application of Community Law, COM (2002)725 final/4, p 11.

[17] These are set out in the Commission's Communication to the European Parliament and European Ombudsman on relations with the complainant in respect of infringements of Community law, COM (2002) 141 final.

at the national level being required directly by EU law itself. In the first case, under the *Greek Maize* case law,[18] a member state's choice of remedies is constrained by the principles of equivalence, effectiveness, and proportionality as well as non-discrimination. A key issue identified by Dougan is the relationship between this basis for criminal sanctions and the closely related *Rewe/Comet* case law concerning the member states' duty to ensure the effective judicial protection of individuals whose rights derive from the Union legal order.[19] Here we have two forms of decentralized enforcement—the public sanction and the private remedy; to what extent can member states meet their Article 4(3) TEU obligations of effective enforcement of Union law by facilitating private remedies?

In the second place, EU law may itself provide that criminal sanctions must be imposed at national level. In order to understand the complexity of the current position, Dougan takes us back to the debates over possible Community competence before the entry into force of the Lisbon Treaty, the evolution of the position both before and after the Maastricht Treaty, the *Environmental Crimes* and *Ship Source Pollution* rulings which established derived Community powers to adopt criminal enforcement measures,[20] and then the effects of the Lisbon Treaty, especially the new legal basis for establishing minimum criminal law measures in order to 'ensure the effective implementation of a Union policy in an area which has been subject to harmonization measures'.[21] As he says, a number of questions remain over the relationship between the derived powers established through the *Environmental Crimes* and *Ship Source Pollution* rulings and the new express power granted by Article 83(2) TFEU. The interplay between these different constitutional frameworks for the imposition of criminal sanctions is also an important factor in considering the safeguards developed by the Court and based on fundamental rights, such as the principle of non-retroactivity, which offer a minimum level of judicial protection for individuals faced with criminal sanctions. As against the risk of application of different standards of judicial protection depending on the constitutional basis of criminal proceedings, Dougan argues that the Court-developed principles of judicial protection are potentially 'a powerful unifying force which is capable of overreaching the underlying constitutional complexities, so as to shield individuals . . . from significant and unjustified differences in the levels of judicial protection guaranteed to them under Union law.' However, as he also argues, real problems exist—from doctrinal uncertainties to broader issues such as the absence of direct external fundamental rights scrutiny (at least until the envisaged future accession of the EU to the European Convention on Human Rights).

The final two chapters in this collection consider the role of national courts in ensuring or inducing (to use the term adopted by Nollkaemper) compliance. Darinka Piqani focuses on national constitutional courts and in particular what

[18] Case 68/88, *Commission v Greece*, [1989] ECR 2965.

[19] Case 33/76, *Rewe-Zentralfinanz v Landwirtschaftskammer für das Saarland*, [1976] ECR 1989; Case 45/76, *Comet BV v Produktschap voor Siergewassen*, [1976] ECR 2043.

[20] Case C-176/03, *Commission v Council*, [2005] ECR I-7879 and Case C-440/05, *Commission v Council*, [2007] ECR I-9097.

[21] Art 83(2) TFEU.

she sees as their role in facilitating compliance by member states. On the one hand the EU law mandate of constitutional courts (as all national courts), based on *Simmenthal*[22] and the *Rewe/Comet* case law,[23] is to ensure the full application of EU law, and on the other hand their national constitutional mandate is to uphold national constitutional provisions—even where in tension with EU law. One aspect of the constitutional courts' management of this dual role is to separate the questions of EU-compliance review and constitutional review. On the one hand, if EU-compliance is not characterized as a constitutional issue per se it may be ensured through ordinary courts as well as constitutional courts, and application of the *Simmenthal* doctrine need not be seen as a constitutional issue. On the other hand, where constitutional limits of both EU law and national law are at stake, constitutional courts have continued to assert the need for a possible review of the application of EU law, whether on grounds of fundamental rights, of limits to EU competence or (in the German Constitutional Court's *Lisbon* judgment) of 'national identity'. To what extent does this review pose a threat to compliance within the EU system? As Piqani points out, 'there is a discrepancy between what courts say and what they in fact do'. The language may speak of constitutional reservations, but in practice EU law itself is not disapplied. She sees this not as sign of weakness or failure of nerve, but rather of a willingness to accommodate and dialogue which—at least potentially and if taken seriously—may improve true compliance. Accommodation may take place via a constitutional critique of the national implementation of an EU measure, or by signalling the need for constitutional amendments. Courts may also play a role in 'judicial harmonization' even before the accession of a candidate state, and Piqani finds a positive correlation between the pre-accession disposition of constitutional courts and their post-accession willingness to reconcile constitutional law with EU law obligations.

André Nollkaemper's contribution in the final chapter assesses the contribution of national courts to compliance, making a comparison between EU law and international law. The value of the comparison rests in the 'common roots' of international and EU law, especially as regards reception into national legal orders, and in the fact that EU law may be seen as a particularly successful (in terms of compliance) form of integration, its techniques offering a possible model, despite the fact that 'there is only limited evidence that it as such has an influence on states or that states intentionally seek that model'. As this perhaps suggests, the classical EU law tools of compliance such as direct effect and primacy are not completely separated from or unknown to international law, although as Nollkaemper demonstrates, many of the classic theories of international law and international relations do not attribute much significance to courts as agents of compliance. One of the key differences, of course, lies in the insistence of the EU Court of Justice that questions concerning the relationship between EU law and national law are to be decided by EU law (and therefore by the Court of Justice itself). As regards international law, on the other hand, practice varies between states, this variation being both a

[22] Case 106/77, *Amministrazione delle Finanze dello Stato v Simmenthal SpA*, [1978] ECR 629.
[23] See note 19.

cause and an effect of its relative weakness. While national courts tend, as regards both international and EU law, to insist on a constitutional reservation protective of fundamental constitutional principles, Nollkaemper argues that 'questions of ultimate authority are not decisive for explaining general patterns of compliance or non-compliance'—a conclusion that reflects Piqani's discussion of the role of constitutional courts in the previous chapter. It needs also to be remembered that EU law itself has an impact on the operation of international law within the legal systems of the EU member states, so that we need to think in terms of a triangular relation between national, international, and EU law.[24] From this point of view, by aligning the positions of at least the EU member states as regards at least some international treaties, the EU Court of Justice has an impact on compliance with international as well as EU law.

[24] S. Besson, 'European Legal Pluralism after *Kadi*', 5 *European Constitutional Law Review* (2009), at 237.

1

Compliance and What EU Member States Make of It

Lisa Conant

1. Introduction: Political Science Perspectives on Compliance with EU Law

The apparent success of the European Union's (EU) legal system inspired political scientists to investigate the sources of compliance in what most assumed should be a typically weak international legal regime. Efforts to explain compliance with EU law originated among international relations (IR) theorists of international organization and regional integration, who focused on the puzzle of how a supranational court could impose its authority over states and thereby transcend national sovereignty. Early debates focused on the traditional divide between 'intergovernmentalist' and 'neofunctionalist' theories of European integration, with more general theorizing from 'rationalist' and 'institutionalist' approaches supporting both positions. More normative theorizing from the 'constructivist' strand of the IR literature has challenged these competing instrumental approaches. Broader debates concerning compliance with international law and domestic judicial politics and public policy have informed political science scholarship on EU law as well, attracting the attention of scholars of comparative politics who have historically focused exclusively on purely domestic political systems. Today most political scientists would agree that the EU legal system boasts a compliance record that is extraordinary by standards used to evaluate international law and probably more appropriately comparable to the compliance situation of domestic legal systems, although disagreement about the cause of this exceptional status remains.

Theoretical disagreements coexist with widely divergent empirical findings of a myriad of types of compliance with EU law. Across existing studies, the 'dependent variable' of compliance is operationalized in many different ways. Much of the literature assesses the transposition of EU directives into national law, with some studies using timely transposition of EU directives as the sole indicator of compliance, while others attempt to examine the extent to which transposition is correct by looking into infringement proceedings that challenge the adequacy of domestic measures. Examinations of aggregate patterns in infringement proceedings, which track cross-national differences in rates of formal letters, reasoned opinions, and referrals to the European Court of Justice (ECJ) are also fairly common, as are studies that focus on compliance with ECJ judgments that result from infringement proceedings. Fewer scholars have investigated the extent to which national courts (1) comply with the preliminary rulings they receive after sending a reference to the ECJ or (2) generally comply with the broader case law of the ECJ. Finally, relatively few studies explore how EU law, whether it derives from member state approved 'legislation' or ECJ interpretation in case law, is applied and enforced in typical practice across the member states. Broadly comparative, quantitative studies are most likely to concentrate on formal, legalistic types of compliance such as timely transposition or official infringement statistics from the European Commission while more narrowly focused qualitative case studies are more likely to provide evidence concerning practical application and enforcement.

Variations in transposition rates and difficulties with excessively late transposition have largely disappeared in recent years. Meanwhile, nearly all studies of practical application and enforcement of EU law identify serious shortcomings. Given this discrepancy between the 'law on the books' and the 'law in action', and the paucity of research on the application of EU law in national courts more generally, I argue that future research on compliance should concentrate on investigation of the practical application of EU law by domestic implementing authorities and national judges. Because this type of research requires labour-intensive field research and case law analysis, qualitative case studies and small 'n' comparisons (2–4 cases) of member states and/or policy areas are likely to be the most productive. Careful research design in selecting cases should yield results that are ultimately more informative than quantitative studies of formal indicators of dubious validity or very limited variation.

2. Theoretical Approaches to Understanding Compliance with EU Law

The dramatic progress in integration associated with efforts to achieve the internal market by the end of 1992 attracted the attention of international relations scholars in the subfield of international organization. Rational choice institutionalists produced the pioneering political analysis of the European legal regime, with explanatory factors and outcomes that are consistent with the intergovernmentalist branch of regional integration theory and ultimately pessimistic about the capacity of the European Commission and ECJ to enforce compliance with EU law when it threatens important national interests. Informed by the substantial body of European legal scholarship, a joint effort by a lawyer and political scientist offered a competing neofunctionalist account of the instrumental and technocratic features of legal integration that encourage compliance with EU law. The theoretical debate among intergovernmentalists and neofunctionalists, which I specify further below, inspired a wave of empirical inquiry that addresses compliance. Contradictory findings and failures to explain cross-national and cross-issue variations in compliance led others to develop more norm-based constructivist accounts and a substantial body of middle range theorizing that focuses on explanatory factors that are either unique to the EU setting or specific to sets of member states or particular types of institutions. In this section, I discuss the major theoretical contributions that political scientists have made to understanding the sources of compliance with EU law.

A. Theories of International Organization and European Integration

IR theorizing in political science values parsimonious explanations of general trends in behaviour among the dominant actors in world politics. With its explanatory focus on variations in the distribution of power among states, 'realism' has long been the approach that frames the puzzles and conventional accounts of international politics. Consistent compliance with any international legal regime is surprising to realists, who expect that states will cheat whenever a rule puts them at a disadvantage relative to their primary competitors. As realism in its simplest formulation cannot explain why states would bother constructing a legal regime as complex and encompassing as the EU, intergovernmentalist integration scholars elaborate on core realist assumptions to account for the extent of the EU's success.

1. Intergovernmentalism

Intergovernmentalists argue that member states remain fundamentally in control of an integration process that they pursue to gain economic benefits that are impossible to achieve independently in the postwar global political economy. In this account member states determine the momentum of the EU, agreeing to all important expansions in the scope of cooperation and ultimately never ceding authority over core areas of state sovereignty such as defence. Integration may extend only to those fields associated with improvements in the quality of life such as the market, environmental protection, and social security. Meanwhile, states ultimately provide for their own security through conventional balance of power considerations that involve important alliances with states outside the EU and the nuclear deterrent.[1] The elaborate institutional structure of the EU derives from the need to manage the 'complex interdependence' of advanced economies in Europe. Bargaining among national governments in the Council of Ministers and European Council establishes the trajectory of integration, while the more supranational European Commission and ECJ merely enforce agreements accepted by states.[2]

States cannot efficiently police rules associated with the economic liberalization that is at the heart of the integration project for intergovernmentalists whereas the European Commission and ECJ can largely specialize in acquiring the expertise to

[1] Hoffmann, 'Obstinate or Obsolete? The Fate of the Nation-State and the Case of Western Europe', 95 *Daedalus* (1966) 3, at 862–915.

[2] A. Moravcsik, *The Choice For Europe: Social Purpose And State Power From Messina To Maastricht* (1998).

identify transgressors and ensure a level playing field. Although intergovernmentalists conceive of enforcement largely as the application of pre-existing rules, they acknowledge that the ECJ also necessarily fills gaps in the 'incomplete contract' of EU law with creative interpretation. In this account, the ECJ elicits a solid record of compliance with its rulings by (1) respecting the preferences of the more powerful member states in most disputes and (2) tolerating periodic non-compliance to ward off efforts to reverse its case law or limit its jurisdiction.[3] Intergovernmentalists further argue that these court-curbing activities were relatively difficult to orchestrate both before the Single European Act (SEA) when unanimous voting prevailed in the Council of Ministers, and in recent years as the increasing power of the European Parliament has created a more genuinely bicameral European legislature that is prone to gridlock.[4] Despite the difficulties associated with actively reversing or reining in the Court, intergovernmentalists expect individual member states to fail to comply with adverse judgments on issues of central importance to the ruling government or key domestic constituencies.

2. *Neofunctionalism*

Neofunctionalists contend that regional integration generates a steady stream of incentives to solve new problems through further cooperation in a process of spillover that erodes the capacity of states to control outcomes. Once technocratic experts begin to take joint action in areas insulated from mass politics, societal actors that benefit from transnational collaboration and exchange redirect their activities toward supranational institutions and promote the deepening of integration in an expanding set of domains.[5]

In the legal realm, the ECJ appeals to shared professional norms and self-interests to co-opt national judiciaries, practising lawyers, and legal scholars. Convincing legal argument legitimates rulings for the legal profession generally, and the creation of a binding system of EU law serves professional interests as well: the supremacy and direct effect of EU law empower national courts to exercise judicial review by testing the compatibility of national and EU law, offer lawyers a new avenue to pursue their clients' interests, and present academics with an entirely new field of inquiry. National governments find themselves trapped into accepting EU law, even when it departs from their preferences, because legal justifications 'mask' the implications of rulings and 'shield' the ECJ from attack.[6] Once supranational rules govern transactions, transnational exchange increases

[3] Garrett, 'International Cooperation and Institutional Choice', 49 *International Organization* (1992) 1, at 533–60; Garrett, Kelemen, and Schulz, 'The European Court of Justice, National Governments, and Legal Integration in the European Union', 52 *International Organization* (1998) 1, at 149–76.

[4] Tsebelis and Garrett, 'The Institutional Foundations of Intergovernmentalism and Supranationalism in the European Union', 55 *International Organization* (2001) 2, at 357–90.

[5] E. Haas, *The Uniting of Europe* (1958); L. Lindberg, *The Political Dynamics of European Integration* (1963).

[6] Burley and Mattli, 'Europe before the Court', 47 *International Organization* (1993) 1, at 41–76; Mattli and Slaughter, 'Revisiting the European Court of Justice', 52 *International Organization* (1998) 1, at 177–209.

and generates new disputes that the ECJ resolves with its case law, which further encourages both more exchange and more supranational legislation to address emerging problems. This process sustains an ongoing expansion in legal integration that is difficult to reverse or stop given the institutional obstacles to treaty revision.[7] National governments find themselves increasingly enmeshed in a web of legal precedents that influence how they can premise, structure, and sequence their arguments in legal proceedings, which promotes the incremental acceptance of once unwelcome rulings.[8] Ultimately, neofunctionalists expect that compliance with EU law and ECJ rulings will be the most common outcome, and many emphasize the role that national courts play in enforcing the substantial docket of preliminary rulings.

3. *Constructivism*

In contrast to these instrumental approaches that focus largely on interests, constructivists emphasize the role that norms, learning, persuasion, and socialization play in encouraging compliance with international institutions. Here compliance with the law is an internalized obligation that actors accept without making cost/benefit analyses. Instead, 'logics of appropriateness' govern behaviour.[9] In some accounts, norms merely constrain elites who cannot ignore the mobilization of opposition to behaviours that violate particular norms. The mobilization of support for norms that shifts elite behaviours can eventually lead to the internalization of new preferences.[10] In other accounts, learning and persuasion occur through social interactions that are not accompanied by political pressure.[11] Persuasion is more likely to lead to changes in preferences when actors (1) are in novel environments that facilitate the reception of new information, (2) have few ingrained beliefs that are inconsistent with the relevant norm, (3) want to belong to the 'in-group' that advocates on behalf of the norm, (4) can participate in serious deliberative argumentation concerning the norm, and (5) deliberate in less politicized and more insular private settings.[12]

Constructivist accounts of compliance with European institutions usually strive to incorporate normative dimensions into explanations that also invoke

[7] Stone Sweet and Brunell, 'Constructing a Supranational Constitution', 92 *American Political Science Review* (1998) 1, at 63–81. And on the constraints associated with treaty revision see also Alter, 'Who Are the Masters of the Treaty?', 52 *International Organization* (1998) 1, at 121–47.

[8] McCown, 'The European Parliament before the Bench', 10 *Journal of European Public Policy* (2003) 6, at 974–95.

[9] March and Olsen, 'The Institutional Dynamics of International Political Orders', 52 *International Organization* (1998) 4, at 943–69.

[10] M. Keck and K. Sikkink, *Activists beyond Borders* (1998); T. Risse, S. Ropp, and K. Sikkink, *The Power of Human Rights* (1999).

[11] Risse-Kappen, 'Democratic Peace—Warlike Democracies? A Social Constructivist Interpretation of the Liberal Argument', 1 *European Journal of International Relations* (1995) 4, at 491–517; M. Finnemore, *National Interests in International Society* (1996); E. Adler and M. Barnett (eds), *Security Communities* (1998); Price, 'Reversing the Gun Sights: Transnational Civil Society Targets Land Mines', 52 *International Organization* (1998) 3, at 613–44.

[12] Checkel, 'Why Comply? Social Learning and European Identity Change', 55 *International Organization* (2001) 3, at 562–3.

instrumental incentives. For some, rationalist conceptions of interest can limit the causal role of norms in situations that are not conducive to successful persuasion.[13] Others see normative constraints to self-interested behaviours and carve out the scope conditions for norms to be definitive in explaining particular outcomes. Constructivists highlight how the instrumental costs of compliance with EU law can be very high, financially and politically, while the sanctions associated with non-compliance are often negligible in comparison. In these cases, the 'normative cost' of non-compliance must be high to encourage compliance. Blatant, public disregard for the law is inconceivable in states where respect for the rule of law is an important tradition, and this can be as true for EU law as it is for domestic law.[14] ECJ judgments empower compliance proponents, which facilitates 'shaming' the government based on the inappropriateness of continued non-compliance. Shaming strategies are most likely to be effective if the legal interpretation in an ECJ judgment resonates well with domestically institutionalized norms, but compliance in response to shaming can remain 'incomplete' in the sense that governments may transform legal acts in a minimalist manner that leads to future infractions, particularly at the stage of practical application. By contrast, 'reframing' strategies that rely on persuasion are more likely to be successful in promoting full compliance when existing policies have become delegitimized.[15] Given the potentially wide range of normative contestation concerning various EU laws across member states and issue areas, constructivist accounts are likely to predict more variation in compliance outcomes than intergovernmentalism, which interprets much compliance as coincident with state interests, or neofunctionalism, which expects compliance in most cases.

B. Theories of International Law and European Integration

In IR subfields that are further removed from a focus on security, political economy approaches of game theory, public (or rational) choice theory, and collective action theory animate IR debates about sources of compliance with international law. The 'enforcement' and 'management' approaches develop expectations about the sources of compliance and non-compliance that derive from rationalist factors highlighted by political economists. Applications of these approaches to the EU setting produce hybrid accounts that combine features from the enforcement and management schools as well as from the theories of international organization and European integration discussed previously.

13 Ibid, at 553–4 or 553–88 for full reference.

14 Beach, 'Why Governments Comply: An Integrative Compliance Model that Bridges the Gap between Instrumental and Normative Models of Compliance', 12 *Journal of European Public Policy* (2005) 1, at 113–42.

15 Panke, 'The European Court of Justice as an Agent of Europeanization? Restoring Compliance in EU Law', 14 *Journal of European Public Policy* (2007) 6, at 847–66; Panke, 'Putting International Legalization to the Test: Differential Paths toward Compliance with EU Law', 14 *Zeitschrift für internationale Beziehungen* (2007) 2, at 289–318.

1. *Enforcement Approach*

Enforcement theorists expect that free-riding is a paramount concern for compliance with international regulation because each state gains most if others comply while it reneges on commitments. The assumption is that states choose to cheat whenever the benefits of shirking outweigh its costs. Because states gain more through compliance with international regulation than unilateral defection in a non-cooperative situation, they have an incentive to create institutions that increase the probability of detection and the costs of cheating. Investing in monitoring and sanctioning helps to expose and punish cheaters, increasing the costs of non-compliance and thereby reducing its incidence.[16]

Assumptions and hypotheses from the enforcement approach are common in empirical accounts of compliance with EU law. More specifically, 'principal-agent' (P-A) analysis often informs the literature on enforcement of EU law. Deployed by intergovernmentalists and neofunctionalists alike, P-A theory also offers a neutral language to evaluate strategic interaction among officials at different levels of governance. Most basically, member states are the 'principals' who might constrain their enforcing 'agent', the ECJ, by (1) specifying law to avoid innovative judicial interpretation or (2) limiting the Court's jurisdiction. Yet the difficulties associated with treaty revision and even ordinary statutory legislation facilitate judicial autonomy that can result in 'agency slippage', where the ECJ takes actions that are unanticipated and unwelcome by its principals. For example, with its rulings of direct effect and supremacy, the ECJ transformed the system of preliminary rulings from a mechanism to challenge EU law into a means of enforcing EU law, which placed the ECJ in the position of a 'principal' with its own 'agents' of enforcement in the national courts.[17] In a more nuanced variant of this approach, member states act collectively as 'principals' to adopt beneficial regulations, the Commission and ECJ act jointly as 'supervisors' who monitor compliance, and the members states act individually as 'agents' of implementation. With two principal-agent relationships that are vulnerable to slippage, the range of strategies to maximize autonomy increases for both the supranational agents of enforcement and the national agents of implementation.[18]

2. *Management Approach*

In contrast to the enforcement approach, management theorists expect that states usually intend to comply with commitments that they undertake in the interests of efficiency and norms. Non-compliance emerges due to capacity limitations and ambiguities of interpretation rather than deliberate defiance. As a result,

[16] M. Olson, *The Logic of Collective Action: Public Goods and the Theory of Groups* (1965); R. Axelrod, *The Evolution of Co-operation* (1984); Axelrod and Keohane, 'Achieving Cooperation under Anarchy: Strategies and Institutions', in K. Oye (eds), *Cooperation under Anarchy* (1986), at 226–54; Downs, Rocke, and Barsoom, 'Is the Good News about Compliance also Good News about Cooperation?', 50 *International Organization* (1996) 3, at 379–406.

[17] Alter, *supra* note 7.

[18] Tallberg, 'Supranational Influence in EU Enforcement: The ECJ and The Principle of State Liability', 7 *Journal of European Public Policy* (2000) 1, at 104–21.

management theorists argue that improvements in economic and political capacity, rule interpretation, and transparency are the best means to promote compliance. Coercive enforcement is not expected to be effective or necessary in most situations.[19]

Expectations from the management approach are often tested alongside those from the competing enforcement approach in studies on compliance in the EU. Despite the apparently competing strategies of these two approaches, application to the EU case suggests that the coercive and cooperative elements are most effective when combined in a hybrid approach. Monitoring, sanctions, capacity building, rule interpretation, and social pressure all coexist in the EU legal system as techniques of improving state compliance. EU infringement proceedings, with their potential for fines, along with incriminating press releases and public score boards, identify, shame, and punish non-complying states. National courts' application of EU law and awards of damages for injuries resulting from states' failures to comply with EU law provide a further, decentralized source of enforcement. Meanwhile negotiation during infringement proceedings, as well as reasoned opinions, ECJ judgments, and the Commission's interpretive guidelines of ECJ case law all serve to reduce the ambiguity of EU rules. Finally, EU level funding helps states build capacity to comply in a variety of areas. Such a dual approach to encouraging compliance is useful because the high economic and political costs associated with implementing some EU policies can inspire both intentional and unintentional defiance.[20]

3. Worlds of Compliance

Another synthetic approach includes the 'worlds of compliance' typology that proposes that different explanatory factors determine compliance processes in different sets of EU member states. First, expectations that are consistent with constructivist IR theory and the management approach in international law characterize the 'world of law observance', which includes Denmark, Finland, and Sweden. In these states, compliance with EU law typically proceeds without difficulty in terms of both the formal 'law on the books' and the practical 'law in action'. An ingrained 'compliance culture' and strong legal and administrative capacity both contribute to the dominant pattern of timely and complete compliance. Second, predictions from the 'liberal' variants of intergovernmentalism that emphasize the responsiveness of national governments to domestic constituencies are parallel to the 'world

[19] Young, 'The Effectiveness of International Institutions: Hard Cases and Critical Variables', in J. Rosenau and E-O. Czempiel (eds), *Governance without Government: Order and Change in World Politics* (1992), at 160–94; P. Haas, R. Keohane, and M. Levy (eds), *Institutions for the Earth: Sources of Effective International Environmental Protection* (1993); R. Mitchell, *Intentional Oil Pollution at Sea: Environmental Policy and Treaty Compliance* (1994); A. Chayes and A.H. Chayes, *The New Sovereignty: Compliance with International Regulatory Agreements* (1995); R. Keohane and M. Levy (eds), *Institutions for Environmental Aid: Pitfalls and Promises* (1996); A. and A.H. Chayes, and Mitchell, 'Managing Compliance: A Comparative Perspective', in E. Brown Weiss and H. Jacobson (eds), *Strengthening Compliance with International Environmental Accords* (1998), at 39–62.

[20] Tallberg, 'Paths to Compliance: Enforcement, Management, and the European Union', 56 *International Organization* (2002) 3, at 609–43.

of domestic politics', which includes Austria, Belgium, Germany, the Netherlands, Spain, and the United Kingdom (UK). Here, governments are much more likely to engage in a cost/benefit analysis before coming into compliance with EU law. Political resistance based on the outcome of this rationalist equation is the source of most violations because these states do not usually have difficulties associated with adequate state capacity to implement. Third, the enforcement approach best explains compliance processes in the 'world of neglect', which includes France, Greece, Luxembourg, and Portugal. Powerful enforcement action by supranational institutions is the most important motivation for compliant behaviour in these states, whereas the absence of enforcement 'sticks' leads to inaction with respect to EU obligations. Neglect can derive from either preferences for national solutions or state capacity limitations, but the source of neglect is responsive to supranational efforts to shame and sanction. Finally, liberal intergovernmentalism accounts for 'law on the books' compliance while the management approach accounts for 'law in action' non-compliance in the 'world of dead letters', which includes the Czech Republic, Hungary, Ireland, Italy, Slovakia, and Slovenia. Responsiveness to domestic constituencies and governing coalition partners can lead to delays in formal legal compliance in a manner similar to the 'world of domestic politics', but severe capacity limitations result in widespread non-compliance at the stage of application and enforcement of law on the ground. In these countries, 'what is written on the statute books simply does not become effective in practice.'[21] Developed inductively on the basis of qualitative empirical research, the 'worlds of compliance' hybrid has inspired ongoing empirical tests of its central propositions. It makes an important contribution to the literature in identifying limitations to research that focuses exclusively on the 'law on the books'.

C. Theories from Comparative Politics

The IR debate on the ECJ as well as a burgeoning interest in the role of courts in postwar democracies inspired scholarship on EU compliance that derives from the subfield of comparative politics. While IR theories had to account for something assumed to be nearly impossible—a solid record of compliance with a demanding system of international law—comparativists set out to account for variations in something assumed to be fairly common place: democratic governments' respect for the rule of law and compliance with its central requirements. Accustomed to exploring more nuanced interactions between law and politics within domestic settings, comparativists largely abandon the national/supranational dichotomy that animates IR debates and focus on factors that affect legal and judicial influence in a variety of contexts. Here, explanations more often examine how legal and political outcomes evolve over time to reflect the impact of different institutional venues

[21] Falkner and Treib, 'Three Worlds of Compliance or Four?', 46 *Journal of Common Market Studies* (2008) 2, at 308. For the development of this typology, see also G. Falkner et al, *Complying with Europe: EU Harmonization and Soft Law in the Member States* (2005) and Falkner, Hartlapp, and Treib, 'Worlds of Compliance: Why Leading Approaches to European Union Implementation are only "Sometimes-true Theories"', 46 *European Journal of Political Research* (2007), at 395–416.

and evolving constellations of interest and power. Comparative politics theories typically develop at the 'middle range', accounting for dynamics in bounded institutional settings, and they do not necessarily present the mutually exclusive understandings of political developments that are characteristic of major IR theories.

1. Judicial Politics

Comparative politics scholars challenged neofunctionalist assumptions about national judicial empowerment by identifying how the EU legal system 'demotes' national supreme courts from the apex of their respective jurisdictions. Serving as the ultimate authority over legal developments within their field is likely to be more important to courts of last instance than the opportunity to review national law for its compatibility with EU law. In the case of constitutional courts, who already enjoy the power of judicial review, EU judicial review merely opens the door to challenges to their authority by lower courts. As a result, high courts' cooperation in the decentralized system of EU law enforcement that proceeds through national courts is a puzzle worthy of explanation. Working within an institutionalist framework, the 'bureaucratic politics' or 'inter-court competition' model proposes that first instance and intermediate appellate courts have the greatest incentives to send references to the ECJ for preliminary rulings (or to apply ECJ precedents) because the EU legal system genuinely empowers these courts. Proponents of this model expect that national supreme courts will initially send fewer references than their lower-court counterparts, with constitutional courts sending the fewest references of all. As lower courts seize the opportunity to send references to the ECJ (or apply ECJ precedent) to achieve legal outcomes that are impossible under national law, bureaucratic-politics scholars argue that national supreme courts will begin to send references in an effort to influence the direction of the ECJ's legal interpretation in ways that are more deferential to national legal traditions.[22] National judges do this by including opinions with their references, while the ECJ tries to maintain legal consistency in its responses by redefining issues and adding or suppressing questions. Bureaucratic-politics scholars anticipate that national judges will usually comply with the preliminary rulings that respond to their references, but they will also evade unwelcome decisions by re-referring issues or reinterpreting the facts of particular cases.[23]

Legal scholars have challenged this strategic account of judicial politics with a 'team model' of judicial behaviour that assumes judges' primary motivations are functional and legalistic. Here, judges at different levels of the national judicial hierarchy conceive of themselves as a team and are sensitive to the signals that other courts are sending about the appropriate application of EU law. As a result, higher courts should cite the ECJ more often, since they direct legal interpretation,

[22] Alter, 'The European Court's Political Power', 19 *West European Politics* (1996) 3, at 458–87; K. Alter, *Establishing the Supremacy of European Law* (2001).

[23] S. Nyikos, 'The European Courts and National Courts', 61 *Dissertation Abstracts International. A, Humanities and Social Sciences* (2000) 6, at 2459-A (available from UMI, Ann Arbor, Michigan. Order No. DA 9975557).

and lower courts should cite the ECJ regularly only after higher courts incorporate the ECJ into the 'team' by acknowledging and following ECJ case law. Courts with more experience with EU law should cite ECJ case law less often and also diverge from ECJ 'precedent' more often because they need less guidance than courts with less experience. National courts are ultimately the primary EU law courts that look to the ECJ periodically because it is a specialized EU law court. As a result, judges will cite the ECJ more often if an area of EU law is governed largely through broad treaty provisions and many ECJ precedents are available. Citations fall in areas of EU law that are heavily codified in specific regulations and directives, which leave less room for divergent interpretation.[24] In sum, issues of legal certainty and knowledge, rather than political preferences and empowerment, explain judicial behaviour in the team model.

2. *Mobilization*

Because courts are reactive institutions, relying on other actors to bring problems to their attention, comparative politics scholars have also concentrated on the role that groups, from civil society and institutional structures to support litigation, play in encouraging compliance with EU law. Informed by literatures on political economy and social movements, this theorizing concentrates on explaining the mobilization of 'compliance constituencies'. In basic terms, actors with the resources and knowledge to litigate strategically, 'shopping' for the most friendly forums among national courts and persisting with 'copy-cat claims', generate the most effective legal pressures to comply.[25] More specifically, mobilization theory grounded in political economy proposes that the magnitude and distribution of consequences associated with EU legal requirements influences patterns of legal and political mobilization that in turn affect the extent to which EU law applies in practice. 'Intense' interest in high-magnitude costs or benefits that are 'concentrated' to affect relatively few actors is likely to inspire collective legal and political mobilization by organized civil society (including business) groups that may ratify—in the case of benefits—or delay and dilute—in the case of costs—EU legal requirements. By contrast, intense interest in high-magnitude costs or benefits that are 'diffused' across a large population is likely to inspire individual legal mobilization that induces compliance only for parties to the litigation. Unless broader institutional support emerges to sustain legal pressures for widespread changes, eg from the Commission's infringement proceedings or other public enforcement agency such as the British Equal Opportunities Commission, compliance with

[24] Ramos Romeu, 'Law and Politics in the Application of EC Law: Spanish Courts and the ECJ 1986–2000', 43 *Common Market Law Review* (2006), at 395–421.

[25] C. Harlow and R. Rawlings, *Pressure through Law* (1992); Alter and Meunier-Aitsahalia, 'Judicial Politics in the European Community', 39 *Comparative Political Studies* (1994) 4, at 535–61; Alter and Vargas, 'Explaining Variation in the Use of European Litigation Strategies: European Community Law and British Gender Equality Policy', 33 *Comparative Political Studies* (2000) 4, at 452–82; Conant, 'Europeanization and the Courts' in M. Green Cowles, J. Caporaso, and T. Risse (eds), *Transforming Europe: Europeanization and Domestic Change* (2001), at 97–115.

legal norms will be narrowly 'contained'.[26] Liberal standing rules, particularly those that allow for group standing and class actions, and tribunals that are readily accessible to average citizens even in the absence of legal representation, are further potential sources of institutional support for litigation that can magnify pressures to implement legal rules more fully.[27]

A variety of social-movements hypotheses also address the EU case. Groups that lack access to policymaking venues are more likely to litigate in efforts to enforce EU law,[28] whereas groups with better access to officials will avoid adversarial proceedings and seek to encourage compliance through negotiation and traditional lobbying activities.[29] With fewer cross-cutting interests, groups with narrower mandates are more likely to litigate as a strategy of enforcement as well.[30] Litigants should disproportionately target states that are non-compliant, whether this entails national standards that are lower or higher than EU requirements, and states that dragged EU law down to a lowest-common denominator position. In this last instance, litigants hope to receive judicial interpretations that expand EU requirements to a more ambitious and widely accepted target.[31] Mobilization is more likely to occur if issues are highly salient to domestic politics,[32] theoretically even in the absence of significant costs and benefits. Groups will be more likely to litigate at the EU level if national levels of litigation are relatively high, whereas groups will be more likely to refrain from litigation in countries where litigation is not typically part of strategies to achieve political change.[33] Finally, the legacies of authoritarian or communist regimes may have a dampening effect on civil society activism of all types for a long period of time.[34]

3. Institutional Opportunities and Constraints

Institutionalist theorizing informs comparative research on compliance that focuses on variables at the level of states and policy sectors. Cross-nationally, a greater number of 'veto points' that allow opponents to obstruct agreements make compliance with EU law more difficult to achieve because states must legislate to comply with EU directives and, in many cases, ECJ judgments that declare

[26] Conant, *supra* note 25; L. Conant, *Justice Contained: Law and Politics in the European Union* (2002).

[27] K. Alter, 'The European Union's Legal System and Domestic Policy: Spillover or Backlash?', 54 *International Organization* (2000) 3, at 489–518; Conant, *Justice Contained, supra* note 26; Kelemen and Sibbitt, 'The Globalization of American Law', 58 *International Organization* (2004) 1, at 103–36.

[28] Alter and Vargas, *supra* note 25; Conant, *Justice Contained, supra* note 26.

[29] Conant, *Justice Contained, supra* note 26; Börzel, 'Participation through Law Enforcement: The Case of the European Union', 39 *Comparative Political Studies* (2006) 1, at 128–52; Mabbett, 'The Development of a Rights-based Social Policy in the European Union', 43 *Journal of Common Market Studies* (2005) 1, at 97–120.

[30] Alter and Vargas, *supra* note 25.

[31] R. Cichowski, 'Integrating the Environment', 5 *Journal of European Public Policy* (1998) 3, at 387–405; R. Cichowski, *The European Court and Civil Society: Litigation, Mobilization, and Governance* (2007).

[32] Alter, *supra* note 27.

[33] Conant, *supra* note 25; Sverdrup, 'Compliance and Conflict Management in the European Union: Nordic Exceptionalism', 27 *Scandinavian Political Studies* (2004) 1, at 23–44.

[34] Börzel, *supra* note 29; Falkner and Treib, *supra* note 21; Sedelmeier, 'After Conditionality: Post-accession Compliance with EU Law in East Central Europe', 15 *Journal of European Public Policy* (2008) 6, at 806–25.

particular violations of EU law. Veto points arise in multiple forms in different national political systems. Federal systems have more veto points than unitary systems since agreement of more than one level of government is at stake in at least some issue areas.[35] Similarly, the centralization of administrative and enforcement agencies allows for easier supervision of implementation.[36] Furthermore, parliamentary systems with proportional representation that produce coalition governments have more veto points than those with single plurality districts that produce single party governments. Bicameral legislatures with joint law-making powers and constitutional systems designed to 'check' the power of each branch of government also generate more veto points. By contrast, fast-track procedures for legislation in certain issue areas may reduce the number of veto points, making formal legal compliance easier to achieve. Systems of interest intermediation also potentially affect veto points, with some scholars arguing that pluralist systems have more than corporatist systems since a greater variety and number of interests need to be mobilized into a supportive coalition.[37] The close and cooperative relationship between the state and interest groups that characterizes corporatism is also expected to improve implementation.[38] Others, however, view the government's need to satisfy its social and economic partners as impediments to effective implementation.[39]

At the level of distinct issue areas, comparative politics scholars have argued that the degree of 'fit' or 'misfit' between EU rules and pre-existing institutional and regulatory traditions determines performance relative to compliance and implementation. Here, EU law confronts deeply entrenched domestic structures. If the EU and national approaches fit well together, adaptational costs are low and implementation should be easy to achieve promptly. If EU law clashes with domestic traditions, adaptational costs will be high and implementation is more likely to be contested, delayed, or incomplete.[40] These comparative institutionalist approaches focus largely on instrumental factors, although some of the proponents of the

[35] Tsebelis, 'Decision Making in Political Systems: Veto Players in Presidentialism, Parliamentarism, Multicameralism and Multipartyism', 25 *British Journal of Political Science* (1995), at 289–325.

[36] Versluis, 'Even Rules, Uneven Practices: Opening the "Black Box" of EU Law in Action', 30 *West European Poliitics* (2007) 1, at 50–67.

[37] Tsebelis, *supra* note 35; König and Luetgert, 'Troubles with Transposition? Explaining Trends in Member-State Notification and the Delayed Transposition of EU Directives', 39 *British Journal of Political Science* (2008), at 163–94.

[38] Lampinen and Uusikylä, 'Implementation Deficit—Why Member States do not Comply with EU Directives', 21 *Scandinavian Political Studies* (1998) 3, at 231–51.

[39] Mbaye, 'Why National States Comply with Supranational Law: Explaining Implementation Infringements in the European Union, 1972–1993', 2 *European Union Politics* (2001) 3, at 271.

[40] Duina, 'Explaining Legal Implementation in the European Union', 25 *International Journal of the Sociology of Law* (1997) 2, at 155–79; F. Duina, *Harmonizing Europe: Nation-states within the Common Market* (1999); Duina and Blithe, 'Nation-states and Common Markets: The Institutional Condition for Acceptance', 6 *Review of International Political Economy* (1999) 4, at 494–530; Knill and Lenschow, 'Coping with Europe: The Impact of British and German Administrations on the Implementation of EU Environmental Policy', 5 *Journal of European Public Policy* (1998) 4, at 595–614; Börzel, 'Why There is No "Southern Problem": On Environmental Leaders and Laggards in the European Union', 7 *Journal of European Public Policy* (2000) 1, at 141–62; M. Green Cowles, J. Caporaso, and T. Risse, *Transforming Europe: Europeanization and Domestic Change* (2001);

fit/misfit approach deploy sociological variants of historical institutionalism that emphasize the importance of ideas and norms rather than rationalist cost/benefit analysis.

4. Political Legitimacy

Comparative theorizing on sources of political legitimacy focuses more directly on normative influences on compliance with EU law. Some scholars argue that the domestic legitimacy of the rule of law and judicial institutions transfers to the EU level. As a result, the more officials in a state respect their own domestic courts' decisions, the more likely it becomes that they comply with ECJ judgments.[41] By contrast, corruption that afflicts national politics will undermine efforts to comply with EU law as well.[42] Furthermore, the more that the general public trusts their national supreme courts, the more likely it is that they trust the ECJ as the supreme court of the EU. This public trust should then generate legitimacy problems for governments who choose to disobey ECJ rulings.[43] Others argue that the ECJ's relative obscurity makes its legitimacy dependent on public views of the EU more generally, and particularly the European Parliament. Because the European Parliament enjoys little legitimacy itself, these scholars argue that the ECJ has few resources to elicit compliance with controversial rulings and is therefore not in a good position to hold states accountable to their legal obligations.[44] The obscurity of EU legal provisions themselves may lead to compliance deficiencies as well since enforcement agencies must prioritize what they monitor, and they are less likely to monitor rules that govern issues of low salience. Only violations that result in crises attracting widespread media attention would be likely to delegitimize a government's lax compliance.[45]

One comparative account argues that conceptions of the appropriate relationship between law and politics influences compliance with EU law. In a national, cross-issue version of the 'fit/misfit' approach, judges and administrators in states characterized by 'constitutional democracy' should comply more readily with ECJ judgments because they are accustomed to having domestic political decisions periodically overturned by constitutional courts. By contrast, judges and administrators in states characterized by 'majoritarian democracy' will be more likely to disregard ECJ interpretations of EU legal obligations that conflict with important national law and policies. In these states, judges and administrators defer to the decisions that majorities of legitimately elected politicians have made and

T. Börzel, *States And Regions in The European Union: Institutional Adaptation in Germany and Spain* (2002).

[41] Alter, *supra* note 27, at 511. [42] Mbaye, *supra* note 39.

[43] A. Grosskopf, 'A Supernational Case', 61 *Dissertation Abstracts International, A, The Humanities and Social Sciences* (2001) 9, at 3750-A. (Available from UMI, Ann Arbor, Michigan. Order No. DA 9985047.)

[44] Caldeira and Gibson, 'The Legitimacy of the Court of Justice in the European Union', 89 *American Political Science Review* (1995) 1, at 356–76; Gibson and Caldeira, 'Changes in the Legitimacy of the European Court of Justice', 28 *British Journal of Political Science* (1998) 1, at 63–91; Carrubba, 'The European Court of Justice, Democracy, and Enlargement', 4 *European Union Politics* (2003) 1, at 75–100.

[45] Versluis, *supra* note 36.

consider any substantial judicial revision of these decisions to be inappropriate.[46] Individuals in these majoritarian democracies may also be less likely to initiate litigation to resolve disputes concerning EU law because the political culture encourages cooperative negotiation and consensus-seeking rather than adversarial legal contests that produce winners and losers.[47]

3. Empirical Findings on Compliance with EU Law

The contending theories reviewed above generate a wide range of propositions about what we can expect to see in the empirical record on compliance with EU law. Empirical findings have mirrored the theoretical diversity to a substantial extent, due in part to variable operationalization of 'compliance', where different scholars are 'testing' propositions with different types of evidence. Much of the empirical record remains inconclusive (because of contradictory results) and there are many remaining 'black holes' where little knowledge exists. In this section, I review the diverse empirical literature on compliance with EU law, identify areas where a nascent consensus is emerging, and outline how future work may contribute to a more comprehensive understanding of compliance.

A. Compliance with the 'Law on the Books'

Much of the empirical literature focuses on formal legal compliance, where data is most readily accessible and quantifiable for broadly comparative study across member states and over time. Such 'law on the books' scholarship is a helpful starting point to assess compliance with EU law because it is plausible to assume that legal compliance is a necessary precursor to practical compliance in any field of activity that actually requires regulation. Inquiry into the law in action, however, suggests that conclusions about compliant behaviours that are based on patterns of legal compliance alone will be highly misleading. As a result, I argue that future scholarship should merge research on the law on the books and the law in action for more useful results.

1. Transposition of Directives

Studies on the transposition of directives into national law are among the most common types of compliance research among political scientists. Data tracking notifications of domestic legislation to implement EU directives has always been among the easiest to gather, originally from published reports by the Commission and more recently from its online 'scoreboard'. Given limited variation in transposition rates, however, it is puzzling that this measure of formal legal compliance has been the focus of so much scholarly attention. Rates of transposition have always been high, averaging over 90 per cent, and have improved from an average of 91 per cent in 1990, to 95 per cent in 1999, and then 98 per cent by 2005. A momentary

[46] Wind, 'The Nordics, the EU, and Reluctance towards Supranational Judicial Review', 48 *Journal of Common Market Studies* (2010) 4.

[47] Sverdrup, *supra* note 33, at 27–8.

dip to 65 per cent in 1991, attributable to the internal market program (where only 24 of nearly 300 directives were transposed by all member states at one point), directed attention to the issue of a possible 'compliance deficit'. Lagging performance by a few member states in 1990—Greece, Italy, and Portugal—also inspired interest in the source of delay. Yet the range between member states decreased from 20 per cent in 1991 to five per cent in 1999 and one per cent by late 2006.[48] Non-compliance at the stage of transposition is highly visible, resulting readily in 'naming and shaming', and no longer a viable option given the financial sanctions introduced by the Maastricht Treaty on European Union. In the long run, changes in government promote compliance in particularly intransigent cases.[49] This convergence in transposition performance stands in stark contrast to the divergence of explanations available for the limited variations that exist. Now that very little variation remains, scholars might more productively explore compliance with any measure other than transposition.

The 'worlds of compliance' typology originated in a quest to account for variations in transposition that prominent institutionalist approaches failed to explain. Patterns of transposition did not substantiate the goodness of fit or veto points propositions: multiple qualitative case studies found that the goodness of fit between EU and national rules was neither a necessary nor sufficient condition for timely transposition and that misfits did not regularly result in substantial delays.[50] Likewise, countries with many veto points are generally able to meet transposition deadlines, while countries with few veto points periodically exceed deadlines for long periods of time.[51] A study of six EU labour law directives in 15 member states found that party political factors could overrule the misfit logic in that governments' interests in major reform may coincide with demanding requirements from EU directives. In other cases, the very fact that a directive required substantial changes led officials to prioritize its transposition. The data from this in-depth qualitative study suggested that different causal factors were important in different clusters of countries, inductively generating the 'worlds of compliance' typology.[52]

Two subsequent quantitative studies of non-transposition rates found weak support for the central claims of the worlds of compliance approach. Patterns of transposition were consistent with the argument in two ways: First, the world of law observance boasts the most consistent performance and the lowest mean and median rate of non-transposition, the world of domestic politics experiences a more variable pattern of transposition and a higher mean rate of non-transposition, and the world of neglect includes the most variable performance with the highest

[48] Börzel, 'Non-compliance in the European Union: Pathology or Statistical Artefact?', 8 *Journal of European Public Policy* (2001) 5, at 814; Mastenbroek, 'EU Compliance: Still a "Black Hole"?', 12 *Journal of European Public Policy* (2005) 6, at 1104; Sedelmeier, *supra* note 34, at 816.

[49] Falkner et al, 'Non-Compliance with EU Directives in the Member States: Opposition through the Backdoor?', 27 *West European Poliitics* (2004) 3, at 467.

[50] Mastenbroek, *supra* note 48 and the literature reviewed there, at 1109–10; Falkner, Hartlapp, and Treib, *supra* note 21 and the literature reviewed there, at 396.

[51] Falkner, Hartlapp, and Treib, *supra* note 21, at 401–3.

[52] Ibid, at 399–400 and 404–5.

mean of non-transposition.[53] Second, world of law states transposed fastest, world of domestic politics states had longer delays, and world of neglect states had the longest delays.[54] Differences in the timing of transposition across countries in different clusters are marginal, however, and results on delays are not statistically significant. These qualifiers are not surprising given that transposition does not vary much in general.

By contrast, the pattern of political party preferences does not have the expected effect in the world of domestic politics and the number of veto players had no impact on transposition performance in any of the country clusters.[55] Another quantitative study based on the original data from the 'worlds of compliance' project found no evidence that effects of variables differed by the cultural context. Instead, this study found that in all worlds of compliance (1) misfit is indeed likely to cause transposition delays, and (2) corporatism contributes to more timely transposition, although neither effect is statistically significant given the small numbers of cases within each sub-group. Other findings from this study include a positive association between a larger degree of discretion within directives and prompt transposition and negative associations between the length of directives and greater decentralization in governments and timeliness. The only variable with effects that varied by world was government efficiency, which had a positive impact only in the world of domestic politics.[56] Disagreement persists concerning whether delays are more likely when states opposed the content of directives at the time of adoption, with one quantitative study finding this effect while another did not.[57] The impact of discretion also remains controversial, as one quantitative study found that more discretion contributed to longer delays in transposition, contrary to the finding mentioned above, but also that discretion was associated with a reduced risk of formal infringement proceedings.[58]

Contradictory findings may be attributed to differences in the samples of directives under consideration, with one study based on the non-representative sample of labour directives from the world of compliance study and another based on a non-representative sample of directives selected for variation in the extent to which states agreed with the contents of directives at the time of adoption. Unfortunately, another quantitative study of timely transposition with the largest sample of all (1590 directives in 15 states from 1986 until 2002), does little to resolve empirical inconsistencies. Testing a laundry list of available propositions, this study demonstrates that timeliness of transposition correlates highly with infringement proceedings: over 47 per cent of Commission referrals to the ECJ between 1992 and

[53] Toshkov, 'In Search of the Worlds of Compliance: Culture and Transposition in the European Union', 14 *Journal of European Public Policy* (2007) 6, at 934.

[54] Thomson, Torenvlied, and Arregui, 'The Paradox of Compliance: Infringements and Delays in Transposing European Union Directives', 37 *British Journal of Political Science* (2007) 4, at 685–709.

[55] Toshkov, *supra* note 53, at 947, 949.

[56] Thomson, 'Same Effects in Different Worlds: The Transposition of EU Directives', 16 *Journal of European Public Policy* (2009) 1, at 13.

[57] Thomson, Torenvlied, and Arregui, *supra* note 54, at 699 and Thomson, *supra* note 56, at 8–9 respectively.

[58] Thomson, Torenvlied, and Arregui, *supra* note 54.

2004 stemmed from a failure to notify transposition measures.[59] Given that a failure to notify is the single easiest transgression that the Commission can identify, this unsurprising discovery contributes little to understandings about compliance. This large-n study also generates its own internal contradictions, with findings that (1) Germany is among the leaders in notification failure, but also has a particularly efficient transposition record among notified measures,[60] (2) Sweden appears more efficient than most in transposing on time, but also has one of the most deviant transposition patterns in terms of notification failure,[61] and most baffling of all (3) national parliamentary involvement, while rarely occurring, contributes to longer transposition delays, but also that a higher share of parliamentary involvement in national transposition does not contribute to increased delays.[62] Meanwhile, federalism and pluralism are associated with longer delays,[63] although no indication is given about how these variables may map onto cross-national variations. For instance, is Germany slow to notify due to its federal structure? But why is it then particularly efficient with respect to notified measures?

Finally, the newest member states' good transposition record has surprised observers who anticipated that post-communist states might lag in implementation once the period of 'conditionality' was over and they could no longer be denied membership for poor performance. Instead, the eight post-communist states that joined in 2004 have consistently outperformed the 'EU 15' of longer-term members since early 2005. Lithuania has nearly continuously boasted the fastest transposition rate among all states since accession, and only the Czech Republic temporarily dipped below the average transposition rate of the EU 15 since 2005. This record is consistent with institutionalist factors: new member states invested in legislative capacity to adopt the massive EU *acquis* as preparation to join, and extensive monitoring during the conditionality phase may have made them more sensitive to the 'shaming' strategies associated with EU law enforcement. Prompt transposition could also be a sign that the 'EU 8' states internalized commitments to EU rules and self-identify as good members who obey the law.[64]

A quantitative study of a random sample of 119 directives in the EU 8 from the late 1990s until 2005 found a number of variations: internal market directives had a better chance of timely transposition than the general population of directives while environmental directives were more likely to experience delays. Political preferences and government capacity—measured in terms of the number of parties in government and their ideological distance from each other—both had an impact on transposition timing, which tended to trump sectoral differences: one-party cabinets transposed environmental directives faster than four-party cabinets transposed internal market directives, and coalition governments that strongly supported integration were more likely to transpose directives on time

[59] König and Luetgert, *supra* note 37, at 163–4.

[60] Ibid, cf discussions at 172 with 189.

[61] Ibid, cf discussions at 172 with 191.

[62] Ibid, cf discussions at 189 with 191. Discussions on 191 alone include contradictory claims about the impact of parliamentary involvement.

[63] Ibid, at 163–94.

[64] Sedelmeier, *supra* note 34, at 812.

than single party cabinets that only moderately favour integration. In terms of preferences, pro-European and right-wing governments were both associated with better transposition performance.[65] This record is most consistent with intergovernmentalist accounts that emphasize government preferences and the costs associated with EU rules, but also more purely institutionalist expectations about veto players. Research on the practical application and enforcement of directives in the EU 8 (discussed below), however, casts serious doubts concerning the significance of this exemplary legislative performance and highlights the limitation of studying only the law on the books.

2. Trends in Infringement Proceedings across all Stages

Data on infringement proceedings, available in the *Annual Reports of the Commission on the Monitoring and Application of Community Law*, provide a more comprehensive view of law on the books compliance than transposition studies and are the focus of a substantial body of scholarship in political science. Tracking the numbers of suspected infringements, formal letters of notice, reasoned opinions, referrals to the ECJ, and proceedings for financial penalties, data on infringement proceedings can serve as indicators of *relative* non-compliance across member states. Comparative studies reveal that complaints about suspected infringements are highest in the five most populous member states, but also that Spain and Greece have a disproportionately high rate of complaints relative to their populations,[66] and that the EU 8 countries have disproportionately low rates of complaints.[67] Neofunctionalism may explain higher rates of complaints in larger states in that the largest markets attract the greatest number of exporters, service providers, entrepreneurs seeking to establish businesses, and workers seeking employment, who may then encounter and contest violations of EU rules. High rates of complaints in Greece and Spain are more puzzling given that this situation does not also characterize Portugal, which would share a recent authoritarian past that may generate distrust of the state, and it does not affect Italy, whose other indicators of non-compliance might suggest that the most non-compliant states may inspire the highest rates of complaints. In the EU 8, there may still be little interest in enforcing EU rules in these countries, or civil society may not yet be effectively mobilized to demand enforcement.

Differences between states are fairly small at the unofficial stage of letters of formal notice, but widen at each of the three subsequent official stages of reasoned opinions, referrals to the ECJ, and ECJ judgments. France and Germany figure prominently in later stages of proceedings, while Portugal and Spain avoid judicial proceedings by settling at the reasoned opinion stage. Cross-national variations are less dramatic with the exclusion of Italy, which is a very exceptional case. Most member states demonstrate a respectable level of compliance, but Belgium, France,

[65] Toshkov, 'Embracing European Law: Compliance with EU Directives in Central and Eastern Europe', 9 *European Union Politics* (2008) 3, at 379–402.

[66] Börzel, *supra* note 48, at 809–10

[67] Sedelmeier, *supra* note 34, at 813–15, 818.

Greece, and particularly Italy show a consistent pattern of non-compliance.[68] Studies focusing on particular sub-groups of states identify distinctive patterns as well. While larger states generally receive more letters of formal notice and reasoned opinions than smaller states, the Nordic states, including European Free Trade Association (EFTA) members, receive far fewer letters of formal notice and reasoned opinions than the EU average, and very few cases from Nordic states end up before the ECJ. The total number of referrals to the ECJ concerning Denmark, Finland, and Sweden from 1995 to 2001 was less than the number referred concerning Italy in a single year.[69] The EU 8 have a similar pattern of early settlement of infringement disputes: while their rate of letters of notice is similar to that of the EU 15, they account for far fewer reasoned opinions and referrals to the ECJ than the EU 15. At these formal stages, Lithuania is the 'top' performer with the fewest infringements of all member states, and six other EU 8 states join Denmark and Cyprus in the 'top' nine. Exceptions include the Czech Republic, whose performance deteriorated in 2005 but improved again in 2006 and 2007, and Poland, whose infringements have been on the rise, especially since 2007.

These aggregate patterns are potentially consistent with multiple theoretical approaches. For larger states, the higher rates of complaints and subsequent infringement proceedings at all stages of the process may simply reflect greater societal demand for the proper application of EU rules in these countries, which increases the chances that implementation burdens rise sufficiently to motivate states to defend suspect practices in the hope of minimizing their burdens. While this interpretation is consistent with neofunctionalism, an alternative intergovernmentalist reading would be that large states are less compliant than smaller states because larger states can get away with non-compliance more easily. Finally, researchers observing the distinctive infringement patterns in the Nordic and EU 8 states have proposed that a tradition of consensual negotiated settlements[70] or greater susceptibility to shaming,[71] respectively, account for early settlements and aversion to referrals to the ECJ.

An important limitation in studies based on infringement proceedings is that published reports on infringements are not a valid indicator of the *absolute* level of non-compliance in the EU because the Commission is not able to monitor compliance systematically and exhaustively, and it may not disclose all cases in which it initiated some type of negotiation concerning compliance. The large body of preliminary rulings, producing approximately half of the ECJ's docket, indicates that non-compliance that escapes formal infringement proceedings occurs regularly. The Commission's goals in enforcing EU law inevitably influence its presentation of data on infringements. It denounced a growing compliance deficit in the 1990s, but statistical analysis of its own data reveal that the level of non-compliance did not increase if the number of legal acts and member states are considered. Infringement proceedings as a percentage of 'violative opportunities' has not increased, and has even decreased if changes in the Commission's enforcement strategy are also taken

[68] Börzel, *supra* note 48, at 812, 819. [69] Sverdrup, *supra* note 33, at 36–8. [70] Ibid.
[71] Sedelmeier, *supra* note 34.

into account.[72] Critics of constructivism respond to this interpretation, however, by observing that the number of opportunities to violate the law should not matter if the internationalization of European norms means that compliance takes on an automatic character over time.[73]

3. *Referrals to the ECJ*

Some scholarship focuses exclusively on the final stages of infringement proceedings, examining disputes that the Commission refers to the ECJ for formal adjudication. Data on ECJ referrals and the resulting judgments are readily available and generate the most comprehensive picture of the interests involved in disputes about compliance with EU law since ECJ judgments are public records and typically include a summary of the major arguments put forward by the contending parties as well as other interested observers. As a result, the reasons a member state contests a particular EU rule are visible, and possible allies and opponents among other states are often evident too. While this accessibility and transparency are useful, the Commission's complete discretion in referring cases to the ECJ introduces a bias within this sample: the Commission is likely to litigate cases that it is confident it can win, whereas it is likely to settle disputes where the law remains more ambiguous. And member states should defend only cases of tremendous importance. A quantitative study of referrals to the ECJ from 1971 to 1993 demonstrates that the ECJ found in favour of the Commission in every single case,[74] suggesting that these two biases were probably at issue most of the time. Meanwhile, the tiny fraction of ECJ referrals relative to letters of notice and reasoned opinions means that the bulk of negotiations concerning compliance takes place at earlier stages of infringement proceedings. Studies of the exceptional disputes that make it all the way to the ECJ uncover a number of patterns, but none conclusively confirm any of the existing theoretical explanations.

The quantitative study of 22 years of ECJ rulings on infringements produces a number of statistically significant results that do not fit within one theoretical approach. States with more efficient bureaucracies and less corruption receive fewer adverse rulings concerning infringements, which is consistent with the management approach to international law. Yet states with greater bargaining power in the Council of Ministers are denounced more often for non-compliance than states with less voting power, which is consistent with intergovernmentalist arguments that more powerful states can more easily choose non-compliance than weaker states. Meanwhile, economically prosperous states commit fewer infractions, which is potentially also consistent with intergovernmentalism in the sense that more prosperous states may more easily succeed in getting their preferred policies, proven effective at the domestic level, adopted at the EU level. The longer a state is a member, the more it infringes EU rules, which may result from more vigorous Commission prosecution of violations that become increasingly 'inexcusable'

72 Börzel, *supra* note 48, at 808, 813, 817.

73 Huelshoff, Sperling, and Hess, 'Is Germany a "Good European"? German Compliance with EU Law', 14 *German Politics* (2005) 3, at 361.

74 Mbaye, *supra* note 39, at 268.

with passing time. Consistent with institutionalist propositions about veto players and federalism, states with high levels of regional autonomy post poorer compliance records than states with more centralized authority structures. Finally, more infringements occur in states where public approval levels for the EU are higher, which is plausibly the result of publics who are dissatisfied with ineffective domestic institutions and look toward 'Europe' for better governance.[75]

An in-depth comparison of ECJ referrals focusing on the relative performance of Germany concludes that constructivist arguments that Germany is a particularly 'good European' lack any empirical foundation. Contrary to the expectations of constructivism, Germany, with its pro-EU identity, has a statistically significant greater number of infringements than the Netherlands, Luxembourg, Denmark, Sweden, and Austria. The German rate of infringement is statistically identical to that of France, which is usually associated with a less cooperative, sovereignty protecting orientation. Denmark in particular is typically evaluated as having a national or at best 'defective' European identity, but has one of the best records of compliance. Meanwhile, only three states often reputed to be laggards—Greece, Italy, and Spain—have significantly more cases brought against them than Germany.[76]

Another study examining general trends in non-compliance with ECJ rulings from 1987 to 2002 found little relationship between instrumental interests and compliance. For instance compliance did not vary according to the extent to which member states benefit from the internal market, measured in terms of their intra-EU exports. The introduction of financial sanctions appeared to have no significant impact on the number of rulings that remained unimplemented throughout the 1990s, although a slight decrease in the number of long-standing cases occurred after the introduction of sanctions.[77] By contrast, a qualitative case study of the British response to the ECJ's ruling on the Working Time Directive suggests that normative interests can lead to compliance even when it involves substantial costs. While the government initially publicly refused to implement the directive, it subsequently began the process of national transposition while it hoped to change unwelcome provisions at the EU level and also delayed completing the transposition process until after upcoming elections were held. Legal defiance never followed loud political defiance because the government ultimately concluded that it could not blatantly and publicly break the law, consistent with the expectations of constructivists.[78]

Another pair of qualitative case studies on compliance with ECJ rulings on infringements shows that the threat of sanctions only induces compliance with the letter of the law when fines are imminent and little domestic resistance to change exists. Meanwhile, violations persist in practice. More complete compliance with the law in practice typically requires that domestic norms and interests be reframed to align with the EU norms at stake, a process that typically only proceeds in the

[75] Ibid, at 274–7. [76] Huelshoff, Sperling, and Hess, *supra* note 73, at 362–4.
[77] Beach, *supra* note 14, at 116, 118–19. [78] Ibid, at 131–4.

aftermath of substantial societal mobilization in support of new norms.[79] These findings are broadly consistent with accounts that emphasize the role of mobilization, albeit with a constructivist emphasis on changes in norms and identity.

B. National Courts and Compliance with EU Law

National courts play a key role in EU legal compliance because they adjudicate far more EU legal claims than the ECJ and are also responsible for referrals to the ECJ and the subsequent application of the ECJ's preliminary rulings. Political science scholarship has focused most of its attention on dynamics related to the reference patterns of national courts and their reception of preliminary rulings. A few scholars have explored national courts' broader pattern of compliance with ECJ case law as they independently resolve conflicts where parties dispute EU provisions. Given that the vast majority of EU legal disputes appear exclusively before national courts, their approach to enforcing EU law independently of references deserves much more scrutiny from lawyers and social scientists.

1. Compliance with Preliminary Rulings

Research on compliance with preliminary rulings and the reference procedure more broadly indicates that national courts are crucial to the decentralized enforcement of EU law, but also suggests that gaps in compliance persist. Interdisciplinary scholarship has traced doctrinal responses to the ECJ's declarations of major principles such as direct effect, supremacy, and liability. It took decades for some national courts to accept these rulings, and multiple constitutional courts justify EU legal supremacy in their own way in order to reassert domestic constitutional norms.[80] Nonetheless, scholars attribute much of the habitual compliance that characterizes the EU legal system, in comparison to international law more generally, to the decentralized enforcement that national courts provide under the auspices of supremacy, direct effect, and references for preliminary rulings.[81] Empirical research demonstrates that national courts that send references typically comply with the preliminary rulings that they receive from the ECJ, but they also evade unwelcome decisions by re-referring issues or reinterpreting the facts of cases to shift outcomes.[82]

Meanwhile, failure to make references in appropriate circumstances obscures judicial sources of non-compliance. The Commission anecdotally reports on cases in which national high courts refrain from making references that are

[79] Panke, 'The European Court of Justice as an Agent', *supra* note 15, at 852–61.

[80] A. Slaughter, A. Stone Sweet, and J. Weiler (eds), *The European Court and the National Courts—Doctrine and Jurisprudence* (1998); Alter, 'The European Court's Political Power', *supra* note 22; Boom, 'The European Union after the Maastricht Decision', 43 *American Journal of Comparative Law* (1995) 2, at 177–226; Conant, *Justice Contained*, *supra* note 26, at 93; Ruggiero, 'The European Court of Justice and the German Constitutional Court', 24 *Studies in Law, Politics, and Society* (2002) 1, at 51–80.

[81] Alter, *Establishing the Supremacy of European Law*, *supra* note 22; Weiler, 'A Quiet Revolution', 26 *Comparative Political Studies* (1994) 4, at 510–34.

[82] Nyikos, *supra* note 23.

theoretically obligatory, and in one unusual incident, charged that Swedish courts systematically sent too few references.[83] The few in-depth inquiries into national referral patterns suggest that failure to refer is an important judicial source of non-compliance. One study of environmental disputes in the UK demonstrated that British judges refrained from sending references when they wanted to shield domestic policy from unwelcome ECJ interference.[84] Surveys and interviews investigating the Danish and Swedish judiciaries indicate that most judges in these countries consider themselves ignorant about EU law, do not think it is legitimate for judges to overturn national law for its incompatibility with EU law, and feel political pressure from superiors to refrain from sending references. Reluctance to refer is particularly likely if a party accuses the state of violations of EU law or if a dispute potentially involves the extension of social rights or changes to sensitive national policies.[85] This research implies that the world of law observance may have some hidden sources of non-compliance lurking below the surface.

2. *Compliance with ECJ Case Law*

Because only a tiny fraction of EU legal disputes involve references for preliminary rulings, compliance with EU law and its interpretations in ECJ case law are ultimately a more meaningful measure of the role of national judicial enforcement. Findings from the few in-depth case studies that consider national judicial behaviour outside the context of references for preliminary rulings uncover substantial sources of non-compliance. A study of all reported UK national court judgments on EU law from 1973 to 1998 found that judges (1) typically apply EU provisions without addressing the status of incompatible national provisions, and (2) had only considered the issue of whether national legislation needed to be overturned in two cases. More specifically, judges were more likely to apply EU law when it extended state powers to control behaviour or reinforced private legal relationships, and they were less likely to apply EU law when it impeded the state's control over immigration, the application of criminal sanctions, or protection of private property rights.[86]

The propensity of national courts in France, Germany, and the UK to interpret EU treaties, regulations, and directives without any explicit reliance on ECJ case law, coupled with the need for more judicial training in EU law, generate wide discrepancies in interpretation rather than consistent compliance with a relatively uniform understanding of the law.[87] For example, courts in France and Germany, including the Conseil d'État as a court of last instance obligated to refer EU law

[83] Conant, *Justice Contained*, *supra* note 26, at 91; Wind, *supra* note 46. The Commission usually refrains from criticizing national courts for their shortcomings in upholding EU law in an effort to avoid political interference with the judiciary and to encourage voluntary judicial cooperation.

[84] Golub, 'The Politics of Judicial Discretion', 19 *West European Poliitics* (1996) 2, at 360–85.

[85] Wind, *supra* note 46.

[86] D. Chalmers, *The Much Ado about Judicial Politics in the United Kingdom* (Harvard Jean Monnet Working Paper No. 1/100, 2000).

[87] Conant, *Justice Contained*, *supra* note 26, at 81–4.

cases, denied EU migrants access to employment in the field of education as they independently interpreted EU law in the years before the ECJ ruled that the public service exception to the free movement of workers must be construed narrowly. The independent national court review here directly contradicted later ECJ rulings that EU nationals could work in the field of education in any member state. German courts continued to rule against EU migrants even after the ECJ had articulated its narrow definition of public service and had specifically ruled that student teaching in Germany must be open to non-nationals.[88] In another field, German courts decided 21 cases on the basis of Association texts with Turkey before the ECJ had ever interpreted or conferred direct effect on any of their provisions. Here, national judges generously set aside national restrictions and directly applied EU provisions to the benefit of Turkish individuals in 16 cases. Yet other courts ruled restrictively in ways that would contradict future ECJ rulings on Turkish Association agreements; once again, courts of last instance would rule restrictively rather than send references to the ECJ for preliminary rulings even though their decisions indicate that the provisions were certainly open to two divergent interpretations.[89]

A study testing a random sample of 475 Spanish court decisions that apply or cite EU law from 1986 until 2000 fails to support any theoretical explanation conclusively, but generates a number of interesting findings about compliance with EU law.[90] For instance, Spanish judges were 11 per cent more likely to comply with ECJ case law when there were reinforcing signals from other national courts, and they were 41 per cent less likely to comply with ECJ decisions when there were contradictory signals from other national courts, indicating that judges will tend to give national case law precedence if it conflicts with ECJ doctrines.[91] Spanish courts were also 15 per cent less likely to comply with ECJ judgments when the government was a party to the case, suggesting that these courts defer to national political concerns to some extent. Moreover, the Spanish Supreme Court and Constitutional Court are 28 per cent less likely to cite the ECJ and 22 per cent less likely to comply with ECJ case law than other Spanish courts,[92] which parallels the less cooperative stance taken by many courts of last instance in other countries as well. Finally, while citation of ECJ case law has historically been low in Spanish courts, it declines further after 15 years of membership,[93] suggesting that legal interpretation across member states can be expected to diverge more and more over time.

[88] Ibid, at 173. [89] Ibid, at 209–10.

[90] Ramos Rameu, *supra* note 24. The author's claims about particular models (neofunctionalist, realist, team, inter-court competition) explaining the most variation are not convincing since each competing model explains a large majority of the variation in decisions. This is mathematically impossible in distinctive and well-specified models, and the author does not explain whether the small percentage differences between the percentage of cases explained by each model are statistically significant.

[91] Ramos Romeu, *supra* note 24, at 412.

[92] Ibid, at 413–15. [93] Ibid, at 409 and 418.

C. Compliance with the 'Law in Action'

Empirical inquiry into the law in action tends to involve more qualitative, 'small-n' case studies given the more labour-intensive data collection demands associated with discovering how laws apply in practice. As a result, much more research to explore this area is necessary to provide a more comprehensive account of the law in action across member states and issue areas. Existing law in action scholarship on compliance with ECJ rulings and EU directives uncovers substantially more variation and evidence of non-compliance than the literature on the law on the books.

1. Compliance with ECJ Rulings

Research grounded in case studies in a number of different policy areas demonstrates that innovative ECJ interpretation does not induce any automatic, broad-based compliance with evolving legal obligations. Member states most commonly comply with the specific terms of a judgment as it relates to the parties to the litigation and subsequently ignore the implications that the judicial interpretation may have for the universe of similarly situated parties. Active legal and political mobilization is usually necessary to override this tendency for 'contained compliance'.[94] For example, ECJ case law that developed the mutual recognition doctrine did not lead to any widespread changes. Instead, parties had to litigate case-by-case to apply the doctrine to 115 different products prior to the passage of the Single European Act. It ultimately took the Commission's advocacy and the broad mobilization of business and civil society groups to promote widespread adoption and compliance with the mutual recognition approach to regulatory harmonization and trade liberalization.[95] Case studies tracing the impact of ECJ rulings that implied the need for significant reforms in the areas of telecommunications, electricity, air transport, public-sector employment, and social benefits involve a similar dynamic, where the implicit requirements of ECJ interpretation remained dormant for long periods until institutional and societal actors mobilized to demand major changes to legislation and practice. Similar to the mutual recognition case, copy-cat litigation before both the ECJ and national courts indicates that member states evaded broad-based compliance with the evolution of EU legal obligations as they were expressed in ECJ rulings.[96]

Research on judicial independence offers indirect inferences about the source of compliance with individual judgments. A study of 293 randomly selected ECJ rulings (including direct actions and preliminary rulings) on the free movement of goods and social provisions supports the proposition that the ECJ gives judgments that avoid non-compliance with its rulings: the probability of the ECJ upholding a contested national rule is only 23 per cent when no states make observations, but increases to 56 per cent when a blocking minority of states makes observations in

[94] Conant, *Justice Contained*, *supra* note 26.

[95] Alter and Meunier, *supra* note 25.

[96] Conant, *Justice Contained*, *supra* note 26, particularly at 210; Conant, 'Europe's No Fly Zone?', in T. Börzel and R. Cichowski (eds), *The State of the European Union* (2003) 6, at 235–54; Conant, 'Contested Boundaries', in J. Migdal (ed), *Boundaries and Belonging* (2004), at 284–317.

support of a national rule, and it increases further to 96 per cent when a simple majority of states makes supportive observations.[97] Another study of all ECJ cases concerning the relationship between trade and environment norms uncovered evidence to support the proposition that the ECJ is a strategic actor that seeks to maintain its legitimacy by avoiding rulings that will be rejected. In this study, the ECJ accommodated political demands when pressures to uphold national measures were high and legal reasons to invalidate measures were weak.[98] These studies suggest that compliance is epiphenomenal of member state interests, consistent with more realist or intergovernmentalist understandings of legal integration. By contrast, another analysis of case law finds that ECJ precedents influence how litigants subsequently premise, structure, and sequence their arguments in legal proceedings, with the result that gradual changes in litigants' positions lead to the incremental acceptance of ECJ rules over time.[99] A further study of preliminary rulings on social provisions indicates that the ECJ declares violations of EU law in a majority of cases against the most powerful member states and becomes even more likely to do so in the event of multiple observations by states.[100] These last two studies remain more compatible with neofunctionalist expectations about legal integration.

2. *Application and Enforcement of Directives*

Scholarship on the application and enforcement of directives tends to paint a more consistently pessimistic assessment of the state of compliance with EU law. An in-depth qualitative case study of the 'street-level' implementation of a single directive concerning safety data sheets uncovered infringements in a majority of inspected facilities in all four member states under consideration: Germany, Netherlands, Spain, and the UK. While all states had transposed the directive late, transposition was nonetheless complete and correct by the time that inquiries into implementation took place, and the language of the law was clear and straightforward. Moreover, none of the states had opposed the directive at the time of its adoption, and none suffered from any serious institutional enforcement deficiencies. Highlighting the lack of issue salience in a world where inspectors have limited time to enforce a multitude of regulations, the study concludes that noncompliance may be the natural state of affairs for non-salient regulatory rules.[101]

In a similar qualitative investigation into the practical implementation of three social policy directives in four new member states, scholars observed that despite a good transposition record,

> The picture changes significantly if we look at the enforcement and application stage. The Czech Republic, Hungary, Slovakia, and Slovenia are all plagued by a multitude of

[97] B. Kilroy, 'Integration through Law' (PhD Dissertation on file at the University of California, Los Angeles) at 405–6, available through UMI, Ann Arbor, Michigan. Order No. AAT 9940492.

[98] Kelemen, 'The Limits of Judicial Power', 34 *Comparative Political Studies* (2001) 6, at 622–50.

[99] McCown, *supra* note 8, at 974–95.

[100] Cichowski, 'Women's Rights, the European Court and Supranational Constitutionalism', 38 *Law & Society Review* (2004) 3, at 489–512.

[101] Versluis, *supra* note 36, at 50–67.

problems that have so far largely prevented the legislation from being realized in practice. The huge gap between the law on the books and the practice on the ground also suggests that the observation of relatively low degrees of adaptation pressure in legal terms needs to be qualified considerably.[102]

For example, many workers voluntarily exceed the limits of the Working Time Directive in order to earn an adequate living, and discriminatory practices toward women and homosexuals, including widespread sexual harassment, render equality in the workplace elusive. Here, institutional deficiencies in labour inspectorates, equal treatment bodies, and the judiciaries play an important role. Of particular importance for legal recourse, lengthy court proceedings and the lack of attention paid to the rulings of other domestic courts impede prompt resolution of claims and result in similar cases being decided differently.[103]

Problems are evident in the area of environmental protection as well. Qualitative research on German and Spanish compliance with EU environmental directives shows that formal compliance is increasingly less of a problem, but that public authorities circumvent or dilute EU rules in their practical application and enforcement. In eight different cases, compliance only improved when domestic actors mobilized to exert internal pressure on public authorities and pushed the Commission to exert external pressures through infringement proceedings.[104] Given the reliance on the domestic mobilization of political pressure and strategic litigation campaigns in national courts, countries where civil society groups have more resources and experience organizing collective action, such as Germany, are in a much better position to encourage compliance than countries where civil society groups remain weak, often due to the lingering legacies of past authoritarian regimes and their closed structures for domestic political participation.[105] Case studies of both southern and post-communist member states conclude that weaknesses in civil society are likely to contribute to practical compliance deficiencies for the foreseeable future.

A study focusing on the efficacy of ECJ rulings in promoting ground-level compliance with EU directives in Germany found that infringement proceedings intended to 'shame', and even the imminent prospect of financial penalties, encouraged only formal, minimalist legal compliance. Meanwhile, the practical application of policies fell far short of the goals articulated in EU rules. By contrast, ECJ rulings could be a useful tool for domestic groups who hope to 'reframe' issues in a way that can shift interests over time. In these cases, ECJ rulings ultimately contributed to full compliance in letter and spirit, but the changes relied on several years of sustained domestic mobilization and the actual transformation of interests and identity among officials.[106] Another study exploring the utility of infringement proceedings against the UK's unwillingness to transpose the Working Time Directive found that the normative costs of

[102] Falkner and Treib, *supra* note 21, at 303. [103] Ibid, at 303–6.
[104] Börzel, 'Why There is No "Southern Problem",' *supra* note 40, at 158 and 160.
[105] Börzel, *supra* note 29, at 146–7.
[106] Panke, 'The European Court of Justice as an Agent', *supra* note 15, at 855–61.

non-compliance—public and blatant defiance of the law—ultimately trumped the normative costs of compliance—adoption of a regulation that defied the government's liberal market philosophy. The context in this case was a direct, highly publicized challenge to a government's legislative stalling, without any consideration of the question of practical application. Given the importance of the rule of law to British political culture that is stressed in this study, one might expect that domestic transposition will result in adequate enforcement, but this issue remains unexamined.[107]

Finally, a qualitative study of compliance with new citizenship norms promoted by both the EU and the Council of Europe in Germany and the Ukraine found another mixed record of compliance. Learning and persuasion influenced elite policymakers in the Ukraine, leading to formal legal compliance with norms concerning dual nationality, but also implementation failure in practice. Meanwhile, interests opposed to change in Germany delayed legal and practical compliance for a long period of time: it was through the mobilization of pressure that coincided with generational change and a subsequent shift in interests that Germany brought its citizenship laws into compliance with the norms of European regional organizations.[108]

4. Conclusion: Variations in Scholarship and Black Holes for Future Research

The discipline of political science, through the lens of international relations, initially approached the subject of EU legal compliance with bewilderment and scepticism. Reports that states complied with an extensive body of international law and obeyed an international court defied the core assumptions of realist international relations theory. As a result, early scholarship focused on explaining the puzzle of states ceding sovereignty and inspired empirical inquiry designed to determine if states or EU institutions were ultimately in control of the evolution of law. Scholars of comparative politics directed attention away from the emphasis on the lack of enforcement mechanisms in the European legal system to a much wider range of factors that influence compliance in domestic settings. Domestically, force is relevant primarily to the criminal justice system, handling a small minority of individuals who are usually at the margins of society. On an international level, analogous 'rogue' states are not permitted entry into the EU, so it is implausible to expect that the EU would ever need coercive enforcement mechanisms. Force is rarely relevant to the broad range of issues considered through the administrative, civil, and constitutional branches of domestic law. If force is necessary in these domains, a state would be facing a severe crisis of legitimacy and high risk of generalized disorder and even popular violence. Theoretical accounts from both the international relations and comparative politics subfields of political science generate a host of

[107] Beach, *supra* note 14, at 129–34. [108] Checkel, *supra* note 12, at 553–88.

instrumental, institutional, and normative explanations for possible variations in EU compliance patterns.

The empirical findings have been as divergent as the theories that animate the research, largely due to the fact that different studies operationalize and measure compliance with distinctive indicators in a variety of issue areas and member states. Quantitative studies have exclusively investigated formal legal compliance with indicators such as transposition rates and infringement proceedings while qualitative studies are much more likely to have explored compliance with the law in action. The literature has quite definitively established that variation in transposition rates has nearly vanished, such that compliance measured in terms of transposition is no longer problematic. Meanwhile, the much smaller set of studies that examine the practical application of the law consistently indicate that non-compliance is an endemic problem, even in wealthier, long-standing member states.

The discrepancy between studies of the law on the books and law in action indicate that much more empirical research is needed to understand dynamics contributing to compliance and non-compliance in the EU. The biggest gaps in research concern the street-level implementation of EU directives and regulations and the application of EU law by national courts. Existing studies represent the tip of an iceberg of possibilities for research in these areas. Empirical inquiry on practical implementation demands labour-intensive field research, while systematic research on national judicial behaviour requires training in both legal interpretation and social scientific methodology. Both require extensive multilingualism for comparisons across different categories of EU member states. Much existing research concentrates on the usual suspects of Germany, Italy, and the United Kingdom, but oddly enough, not France.[109] Small states tend to receive very little attention and get included primarily in large-n quantitative studies, although the Nordic states and a handful of newer post-communist member states have attracted relatively more attention than other smaller states. Survey research akin to the studies of the Swedish and Danish judiciaries and their attitudes toward EU law and references for preliminary rulings could be very fruitfully pursued all over the EU and extended to many other categories of legal professionals, officials, and citizens including private and government lawyers, bureaucrats implementing EU laws, and law students. Given the central role of mobilization in many accounts of the law in action, the activities of organized civil society deserve much greater scholarly attention as well. Studies of legitimacy could be improved with more precise survey instruments than that which is currently available from sources including Eurobarometer and the World Values Survey. Pursuing this survey data, as well as the data required for much of this research agenda, ultimately entails large-scale social scientific empirical inquiries that require substantial funding and large teams of researchers coordinating their work to generate comparable and systematic types of evidence.

[109] Mastenbroek, *supra* note 48, at 1112.

2

The Governance of Compliance

Edoardo Chiti

1. Purpose

Compliance is usually associated with those means of enforcement based upon coercion. In the European Union (EU) legal order, compliance with EU law by the addressees of EU law and policies—both private actors and national public powers—typically refers to means of enforcement, such as administrative control and litigation in the courts, followed by sanctions. These instruments are exemplified by the infringement proceedings and by judicial review through national courts, where doctrines such as direct effect and supremacy apply.

Yet, compliance by the addressees of EU law and policies cannot be confined within the strict boundaries of coercive means of enforcement. Admittedly, compliance increasingly involves steering and governing instruments, which seek to accommodate behaviours of national public powers and private parties with existing EU law and policy targets. Such steering and governing instruments may be very different one from the other. What they have in common, however, is the circumstance of being qualitatively different from coercive means of enforcement. Steering or governing instruments do not identify a number of techniques aimed at ensuring obedience through simple coercion. Rather, they refer to a more complex and articulated set of instruments. Such instruments combine in a variety of different ways traditional techniques based upon coercion and authority, with non-coercive, non-authoritative instruments (such as incentives or non-binding measures). And they often rely not only on public powers, but also on private actors' action.

The title of this chapter points precisely to such steering or governing instruments. It therefore focuses on the variety of steering mechanisms that combine authority with non-coercive elements. The EU is developing these mechanisms with a view to accommodating behaviours of national public powers and private parties with existing EU law and policy targets and to increasing compliance by the addressees of EU law and policies.

In this context, the notion of compliance is used to denote not only an outcome, but also a process—and in particular the whole of ongoing negotiations, political and legal processes, and institutional change that are involved in the execution of EU law and policies and are functionally orientated to give EU law and policies full effectiveness. Somewhat loosely, compliance does not refer to the simple result of obedience, but to the overall process through which obedience is gradually constructed. As for governance, the way in which such term is used in this chapter lies between the two extremes of the political and academic discourse on EU governance. It is not a secret that the concept of governance is an imprecise term used in a variety of ways.[1] At one end of the spectrum, governance is simply defined as every form of ordered rule to achieve policy results by public and/or private actors: a prominent example of such understanding of governance is provided by the Commission White Paper on Governance, where the Commission (in a footnote!) clarifies that the term governance 'means rules, processes and behaviour that affect the way in which powers are exercised at European level, particularly as regards openness, participation, accountability, effectiveness and coherence'.[2] At the opposite end, governance is used to describe a very particular form of steering, in which public and private actors interact in an open way in order to reach common public policy aims; or even to describe those governing mechanisms which do not take recourse to public authority and the sanctions of government.[3] In between these two extremes, the term governance is used in this chapter to denote mechanisms of governing or steering that may involve public bodies as well as private actors, formal or informal instruments (for example, legally binding acts and soft law), assuming that the links between public and private may take a great variety of forms and technical solutions.

This chapter points to the governing and steering instruments that specifically concern the policy phase of administrative implementation. Such clarification is important because governance is a notion normally used to refer to the policy cycle as a whole: from the formulation of a policy—normally, but not necessarily, leading to binding decisions or to legislation—to implementation, both normative and administrative. The main reason for concentrating on the administrative implementation phase of the EU policy cycle is that it is in this phase that compliance becomes directly and immediately relevant.

Four main sets of questions will be tackled.

1. Which steering instruments have emerged and consolidated in the last two decades, in order to manage the legal and political processes underlying the administrative implementation of EU law and policies?
2. Do they represent 'old' or 'new' modes of governance? Admittedly, there has been a strong tendency in European scholarship to welcome the emerging

[1] As argued by C. Harlow, *Accountability in the European Union* (2002), at 178; on the notion of governance see C. Joerges, *Integration through de-legalisation? An irritated heckler* (European Governance Papers, No. N-07-03), at 6 *et seq.*; as well as the recent account provided by O'Mahony and Ottaway, 'Travelling Concepts: EU Governance in the Social Sciences Literature', in B. Kohler-Koch and F. Larat (eds), *European Multi-level Governance* (2009).

[2] Commission White Paper on European Governance of 25 July 2001, COM (2001) 428 final, see in particular at 8.

[3] See, eg, A. Héritier (ed), *Common Goods: Reinventing European and International Governance* (2002).

steering mechanisms as genuinely new modes of governance. Yet, normative reflection has been given prominence over empirical research, and the discussion of how things should go has kept in the background the actual features of legal and institutional reality. To what extent, therefore, do the steering instruments that have been actually developed represent a true change with national and EU traditions? And to what extent do they combine new forms of action with traditional command and control techniques?

3. Does the emerging 'governance of compliance' raise significant problems? Even assuming that the lack of empirical information prevents, for the time being, a thorough assessment of its effectiveness and legitimacy, is it possible to identify certain critical issues underlying the functioning of the emerging governance of compliance?
4. Finally, what are the perspectives of development for such governance of compliance? Does the current state of affairs tell us anything about the future of these steering and governance mechanisms?

The order in which these questions have been presented corresponds to the order that will be followed in the chapter. The next two sections will identify the steering instruments that have emerged and consolidated in the last two decades (Section 2), and will assess their novelty as modes of governance (Section 3). Then, some of the problems raised by the functioning of the emerging governance of compliance will be discussed (Section 4). The final part of the chapter will be devoted to the perspectives of development of the governance of compliance (Section 5).

2. The European Administrative System as a Machine for Compliance Building

The provision of steering or governing instruments in the EU legal order has gradually become the subject of a specific and well-established narrative, developed by European scholarship in the last 15 years.

Such narrative traces the emergence of the governing instruments back to the early 1990s, when EU political institutions increasingly worked out policymaking processes capable of addressing rapidly and appropriately the problems of the socio-economic European space. This led to a series of innovations in the regulatory techniques used by the EU political decision-makers: from harmonization, realized through legally binding measures, to less straightforward political objectives and more flexible instruments, centred upon mutual learning, cross-fertilization, and exchange of best practices. Crucially, these new modes of governance seek to rely on self-regulation, co-regulation, and other techniques of policy formulation different from the traditional modes of governance based on legislative processes. This change in the regulatory techniques used by European political decision-makers implies also an evolution in the implementation techniques. At the implementation level, the so-called new modes of governance rely on non-hierarchical and informal instruments, based upon mutual learning, persuasion, and administrative coordination.

This development is usually illustrated by a number of well known examples. This is the case of the so-called European regulatory agencies, developed by Majone and others in a successful line of research.[4] This mode of governance is centred upon the delegation of tasks to regulatory agencies in policy formulation in specific and clearly defined sectors. Such agencies should be granted the power to take regulatory measures and, in application of such regulatory measures, individual decisions. And they should operate with a degree of independence and within a clear framework (setting out the limits of their activities and powers) established by the legislature. A second popular example is that of the open method of coordination (OMC), based on a combination of guidelines, monitoring, peer review, cooperation, and limited harmonization.[5] Other examples of the new modes of governance include governance by committees (including the Lamfalussy type procedures), governance by administrative networks, and governance by private parties acting as recipients of delegation (such as technical standards).[6]

The narrative goes on by saying that the Commission, in its 2001 White Paper, has completely failed to understand the potentialities of the emerging new modes of governance. In particular, it has failed to understand its own position at the centre of a set of transnational and subnational administrative networks. And it has concentrated on a 'reinvigoration of the Community method', re-stating the Commission's role in European governance as far as the existing functions are concerned: policy initiation, execution, guardianship of the Treaty, and international representation of the EU.[7]

This classic account, developed over the years in the legal and political science literature, has provided several valuable insights on the governance of compliance.

First, it has revealed and enlightened the development, since the early 1990s, of a number of governance instruments not only in the phase of policy formulation, but also in the phase of policy (normative and administrative) implementation. Such instruments combine in a variety of ways traditional techniques based upon coercion and authority with non-coercive, non-authoritative instruments, such as incentives or non-binding measures, and they often rely not only on public powers,

[4] See, eg, G. Majone (ed), *Regulating Europe* (1996); and D. Gerardin, R. Muñoz, N.Petit (eds), *Regulation through Agencies in the EU. A New Paradigm of European Governance* (2005).

[5] See, in particular, Hodson and Maher, 'The Open Method as a New Mode of Governance: The Case of Soft Economic Policy Co-ordination', 39 *Journal of Common Market Studies* (2001) 4, at 719 *et seq*; C. de la Porte and P. Pochet (eds), *Building Social Europe through the Open Method of Co-ordination* (2002); J. Zeitlin and D. Trubek (eds), *Governing Work and Welfare in a New Economy: European and American Experiments* (2003); and P. Craig, *EU Administrative Law* (2006), at 191 *et seq*.

[6] For an overall framework on these forms of governance, see H.C.H. Hofmann and A.H. Türk (eds), *EU Administrative Governance* (2006), and in particular in the same volume Hofmann and Türk, 'An Introduction to EU Administrative Governance', at 1 *et seq*.

[7] For a radical critique to this self-representation of the Commission see Harlow, *supra* note 1, at 181 *et seq*; and Metcalfe, 'Reforming the European Governance: Old Problems or New Principles?', 67 *International Review of Administrative Sciences* (2001), at 415 *et seq*.

but also on private actors. With the development of such mechanisms, compliance with EU law ceases to be in all cases a matter of pure coercion.

Secondly, the account developed in the last two decades has clarified that implementation instruments depend on the regulatory techniques used by the EU political institutions and on the type of measure which has to be implemented. EU measures are not always normative provisions and binding decisions. They increasingly tend to take different characters, and their implementation is strictly connected to such characters. It is one thing is to comply with a detailed, fully accomplished EU regulation. It is quite another thing to comply with an EU measure laying down a general principle and delegating administrative authorities to implement it.

However, the recalled narrative also has several shortcomings.

For example, it tends to over-emphasize the non-coercive and non-authoritative character of these steering instruments, and to assume that they represent new modes of governance, clearly distinct from traditional techniques based upon coercion: a representation which may raise the scepticism of those who believe that complex instruments may combine coercion with non-coercive techniques.

A second shortcoming lies in its strong normative foundation. The account of the emergence of EU governance instruments brings into the foreground functional and political preferences, depicting EU governance in the way it should be instead of as it actually is developed by the European political institutions. Regulatory agencies, for example, may well be an important option for EU administrative governance. But the way in which Majone understands them is far from the legal and institutional reality of current European agencies.[8]

Some room is therefore left for other interpretations of the features of the steering instruments that have been developed in order to manage the legal and political processes underlying the administrative implementation of EU law and policies. It is not a matter of providing an *alternative* story: admittedly, many intuitions and analytical insights of the traditional narrative last over time and provide a strong foundation for further reflection. It is rather a matter of stressing some particular elements and providing a more focused and balanced picture of the governance instruments specifically aimed at ensuring compliance by the addressees of EU law and policies.

The overall picture may be sketched as follows: the governing instruments that the EU has gradually developed with a view to enhancing compliance in the phase of the administrative implementation of EU law and policies are basically administrative instruments, operating within the context of an emerging European administrative system.

The key point, obviously, is not that EU measures need to be implemented also through administrative activities. This has always been true, and national public administrations have been since the very beginning called to implement EU

[8] For a reconstruction of the current features of the agencification process in the EU, see Chiti, 'An Important Part of the EU's Institutional Machinery: Features, Problems and Perspectives of European Agencies', 46 *Common Market Law Review* (2009) 5, at 1395 *et seq.*

legislation. The key point is rather that the effective implementation of EU law by national administrations—and therefore their compliance with EU law—is not only controlled 'externally' by the Commission or by litigants before a court. The effective implementation of EU law by national authorities and private actors is rather driven and structured 'within' a European administrative system.[9] Such a European administrative system obviously aims at carrying out the various public functions exercised by the EU, from the management of the internal market to social regulation and to the emerging core of welfare and security activities. What is relevant for our purposes, however, is that the European administrative system also operates as a set of governance instruments aimed at enhancing compliance by the addressees of EU policies through the facilitation and institutionalization of negotiation, cooperation, and mutual learning among the national public powers and private actors to which EU law and policies are addressed. Compliance is 'internalized' in the European administrative system, which works, among other things, also as a machine for a gradual development of obedience by national public powers and the relevant private actors.

This point may be illustrated by highlighting five main aspects of the European administrative system: (1) its composite character; (2) the central role of its supranational component; (3) the techniques through which national administrations are 'captured' within the European administrative system; (4) the participation of private actors in the European administrative system; (5) the variety of steering modes characterizing the governance instruments.

(1) The European administrative system that the EU is gradually building is not a fully supranational system, centred upon a number of truly supranational, Commission-like administrations. Rather, it is a composite European administrative system, made up of several qualitatively different components. At least three main types of public administrations may be identified: (i) supranational public powers (the Commission), (ii) national public powers, (iii) and mixed or composite public bodies, ie, bodies composed of representatives of the two levels of authorities (the classic example is that of comitology, but European agencies provide a further significant case of composite European administrations). Most importantly, these three components of the European administrative system are in most cases called to participate *jointly* in the administrative implementation of EU law and policies. In the last two decades, purely direct implementation (through the Commission) and purely indirect implementation (through national administrations only) have become quantitatively marginal. And administrative implementation of EU law and policies has become essentially a matter of joint action by national,

[9] The notion of an administrative system has been developed, with reference to the Italian legal order, by S. Cassese, *Il sistema amministrativo italiano* (1983) and recently reaffirmed by the collective work L.Torchia (ed), *Il sistema amministrativo italiano* (1999). Differently from the traditional understandings of administrations and administrative law, the notion of an administrative system emphasizes the policymaking dimension of the administrative action, the dynamic aspects of the functioning of the administrative machine, the interdependence and the thick web of interactions among the various administrative components (structures, activities, officials, etc), as well as the tensions inherent in such interactions.

supranational, and mixed authorities.[10] The most noticeable institutionalization of such a move towards the joint administrative exercise of European public functions is the establishment of administrative networks operating in specific sectors, ranging from price stability to food safety, public health, civil aviation, and so on. The recognition of this character of the European administrative system is crucial because joint administrative execution implies the provision and functioning of joint processes and structures whereby the various positions of the member states' authorities can and should be accommodated and reciprocally adjusted. In this way, compliance by national administrations with EU law is not exclusively left to the initiative of the single relevant national authorities, and subsequently checked through the 'external' controls of the Commission and the competent courts. Rather, compliance by national administrations with EU law is also internalized in the European administrative system, in so far as joint execution allows exchange, adjustments, and accommodation among the national public powers.

(2) Despite the complexity of the European administrative system, its supranational component plays an essential role. The Commission is currently at the centre of the emerging European administrative system.[11] It is directly or indirectly involved in most of the existing sectoral networks. An example of indirect involvement is provided by the networks coordinated by the European agencies, which are in their turn subject to a number of prerogatives of the Commission. As for direct involvement, one may refer to the case of competition law, where no European agency has been set up and the Commission itself is the coordinator of the network by sector. The central role played by the Commission within the European administrative system should not be overlooked. The joint proceedings and structures through which the positions of the national authorities are accommodated and reciprocally adjusted do not operate in a purely transnational fashion. Rather, they are directly or indirectly influenced by the Commission, whose preferences

[10] For a different view, asserting that administrative implementation in the EU legal order is still essentially a matter of direct and indirect execution, see for example Kadelbach, 'European Administrative Law and the Law of a Europeanised Administration', in C. Joerges and R. Dehousse (eds), *Good Governance in Europe's Integrated Market* (2002), at 167 *et seq*; Ziller, 'Introduction: les concepts d'administration directe, d'administration indirecte et de co-administration et les fondements du droit administrative européen', in J.-B. Auby and J. Dutheil de la Rochère (eds), *Droit Administratif Européen* (2007), at 235 *et seq*.

[11] The peculiar position of the Commission has been legally theorized by the Commission itself, which has on several occasions stated the principle of 'the unity and integrity of the executive function'. The Commission has formulated such a notion in the terms of a legal principle. In its 2002 communication on The Operating Framework for the European Regulatory Agencies (COM (2002) 718 final), the Commission linked the functional and normative foundations of the Community legal order to the unity and integrity of the executive function. Thus 'the legitimacy, effectiveness and credibility of the Community depend on preserving, even reinforcing the unity and integrity of the Community executive function and ensuring that it continues to be vested in the head of the Commission, if the latter is to have the required responsibility vis-à-vis Europe's citizens, the Member States and the other institutions'. This statement was reiterated in the 2005 proposal for a draft inter-institutional Agreement concerning regulatory agencies (COM (2005) 59 final). For a convincing critique of such principle see Everson, 'Agencies: the "dark hour" of the executive?', in H.C.H. Hofmann and A.H. Türk (eds), *Legal Challenges in EU Administrative Law. Towards an Integrated Administration* (2009), at 116 *et seq*, at 118 *et seq*.

and orientations contribute to shaping the processes of exchange, adjustments, and accommodation among the national public powers underlying the joint execution of EU law.

(3) The joint proceedings and structures through which the positions of the national authorities are accommodated and adjusted may take many different forms. National administrations are actually 'captured' within the European administrative system through a huge variety of institutional arrangements. Beneath the surface of differentiation, however, three main institutional arrangements can be identified: first, the setting up of mixed or composite authorities, aimed at expressing both the voice of national authorities and the voice of the Commission (and sometimes also that of other EU institutions); secondly, the provision of administrative proceedings through which the interaction and integration among the various competent bodies (national, mixed, and supranational) is made possible; thirdly, the *mise en place* of non-formalized and non-binding measures of 'administrative integration'. These arrangements are the deep channels through which the European administrative system is actually capable of structuring and managing negotiation, cooperation, and mutual learning among the national public powers, and of operating as a machine for the gradual development of obedience by the latter.

As for mixed bodies, a clear example is provided by the European agencies, which are designed as bodies aimed at establishing and managing a plurality of cooperative relationships involving the Commission and member states' administrations. Such relationships take place within the context of the main internal collegiate bodies of European agencies. In particular, European agencies are governed by a management board responsible for ensuring that the agency performs the tasks set out in the establishing regulation and is usually composed of one representative for each member state and one or two representatives of the Commission. In addition, executive boards, where envisaged, are made up of a limited number of members of the management board and one representative of the Commission.[12]

[12] See, eg, Art 13 of Council Regulation 168/2007 of 15 February 2007 establishing a European Union Agency for Fundamental Rights, OJ 2007 L 53/1. The situation is slightly different as far as scientific collegiate bodies are concerned. The internal organization of certain European agencies also provides one or more scientific collegiate bodies, instrumental to allowing discussion among experts on specific technical matters: this is the case, for example, of the European Centre for Disease Prevention and Control, the European Environment Agency, and the European Monitoring Centre for Drugs and Drug Addiction (see, respectively, Art 18 of Regulation 851/2004 of the European Parliament and of the Council of 21 April 2004 establishing a European Centre for Disease Prevention and Control, OJ 2004 L 142/1; Art 10 of Council Regulation 1210/90 of 7 May 1990 on the Establishment of the European Environment Agency and the European Environment Information and Observation Network, OJ 1990 L 120/1; and Art 13 of Regulation 1920/2006 of the European Parliament and of the Council of 12 December 2006, on the European Monitoring Centre for Drugs and Drug Addiction, OJ 2006 L 376/1). Analogously to the management board, such bodies aim at structuring cooperation among experts from all member states. The cooperation, however, cannot be interpreted in terms of composition of national interests. Due to the technical nature of the matters at stake, cooperation has to respond to the criteria of the best knowledge and scientific excellence in the field. This explains why the scientific internal bodies of European agencies are not always composed of one member nominated by each of the 27 EU member states.

The second technique of administrative integration, which reflects the traditional experience of national administrative law, is based on the proceduralization of the function.[13] In this case, European administrative proceedings are established by the EU legislator. Such proceedings are composite proceedings, both in structural terms (as they involve national, supranational, and mixed authorities) and in regulatory terms (as their single steps may be regulated by different sources, from EU law to national law). This approach is adopted, for example, in the case of the European common systems for pharmaceutical products, for the Community trade marks, and for plant variety, where a large number of administrative proceedings are envisaged.

The third technique of administrative integration has a different structure. In this case, the effect of administrative integration is not pursued through the provision of highly formalized and structured patterns, such as composite administrative proceedings. Rather, the effect of administrative integration is achieved through non-formalized and even non-binding measures. More precisely, a specific coordination and planning function is conferred on the coordinator of the European network. In order to perform such a function, non-binding, soft law instruments are provided, aimed at achieving in a non-coercive way a stabilization of the conduct of the various competent bodies and at achieving expected standards of behaviour.[14] This is what happens in the administrative networks responsible for the production and dissemination of high-quality information in certain fields of EU action, where stabilization of administrative behaviours is pursued essentially through the instrument of the work programme adopted by the relevant European agency.

(4) The composite proceedings and structures through which joint administrative execution of EU law and policies takes place, are not a matter for public authorities only. Rather, they also involve private actors, from national and transnational firms to sectoral interest groups, non-profit bodies, and ordinary citizens and individuals.

Private actors participate in the implementation of EU law in several different ways.

An example is provided by the European Food Safety Authority Scientific Committee, composed of six 'independent scientific experts' appointed by the Management Board, acting upon a proposal from the Executive Director, on the basis of an open application procedure (see Art 28 of Regulation 178/2002 of the European Parliament and of the Council of 28 January 2002, laying down the general principles and requirements of food law, establishing the European Food Safety Authority and laying down procedures in matters of food safety, OJ 2002 L 31/1).

[13] On the notion of composite proceedings see, in particular, Cassese, 'European Administrative Proceedings' and della Cananea, 'The European Union's Mixed Administrative Proceedings' both in F. Bignami and S. Cassese (eds), 'The Administrative Law of the European Union', 68 *Law and Contemporary Problems*, (2004) 1, respectively at 21 *et seq* and at 197 *et seq*.

[14] From the perspective of administrative science, the point is further developed in Chiti, 'On European Agencies', in E.O. Eriksen, C. Joerges and J. Neyer (eds), *European Governance, Deliberation and the Quest for Democratisation* (Arena Report No. 2, 2003), at 275 *et seq*; see also Metcalfe, 'Etablissement de liens entre les différents niveaux de gouvernance: intégration européenne et mondialisation', 66 *Revue internationale de sciences administratives* (2000), at 139 *et seq*.

First, private actors may take part in the various decision-making processes encompassing the implementation phase. In this case, European administrative proceedings are based on the participation not only of (national, supranational, and mixed) public bodies, but also of private subjects, through procedural guarantees such as consultation, good administration institutes, and the like. It should also be noted that procedural guarantees may have different purposes, ranging from defence to collaboration with public powers, according to their features and the context in which they are envisaged.[15]

A second mode of involvement of private actors in the implementation phase is organizational rather than procedural. In this case, private actors do not participate in administrative proceedings. Rather, they take part, through their representatives, in collegiate offices that are internal offices of (national or European) public bodies provided with legal personality and normally granted advisory powers. The internal organization of the European Network and Information Security Agency, for example, includes a 'Permanent Stakeholders' Group' composed of experts representing the relevant stakeholders, such as the information and communication technologies industry, consumer groups, and academic experts in network and information security, and these experts are responsible for advising the Executive Director in the performance of his duties, in drawing up a proposal for the Agency's work programme, as well as ensuring communication with stakeholders on all issues related to the work programme.[16]

A further hypothesis is that of European public bodies making recourse to private bodies for the exercise of specific tasks and functions. This is the case, for example, for standardization, where technical standards are adopted by bodies such as Cen and Cenelec on the basis of a mandate of the Commission.[17]

Admittedly, the involvement of private actors is very different in the three hypotheses. In all cases, however, private actors are brought into the making of administrative action. This does not exclude litigation before courts after the implementing measures have been adopted. But it certainly triggers processes of identification for private interests and exchange of reasons between private actors and public authorities, whose overall effect may be the build-up of consent and compliance by private actors to which EU law and policies are addressed.

(5) The governance instruments concerning the policy phase of administrative execution have different steering modes.

[15] In the Italian literature, the variety of functions that may be carried out by procedural guarantees has been explored by Sabino Cassese; see, eg, his pioneering essay 'Il privato e il procedimento amministrativo. Una analisi della legislazione e della giurisprudenza', *Riv it sc giur* (1971), at 25 *et seq.*; for an attempt to develop this perspective taking into account the recent developments of national and European administrative law, see Chiti, 'La dimensione funzionale del procedimento', in M. Marco et al, *Le amministrazioni pubbliche tra conservazione e riforme* (2008), at 211 *et seq.*

[16] See Art 8 of Regulation 460/2004 of the European Parliament and of the Council of 10 March 2004, establishing the European Network and Information Security Agency, OJ 2004 L 077.

[17] On standardization as a specific form of administrative integration, see Chiti, 'La normalizzazione', in S. Cassese (ed), *Trattato di diritto amministrativo. Diritto amministrativo speciale vol. IV* (2003, 2nd edn), at 4003 *et seq*, where the distinguishing features of the European common administrative system responsible for standardization are analytically reconstructed.

At one end of the spectrum, we find mainly hierarchical modes of steering, based on a clear division of labour, relationships of reciprocal auxiliarity (in the sense that the various competent bodies are, in turns, the principal and the auxiliary subject of the proceedings), and a role of prominence conferred on a European body in case of conflict between national administrations. An example is provided by Council Regulation No. 1/2003, concerning the implementation of Treaty rules on competition, where the Commission's monopoly in the enforcement process has been substituted by a mechanism of joint execution. This mechanism is managed by a common system resulting from the interconnection of the national competition authorities and the Commission and coordinated by the latter, which is placed in a position of functional prominence over the other components of the 'network'.[18]

At the opposite end, we find mainly horizontal modes of steering, centred upon learning, persuasion, non-manipulative use of arguments, and the search for a reasoned consensus. The most obvious example is provided by the networks responsible for the production and dissemination of high-quality information in certain specific sectors, such as environmental information, vocational training, life and work conditions, and drugs and drug addiction, where the implementation of EU law ultimately depends on a host of legally non-formalized interpretative processes.

In between the two ends of the spectrum, we find a great variety of combinations of hierarchical and horizontal steering modes, characterized by bargaining and negotiation. An example is provided by competition among public powers and regulatory regimes. This happens in the decentralized procedure of authorization of pharmaceutical products, currently regulated by Directives 2001/82 and 2001/83, on the Community codes relating to veterinary medicinal products and to medicinal products for human use.[19] In these hypotheses, regulatees may exploit the opportunities resulting from multiple regulators and play various types of strategic games, ranging from the choice of the best national administration to establishing 'alliances' with some authorities to the detriment of other regulators and

[18] For a short account of the mechanisms of administrative integration in the field of competition, see Chiti, 'Les "systèmes communs" européens de pouvoirs publics indépendants', in P. Pavlopoulos and S. Flogaitis (eds), *Governance multiniveau et réforme administrative au XXIème siècle* (2008), at 145 *et seq*. The general discussion on the modernization of EC antitrust law has been too wide to be usefully recalled here; among the contributions more directly concerned with the organizational aspects of the new regulation, see Pera and Falce, 'The Modernization of EC Competition Law and the Role of National Competition Authorities—Revolution or Evolution', 8 *Il diritto dell'Unione europea* (2003) 2/3, at 433 *et seq*; P. Fattori and M. Todino, *La disciplina della concorrenza in Italia* (2004), at 323 *et seq*; Türk, 'Modernization of EC Antitrust Enforcement', in Hofmann and Türk (eds), *supra* note 6, at 215 *et seq*.

[19] Directive 2001/82 of the European Parliament and of the Council of 6 November 2001 on the Community code relating to veterinary medicinal products, OJ 2001 L 311/1, and Directive 2001/83/EC of the European Parliament and of the Council of 6 November 2001 on the Community code relating to medicinal products for human use, OJ 2001 L 311/67. The decentralized procedure of authorization of pharmaceutical products, which applies to the majority of commercial pharmaceutical products, leaves the regulatees the possibility to choose the national regulator that they may consider as the most favourable with respect to their interest and expectations. National laws, therefore, compete within the decentralized procedure.

other regulatees, without excluding even a preference for the less efficient national administration.[20]

Crucially, the various steering modes normally combine one with the other, giving place to complex mixtures. Thus, governance mechanisms are normally based on a variable combination of hierarchy, negotiation, and persuasion. An example is provided by certain procedural arrangements established by various EU sectoral regimes, such as the 'notice and comment' type procedure imposed on national independent authorities in the field of telecommunications. In this case, the steering instruments imply a mix of negotiation and persuasion between regulatees and regulators as well as among regulators (national and European) and among the regulatees (who are competitors in a specific market), within the context of a formalized structure (the administrative proceedings).

3. The European Administrative System between Institutional Novelties and Old Techniques

In the previous pages, we have tried to sketch an overall picture of the governance instruments that the EU has gradually developed with a view to enhancing compliance in the phase of the administrative implementation of EU law and policies. Admittedly, the picture lacks many details and should be further elaborated in several regards. Its general outline, however, is clear enough. The emerging governance of compliance is essentially a matter of administrative law. More precisely, the European administrative system operates as a set of steering instruments aimed at enhancing compliance by the addressees of EU policies through the institutionalization of negotiation, cooperation, and mutual learning among the national public powers and private actors to which EU law and policies are addressed.

Following the programme indicated at the beginning of this chapter, we can now ask whether such governance of compliance, developed within the context of the emerging European administrative system, represents a new type of governance or whether it rather combines new forms of action with traditional command and control techniques.

The answer should be, in this author's opinion, nuanced. Despite the mainstream interpretations, often asserting the original features of the 'new modes of governance', the European administrative system is based on a mix of institutional novelties and old techniques. When compared both with the national experience and with the practice of other international regulatory systems, it reveals its hybrid, partly new and partly derivative, nature.

The European governance of compliance presents several similarities and some differences with national experiences.

[20] The 'games with the rules' connected with the multiplication of the regulators and with the competition among regulatory regimes are discussed by Cassese, 'Dalle regole del gioco al gioco con le regole', 2 *Mercato concorrenza regole* (2002), at 275 *et seq*; see also M. Gnes, *La scelta del diritto. Concorrenza tra ordinamenti, arbitraggi, diritto comune europeo* (2004).

Administrative networks, composite proceedings, procedural guarantees, and modes of governance combining hierarchy, negotiation, and persuasion are not at all a peculiarity of the European administrative system. For example, many national legal orders, such as the German legal order, are traditionally based on cooperative federalism, that is on a variety of cooperative relationships among different levels of public agencies, sometimes formalized in collegiate bodies where different authorities are represented. Procedural guarantees are an increasingly important phenomenon in all member states' administrative laws. And national administrative laws have gradually attenuated, over the second half of the 20th century, their purely hierarchical dimension and the special prerogatives over private actors, to become more complex machines, based also on non-coercive modes of governance.

What is peculiar to the European administrative system is the complication of the relationships among the various actors. National administrative laws are traditionally developed around two poles, that of public powers and that of private parties, subject to different laws and governed by two different and, at times, conflicting rationales. The European administrative system, instead, is based on a more complex web of relationships: EU law is addressed not only to private subjects, but also to national administrations; and both national administrations and private actors are called to participate, with different modes of action, in the implementation of EU law. This opens the way to a genuinely new space for interactions among the various subjects of the administrative system. An example is provided by the triangular relations characteristic of several regulatory regimes, where private regulatees, national regulators, and European regulators interact with one another, playing a great variety of games.[21] It is at this level, ie at the level of the many possible interactions among the various actors of the European administrative system, that we find something really peculiar with respect to the national experiences. Compliance is 'internalized' in the European administrative system through a variety of channels that are quantitatively and qualitatively more complex than those on which national administrative systems rely.

The hybrid nature of the European administrative system, based on a mix of institutional novelties and old techniques, results also from a comparison with the practice of other international or global regulatory systems.

The latter are increasingly establishing their own sectoral administrative systems. This development is taking place in tight connection with the process of significant reinforcement of the powers exercised by international regimes. While traditionally constructed in order to simply coordinate member states' activities or as non-binding regulatory powers, the powers granted to international bodies have become subject to a remarkable change: they tend in practice to go well beyond mere coordination, as exemplified by the case of the World Heritage system,[22] and

[21] The clearest representation of this situation is provided by Cassese, 'L'arena pubblica. Nuovi paradigmi per lo Stato', 3 *Rivista trimestrale di diritto pubblico* (2001), at 601 *et seq*.

[22] The World Heritage Convention is often defined, on the basis of the text of the Convention, as 'a system of international cooperation and assistance designed to support States Parties in their efforts to conserve and identify the world heritage', essentially through the management of a World

even to gain a truly binding regulatory character, as for example in the case of the Codex Alimentarius Commission's standards.[23]

The emerging administrative systems of the relevant international regulatory regimes share with the European administrative system at least two features.

First, analogously to the European administrative system, they are designed as mechanisms for administrative integration. As has been observed by several global administrative law studies,[24] global and national administrations have not developed as two distinct and separate sets of bodies. Rather, they may be seen as two interlinked 'levels', communicating one with the other in at least two main ways: through a thick web of mixed collegiate bodies, established at the global level but composed of national representatives; and through more complex 'common systems' composed of national, mixed, and global administrative bodies. An example of mixed collegiate bodies is provided by the World Trade Organization (WTO) committees. These are plenary transgovernmental collegiate bodies, provided with different tasks: tasks of internal administration (this is the case of the Budget, Finance and Administration Committee); tasks of study and coordination with other international bodies (as with the Committee on Trade and Environment); and tasks of implementation and supervision of the agreements stipulated within the WTO framework (the committees operating in the context of the multilateral agreements on trade in goods).[25] An example of more complex 'common systems' is that of the network responsible for the implementation of the International Plant

Heritage List and the allotment of international assistance, financed by the World Heritage Fund (Art 7 of the Convention Concerning the Protection of the World Cultural and Natural Heritage). The Operational Guidelines adopted in the nineties and their subsequent revision and application, however, show that inscription of a property on the List of World Heritage in Danger may take place without the request of the relevant state party and on the basis of the initiative taken by another state or by a private group, and even against the express wishes of the relevant state party; and it may be accompanied by a number of suggested measures to be adopted by domestic authorities. Thus, inscription of a property on the list is a measure directed to protect a common good against the wish of the state in which the property is located: an evolution which turns the World Heritage Convention from a case of international coordination to a system aimed at taking binding, unfavourable measures against a state and at ensuring member states' compliance with the World Heritage regime. On this evolution see in particular S. Battini, *Amministrazioni nazionali e controversie globali* (2007), at 95 *et seq*.

[23] The Codex Alimentarius Commission (CAC)'s standards are formally non-binding standards. However, they have gradually gained a quasi-mandatory effect via the interpretation of the SPS Agreement (the WTO Agreement on the Application of Sanitary and Phytosanitary Measures) by the WTO Appellate Body, that has made member states' discretion to deviate from international standards subject to very strict limitation. For an account of this evolution, see Pereira, 'Why Would International Administrative Activity Be Any Less Legitimate?—A Study of the Codex Alimentarius Commission', 9 *German Law Journal* (2008) 11, at 1693 *et seq*, at 1703 *et seq*; Bevilacqua, 'Il principio di trasparenza come strumento di accountability nella Codex Alimentarius Commission', 3 *Rivista trimestrale di diritto pubblico* (2007), at 651 *et seq*, at 657. In general terms, Cassese, 'Global Standards for National Administrative Procedure', 68 *Law & Contemporary Problems* (2005), at 109 *et seq*, at 117–18.

[24] See, in particular, Cassese, 'Il diritto amministrativo globale: una introduzione', in S. Cassese, *Oltre lo Stato* (2006), at 38 *et seq*, at 51 *et seq*, and Kingsbury, Krisch, and Stewart, 'The Emergence of Global Administrative Law', 68 *Law & Contemporary Problems* (2005), at 15 *et seq*, at 20 *et seq*.

[25] A classification of global committees is provided by H.G. Schermers and N.M. Blokker, *International Institutional Law* (3rd edn, 2004), at 293 *et seq*; see also Savino, 'The Role of Transnational

Protection Convention, which is composed of a Commission on Phytosanitary Measures, several national offices, and a number of multinational bodies established on the initiative of member states themselves. In addition to this, there is a clear tendency in the global legal space toward interconnection among various global administrations by sector. This is the case, for example, for the so-called NATO-EU Ad Hoc Working Groups, aimed at discussing security issues, modalities for EU access to NATO facilities, and the operating capability of both organizations.[26]

Secondly, the administrative systems of the relevant international regulatory regimes are similar to the European administrative system also in so far as the involvement of private actors is concerned. Involvement of private actors in the exercise of global administrative functions is a general tendency in the global administrative space.[27] Quite often, private actors participate in the functioning of a global public body through the exercise of certain procedural guarantees in the relevant administrative proceedings, as well as through formal representation in collegiate offices of certain international bodies. Modalities of participation obviously vary from case to case. Yet the role of private actors is often limited to the exercise of non-binding advisory powers or to that of simple observers. For example, representatives of non-governmental organizations may attend the meetings of the General Assembly of the International Civil Defence Organization on the basis of an invitation of the latter and without the right of vote. Yet this is not the only way to guarantee involvement of private actors in the exercise of global administrative functions. A common situation is that of global bodies having a private, not public, nature, but subject to a strong public influence. An example is provided by the World Anti-Doping Agency (WADA): a private body in which a number of public bodies participate and that is made subject to public law rules and principles, such as due process.[28] A different hypothesis is that of global public bodies having recourse to private bodies for the exercise of specific tasks and functions. This type of relationship can be highly complex. One example is provided by the relations among global regulators in the financial sector, such as the Basel Committee on Banking Supervision (BCBS), the International Organization of Securities Commissioners (IOSCO), the International Association of Insurance Supervisors (IAIS), and the International Federation of Accountants (IFAC), an international organization composed of private entities that establishes educational, ethical, and professional standards for auditors. The relations between these two groups of bodies involve a Public Interest Oversight Board (PIOB), a non-profit

Committees in the European and Global Orders', 6 *Global Jurist Advances* (2006) 3, art five, available at <http://www.bepress.com/gj/advances/vol6/iss3/art5> last accessed 19 October 2011.

[26] See E. Chiti, *The European Security and Defense Administration Within the Context of the Global Legal Space* (New York University School of Law, Jean Monnet Working Paper, No. 7, 2007).

[27] On such general tendency, often recognized as a distinguishing feature of the global administrative space, see for example Kingsbury, Krisch, and Stewart, *supra* note 24, at 22–3.

[28] In the abundant literature on WADA, see A. Van Varenbergh, *Regulatory Features and Administrative Law Dimensions of the Olympic Movement's Anti-Doping Regime* (International Law and Justice, Global Administrative Law Series Working Paper 2005/11); for a general framework of the subject-matter, see the contributions collected in L. Allison (eds), *The Global Politics of Sport. The Role of Global Institutions in Sport* (2005).

Spanish foundation, comprising eight members who are nominated by the BCBS, the IOSCO, the IAIS, the Financial Stability Forum, and the World Bank, that is responsible for the oversight of all of the IFAC's 'public interest activity committees' which establish standards.[29]

Admittedly, the emerging overall design of the administrative systems of the relevant international regulatory regimes responds to a compliance rationale that is not really different from that underlying the European administrative system. The double movement that has been highlighted—of 'vertical' administrative integration in the global legal space, and of inclusion of private actors in the exercise of administrative functions—has a functional explanation. It allows at the same time the reinforcement of global public powers, the safeguard of member states' prerogatives, and acceptability by the private sector. International or global composite administrative systems inform and structure dialogue among the top institutions of the relevant regulatory regimes and domestic administrations, as well as, although to a more limited extent, with private actors. Compliance is internalized and gradually constructed through participation and co-responsibility. Not differently from the practice of the European administrative system, the emerging global administrative systems tend to work as machines for the gradual development of obedience by national public powers and the relevant private actors.

These significant similarities between the European and the global experience, however, should not hide the equally important differences. The European governance of compliance, in particular, presents certain remarkable specificities, the most important of which is the existence and relevance, in the European administrative system, of a supranational component. Actually, the emerging global administrative systems do not include a supranational component functionally equivalent to the EU Commission. International secretaries enjoy a certain degree of autonomy from the member states, but this is not yet real independence vis-à-vis domestic authorities. Moreover, and in spite of all the fragilities of European constitutionalism, the European administrative system is provided with a constitutional anchorage that is missing in global administrations. Global regulatory regimes are sub-governments by sector, aimed at pursuing specific objectives outside of an institutional relationship with a higher global institution having sovereignty features. The European administrative system, instead, is made dependent upon a fragmented but nevertheless existing executive power[30] composed of an intergovernmental institution (the Council) and, where envisaged by the Treaty

[29] For an analysis of such architecture, see Loft, Humphrey, and Turley, 'In Pursuit of Global Regulation: Changing Governance and Accountability Structures at the International Federation of Accountants (IFAC)', 19(3):24 *Accounting, Auditing & Accountability Journal* (2006) at 428 *et seq.*; and Rotolo, 'La regolazione globale del settore contabile: International Accounting Standards Board (IASB) e International Auditing and Assurance Standards Board (IAASB)', in S. Battini (eds), 'La regolazione globale dei mercati finanziari', 4 *Rivista trimestrale di diritto pubblico* (2007), at 241 *et seq*, at 258 *et seq.*

[30] On the features of the European executive power see, in particular, the recent and overall reconstructions by Dann, 'The Political Institutions', in A. von Bogdandy and J. Bast (eds), *Principles of European Constitutional Law* (2006) and D. Curtin, *Executive Power of the European Union. Law, Practices, and the Living Constitution* (2009).

or by the Council itself, a supranational institution (the Commission), as well as of the member states, to which the implementation of EU law and policies is in principle reserved.

4. A Problematic 'Gravitational Field'

The establishment of a European administrative system is often considered as a positive development. There is little discussion on the need to set up a European composite administrative system, relying on a multiplicity of qualitatively different administrations, including a supranational authority, and on a variety of techniques of administrative integration. Its functional and normative features are often presented in a rationalized way, aimed at highlighting the potentialities of the emerging European administrative system. And it is a shared opinion that member states' administrations tend at the same time to benefit from and to respond positively to their aggregation in the sectoral networks composing the European administrative system.

And yet, it should be recognized that no sufficient data are currently available to allow a sound assessment of the effectiveness and legitimacy of the European administrative system as a machine for compliance. The real capacity of the European administrative system to develop obedience gradually by national public powers and the relevant private actors is an almost unexplored field of research. We still lack a consistent set of thorough empirical analyses by sector, conducted through the instruments of disciplines such as political science, administrative science and law, and economics. The functioning of the various elements of the European administrative system remains uncertain in many regards. And it is not even clear on the basis of which parameters compliance by the addressees of EU law and policies may be measured.

While it is therefore advisable to defer a discussion on the effectiveness and legitimacy of the emerging governance of compliance, it may be nevertheless useful to point to certain issues underlying its functioning. It is not a matter of providing a full account of the functional and normative problems raised by the European administrative system, which goes well beyond the scope of this contribution. It is rather a matter of focusing on certain critical issues capable of exemplifying the ambiguity and tensions of the European administrative system.

To this end, three critical issues, in particular, may be recalled.

The first is that of the effective capacity of national administrations to adapt to the new institutional context. The possibility for the European administrative system to operate as a compliance machine largely depends on the capacity of the national administrations to react positively to their aggregation in the European administrative system, that is to reorganize themselves in such a way as to participate effectively in the processes of negotiation, cooperation, and mutual learning that are triggered within the European administrative system. Yet, such capacity cannot be taken for granted.

On the one hand, certain encouraging elements can be highlighted. The most obvious is the effort of national administrations to modify their structures according to the European functional needs. For example, national offices have often been internally restructured and equipped in order to respond to the new European challenges: a typical example is the setting up of offices internal to the single national administrations specialized in the management of 'European affairs'. Moreover, several new administrations, usually characterized by a high degree of expertise and technical specialization, have been set up. Among the various examples, one may refer to the case of the Italian administrative system, which has been the subject of a broad research project[31] and where various agencies have been established in order to respond to the functional needs of the European sectoral networks: see, for instance, the *Agenzia per la protezione dell'ambiente e per i servizi tecnici*, set up in 1994 and reformed in 1999 and 2008, and the *Agenzia italiana del farmaco*, the purpose of which is to act in a coherent manner with the wider European administration for pharmaceutical products.[32]

On the other hand, other elements suggest that adaptation by national administrations to the new institutional context may be a problematic process. As for efforts on the part of national administrations to modify their structures according to European functional needs, for example, the institutional adjustment of domestic bodies is not always appropriate. An example is provided by the *Agenzia italiana del farmaco*, previously cited: this agency certainly responds to the need on the part of the European administration for pharmaceutical products to have a clearly identifiable and specialized focal point at the national level; but this focal point at the national level is ambiguously designed, since the Italian agency is exposed to the risk of capture by the regulatees, which are in this sector particularly aggressive.[33] In other cases, adaptation by national administrations to the new institutional context is less proven than it is usually assumed. An example is that of the effects of competition among member states' administrations. As has been previously noted, the conduct and performance of national administrations may on certain occasions be compared by regulatees. In those sectors in which competition among regulatory regimes is provided, regulatees may exploit the opportunities resulting

[31] See L. Torchia (eds), *Il sistema amministrativo italiano* (2009), and in particular the chapter by Chiti, 'La dimensione europea e globale', at 395 *et seq.*

[32] In addition to this, and on a much less verifiable and visible level, national administrations are often said to be generally open to the process of mutual learning that should be triggered within the European administrative system. In particular, it is argued that the functioning of the European sectoral networks determines a gradual homogenization of administrative practices among the (national, mixed, and European) bodies composing the various sectoral networks. The content of such homogenization cannot be precisely defined. Admittedly, homogenization varies considerably from case to case and it is excessively complex to measure the influence of the network structure and functioning on national administrative behaviours. Yet, national administrations are said to be generally open to the sharing of information, comparing among national administrative practices and possible convergence on common options that are inherent in the participation to mixed bodies and procedures.

[33] On the one side, the *Agenzia italiana del farmaco* is provided with powers previously exercised by the health ministry. On the other hand, it is not granted genuine independence from the executive, being subject to the direction of the health ministry and to the control of the ministry for economic and financial affairs.

from multiple regulators and play various types of strategic games.[34] Such games are usually presented as a physiological phenomenon, aimed at the optimization of the Community public interests. Yet, it has not been demonstrated at all that national administrations are induced to modify their practice in relation to the behaviour and mobility of the regulatees. Nor has it been shown that the polycentric structure of the regulatory system opens the way to a race to the top.

A second critical issue underlying the functioning of the governance of compliance is the uneven development of the administrative rule of law, broadly meant on the one hand as the whole series of rights of participation of the (private but also public) regulatees in administrative decision-making, and on the other hand, as the whole of the procedural duties to which administrations are subject, such as the duty to give reasons.[35] The administrative rule of law is usually well developed with respect to the procedural position of national administrations, while it is not always sufficiently elaborated as far as the procedural guarantees of private actors are concerned.

An example of a sector in which procedural guarantees of private actors are adequately recognized is provided by the Community trade mark. In this field, the implementation of European regulation takes place through a complex administrative network composed of national administrations and coordinated by the Office for Harmonization in the Internal Market, which manages the procedures for Community trade marks and registered designs. Crucially, the activity of this administrative network is fully subject to the administrative rule of law. The provisions governing administrative procedures may be considered as specific applications of the so-called 'interest representation model': a great deal of attention is devoted to the emergence of interests which might influence public decisions; and these interests are not hierarchically ordered by the European legislator, but are rather balanced in the framework of the administrative law procedure, in order to ensure 'decisions grounded on the knowledge of facts and on a reasonable and justified balance of the interests'.[36]

An example of much more limited procedural protection of private actors is provided by the European administrative networks responsible for the production and dissemination of high-quality information in certain specific sectors, such as the environment, drugs and drug addiction, safety and health at work, and the like. These administrative networks tend to escape the administrative rule of law, as the exercise of tasks of their various components is normally not proceduralized. This could be considered an obvious consequence of the functional specificities of the relevant administrative networks. The making and dissemination of information is a technical exercise, which does not normally imply the adoption of binding

[34] See *supra*, Section 2.

[35] On the principle of the rule of law in the European legal order see Lenaerts, 'The Rule of Law and the Coherence of the Judicial System of the European Union' 44 *Common Market Law Review* (2007), at 1625 *et seq*; Azoulay, 'Le principe de légalité', in Auby and Dutheil de la Rochère (eds), *supra* note 10; and von Bogdandy, 'Constitutional Principles', in von Bogdandy and Bast (eds), *supra* note 30.

[36] Cassese, 'Il diritto amministrativo europeo presenta caratteri originali?', 1 *Rivista trimestrale di diritto pubblico* (2003), at 35 *et seq*, at 47.

measures but the carrying out of a research activity which is, as such, informal. Yet, the lack of formalized procedures and of rules and principles of administrative action is surprising. The drugs and drug addiction sector, where no provisions are envisaged regarding anonymity, analysis, and selection of data in the information production process from sources such as hospitals, law courts, prisons, and police stations to the members of the Reitox network (ie the European Information Network on Drugs and Drug Addiction), provides a clear illustration of the point and exemplifies the need to subject even information agencies to the administrative rule of law.

More generally, the variable degree of elaboration of the administrative rule of law in the various sectors may be on certain occasions explained as an obvious consequence of the functional differentiation of the European administrative system. The various components of the European administrative system are kept under control through several instruments, ranging from the rule of law to institutional and inter-institutional control. And the actual combination of such instruments is a matter of pragmatism and adaptation to the functional needs at stake in the various cases. At the same time, however, the uneven development of rules and principles of administrative action is not always justifiable on the basis of the differences among the various sectors of operation of the European administrative system.

A third and final critical issue, capable of illustrating the ambiguity of the European administrative system, is that of the 'unintended consequences' of the emerging governance of compliance. An example of an unintended consequence is that of the centrifugal tendencies connected with the development of sectoral European administrative networks. European administrative law typically proceeds by fragmenting member states' public powers and restructuring them in composite organizations and procedures. As has been noted, the joint administrative execution of EU law and policies allows exchange, adjustments, and accommodation among the national public powers, and in this sense it is functional to the gradual development of compliance by member states' administrations with EU law. Joint execution, however, has a marked sectoral character: the public powers of member states are fragmented and recomposed in networks by sector, ie, related to specific fields such as environmental protection, public health, competition, and the like. The participation of national administrations in European administrative networks, then, may have the effect of triggering centrifugal tendencies and makes uncertain the order and stability of national administrative systems. In addition to this, administrative order and stability are not adequately recovered at the European level, as the recomposition of national administrations in European networks does not determine their dependence on the European executive power, but constitutes only an anchorage to sectoral sub-systems governed by a specialized coordinator. There are, of course, some encouraging attempts to limit these shortcomings through the formation of a well-equipped senior civil service. For example, the mid-term programmes for cooperation among public administrations elaborated since 2004–2006 constitute the basis of a project of transnational reform of the public function that is likely to be developed and enriched with new ambitions. But there is a need to recognize honestly that the sectoral fragmentation of domestic administrations, inherent to the structural features of the emerging European administrative system, is accompanied by the risk of priming centrifugal tendencies potentially capable of jeopardizing the order and stability of national administrative systems.

5. The Perspectives of the Governance of Compliance

The inquiry carried out in this chapter concerns the features, originality, and problems of what has been labelled the 'governance of compliance'.

The basic premise of this essay has been that compliance by the addressees of EU law and policies cannot be confined within the strict boundaries of coercive means of enforcement. Compliance increasingly involves steering and governing instruments, which combine in a variety of ways traditional techniques based upon coercion and authority with non-coercive, non-authoritative instruments, relying not only on public powers but also on actions by private actors.

Relying upon this premise, it has been argued, first, that the emerging governance of compliance is essentially a matter of administrative law; in particular, the European administrative system in the process of being established operates as a set of steering instruments aimed at enhancing compliance by the addressees of EU policies through the institutionalization of negotiation, cooperation, and mutual learning among the national public powers and private actors to which EU law and policies are addressed. Secondly, such governance of compliance does not represent a genuinely new type of governance, but rather combines new forms of action with more traditional techniques used both in the experience of the member states and in the practice of other international regulatory systems. Thirdly, although the lack of sufficient empirical information precludes a sound assessment of the effectiveness and legitimacy of the emerging governance of compliance, the latter should not be seen as a smoothly functioning system but as an inherently problematic gravitational field.

The limits and shortcomings of such observations are self-evident. As has been previously recognized, the picture lacks many details and should be developed further in several regards. And the real capacity of the European administrative system to gradually develop obedience by the addressees of EU law and policies is an almost unexplored field of research that could be usefully developed by carrying out substantial empirical research.

The theses that have been proposed, nevertheless, are in our view of some relevance to a reflection on the issue of compliance with EU law. They contribute to demonstrating that compliance with EU law goes well beyond the boundaries of purely coercive means of enforcement, being pursued also through steering and governing instruments seeking to accommodate behaviours of national public powers and private parties with existing EU law and policy targets; that such instruments are partly new and partly derivative with respect to the national and international experience; and that they represent an attempt to challenge the compliance issue, but are in their turn inherently problematic.

In addition to this, the proposed theses may be of some relevance also beyond the issue of compliance, in two main directions. On the one hand, they may contribute to the advancement of a reflection on European governance by shedding light on the features and functioning of the steering instruments specifically concerning the policy phase of administrative implementation. On the other hand, they could step up a reflection on European administrative law by highlighting that the European administrative system is not only called to carry out the various material public functions exercised by the EU, such as those of social regulation, economic regulation, and the like, but it also carries out a further, instrumental function, that of enhancing compliance by the addressees of EU policies through the facilitation and institutionalization of negotiation, cooperation, and mutual learning among the national public powers and private actors.

While leaving to further research the implications of the proposed theses on the governance debate and on European administrative law studies, it seems appropriate to dedicate some final remarks to the perspectives of the governance of compliance. Building upon current institutional debates and recent reform processes, two main possible lines of development may be identified.

A first possible line of development concerns the limitation of the Commission's capacity to influence the governance of compliance.

It has been previously argued that a distinguishing mark of the European administrative system lies in the essential role played by its supranational component. The Commission is directly or indirectly involved in most of the existing sectoral networks and it influences the functioning of most of the joint proceedings and structures through which the positions of the national authorities are accommodated and reciprocally adjusted. The governance of compliance, thus, is built upon processes that do not operate in a purely transnational fashion, since the processes of exchange, adjustment, and accommodation among national public powers underlying the joint execution of EU law are shaped also by the preferences and orientations of the Commission.

Some recent institutional developments, however, suggest that the Commission's sphere of influence within the European administrative system is subject to a process of slow but progressive limitation.

The clearest example of this tendency is provided by the gradual emergence of a new type of European agency, fully independent vis-à-vis the market and EU political institutions, including the Commission. This is the case, in particular, with the new governance of the energy sector and the reform of financial supervision. Analogous to the existing European agencies, both the Agency for the Cooperation of Energy Regulators and the European supervisory authorities established in the field of micro-supervision are designed as mechanisms for administrative cooperation. Yet, differently from the practice of existing European agencies, such cooperation takes place among independent, non-ordinary authorities. Moreover, and crucially, the Agency's autonomy vis-à-vis the Commission shows a shift towards genuine independence.[37]

The developments in the energy and financial supervision sectors are of particular relevance as they illustrate that the Commission, in certain key fields of the European legal and economic space, accepts the establishment of sectoral networks coordinated by public bodies that tend to erode or limit its position of functional prominence. The gradual emergence of a new type of European agency, fully independent from the EU political institutions, including the Commission, suggests that the latter will no longer be at the centre of the transnational administrative networks established in certain crucial sectors of the European space.

Admittedly, it would not be sound to derive from these specific cases the general conclusion that the Commission is in the process of losing its overall capacity to influence the governance of compliance. Even if we admit that such a process is at work, moreover, the limitation of the Commission's sphere of influence should obviously be meant as a problematic and highly complex process, the final result and implications of which should not be taken for granted or presented in a simplified way.

Should this tendency be confirmed by further developments in other sectors, however, the role and position of the Commission within the European administrative system might be substantially attenuated. And the governance of compliance might consequently take a different direction to that followed so far; turning from a set of cooperative mechanisms combining transnational and supranational features into a set of cooperative mechanisms in which the supranational component is less influential and capable of orienting the processes of exchange, adjustment, and accommodation among the national public powers. This shift is one that could deeply reshape the character of the governance of compliance, opening the way to a fully new 'game of forces'.

A second possible line of development of the governance of compliance, qualitatively different from the previous one, is the enhancement of administrative cooperation following the new provisions of the Lisbon Treaty.

Part three of the consolidated version of the Treaty on the Functioning of the European Union (TFEU), dedicated to Union policies and internal actions, ends with a title on 'administrative co-operation'.[38] This title, made up of one single

[37] For a more detailed discussion of the gradual emergence of independent European agencies, see Chiti, *supra* note 8, at 1424 *et seq*. The proposed EU reform of financial supervision is currently subject to an ever-increasing academic interest; see, among the best pieces on the topic, F. Recine and P.G. Teixeira, *The New Financial Stability Architecture in the EU* (Institute for Law and Finance, Working Paper Series No. 110, 12/2009), available at <http://www.ilf-frankfurt.de/uploads/media/ILF_WP_110.pdf> last accessed 1 November 2011.

[38] This is one of the three main profiles of relevance of the administrative issue within the Lisbon Treaty. The other profiles concern: the features of the European administration, which is called to be 'open, efficient and independent' (see Art 298 of the Consolidated Version of the Treaty on the Functioning of the European Union, OJ 2010 C83/47); and the rights to good administration envisaged by Art 41 of the Charter of Fundamental Rights of the European Union OJ 2007 C 303, which has now the same legal value as the Treaties. As for the title devoted to administrative cooperation, Art 197 repeats without variations what was envisaged by the project of Constitutional Treaty and lays down three main provisions. First, effective implementation of Union law by the member states,

article (Article 197), represents a genuine novelty in the European 'constitutional' architecture. In the previous setting, administrative cooperation was not envisaged among the matters conferred to the European Union, indeed it seemed even excluded by certain specific Treaty provisions.[39] The new Article 197, instead, explicitly confers on the EU the power to intervene in administrative cooperation, to be broadly meant, coherently with the overall objectives of the EU, as cooperation taking place both among the national administrations and the European bodies with a view to improving the capacity of national administrations to implement EU law effectively.

The inclusion of administrative cooperation among the competences of the Union is somehow an unattended consequence of a discussion originally having a different subject.[40] The discussion within the Convention concerned in the beginning the good governance, efficiency, and transparency of the European public powers' action, but it was rapidly extended to cooperation among national administrations and among the latter and the European authorities, to which a specific Treaty provision was then dedicated. From the quality and legitimacy of EU institutions and bodies, the discussion turned to the capacity of member states' administrations to guarantee the full and effective implementation of European law.

Administrative cooperation falls within the category of EU competences to carry out actions to support, coordinate, or supplement the actions of the member states.[41] While such a category of EU competences is not a true innovation of the

which is essential for the proper functioning of the Union, is qualified as a matter of common interest. Second, it is provided that the Union may support the efforts of member states to improve their administrative capacity to implement Union law, and the modalities and limits of such support are clarified. Third, it is provided that the EU competence on administrative cooperation is without prejudice to the obligations of the member states to implement Union law, to the prerogatives and duties of the Commission, or to other provisions of the Treaties providing for administrative cooperation, as in the area of freedom, security, and justice.

[39] Such as, for example, the EC Treaty provision concerning the approximation of national laws, regulations or administrative provisions, which implicitly assigns to member states' authorities the responsibility for the administrative implementation of European legislation.

[40] The issue arose in the debates of the Convention on 17 July 2002, when Mrs Hjelm-Wallen, representative of the Swedish government, proposed, in a meeting of Working Group V, to envisage in the new Treaty a provision on good governance, efficiency, and transparency: the improvement of administrative principles would reinforce the legitimacy and democratic foundation of the European bodies, as required by the Laeken declaration (see the summary of the meeting on 17 July 2002 of Working Group V, CONV 209/02, available at <http://register.consilium.europa.eu/pdf/en/02/cv00/cv00209.en02.pdf> last accessed 19 October 2011; see also the Working Document No. 13 of 30 July 2002, WD 013—WG V, *Note by Mrs Hjelm-Wallen on 'Good administration, efficiency and openness'*, available at <http://european-convention.eu.int./docs/wd5/1931.pdf> last accessed 19 October 2011). The point was upheld and extended by the President of the Group, who proposed to consider the provision of a European complementary competence enabling the EU to encourage cooperation among member states' administrations, in order to strengthen the administrative capacities and qualities that are necessary to ensure an effective implementation of EU law (see Working Document No. 21 of 4 September 2002, WD 021—WG V, *Proposal by Mr Gérard Druesne, transmitted by Mr Henning CHRISTOPHERSEN, on a new article on Public administration*, available at <http://european-convention.eu.int./docs/wd5/2374.pdf> last accessed 19 October 2011). This proposal provided the basis for the final report of Working Group V, subsequently approved by the plenary session of the Convention, while a different provision was dedicated to the European administration, that is called to be 'open, efficient and independent'.

[41] Arts 2(5) and 6 of the Treaty on the Functioning of the European Union.

Lisbon Treaty,[42] the Lisbon Treaty, as is well known, formalizes this category of EU competences, at the same time increasing the number of sectors in which the Union may take measures to support, coordinate, or supplement the actions of the member states. As for administrative cooperation, the substance and boundaries of EU intervention are sketched in Article 197. This Article provides that possible interventions may include facilitating the exchange of information and of civil servants as well as supporting training schemes. Moreover, it clarifies that the EU measures in this area will be regulations adopted by the European Parliament and the Council, acting in accordance with ordinary legislative procedure. In addition to this, the limits of EU intervention are specified: any harmonization of the laws and regulations of the member states is excluded, and no member state is obliged to avail itself of the EU support.

Though presented in the reports of Working Group V as a qualitative change, the new EU competence on administrative cooperation is perfectly in line with the administrative *acquis* of the Union. As has been highlighted throughout the previous paragraphs, administrative cooperation is a distinguishing mark of the European administrative system. Article 197, therefore, does not open the way to an entirely new line of EU action. More modestly, it provides a specific legal basis that could be usefully exploited by the EU in order to carry out interventions directly focusing on administrative cooperation among national bodies and among the latter and the European authorities.

The key issue, however, is to assess whether the new legal basis will have the effect of slowing down the process of administrative integration within the European legal order or whether it will rather provide new momentum for further administrative integration. In the first case, the development of the governance of compliance, strictly dependent upon administrative integration, could be weakened or made more difficult. In the second case, it could find new paths for stabilization and growth.

A number of elements suggest that the new competence could result in an obstacle to further administrative integration. The principle of indirect execution, through national administrations, is implicitly reaffirmed by Article 197 of the TFEU as the general pattern of administrative implementation of EU laws and policies. And the exercise of EU competence in the area of administrative cooperation is bounded in several ways. Such construction, fully coherent with Declaration No. 19 on the implementation of Community law annexed to the TEU, might imply that the EU is entitled to intervene in the functioning and organization of national administrations only so far as its action is necessary to reinforce the national administrations' capacity to implement EU law, and through the limited mechanisms of a support

[42] In certain sectors, in fact, the EC Treaty already permitted the Community a more limited action than that made possible in the areas of exclusive and shared competences. The Community, in particular, could take measures aimed at co-ordinating the action of the member states, without proceeding to any type of harmonization of national laws. In the public health sector, for example, Art 152 of the EC Treaty envisaged a Community action complementing national policies, encouraging cooperation between the member states and, if necessary, lending support to their action.

competence. A strict interpretation of Article 197, for example, could preclude the possibility for the EU political institutions to adopt measures of harmonization in certain sectors envisaging, together with the harmonization of substantial rules, also instruments of cooperation among national administrations and the EU authorities. Should this interpretation be accepted, the process of administrative integration would not be stopped, but it could take place only through the narrow channel of the support competence provided for by Article 197.

Such interpretation, however, may be countered with the impressive amount and degree of elaboration of EU legislative measures that already develop cooperation among national administrations and among the latter and the EU authorities in specific sectors. The provision of mechanisms for administrative cooperation in substantial EU legislation is a well-established regulatory technique,[43] which the new Article 197 could hardly overthrow. The most reasonable solution, then, is to interpret Article 197 as a legal basis adding to the legal bases already existing and usefully exploited by the EU political institutions to establish and deepen administrative cooperation. The legal bases already existing are provisions laying down material competences and relate to specific fields of action. The legal basis provided by Article 197, instead, has an institutional content and is not linked to a specific sector.

The emergence and consolidation of the governance of compliance, therefore, may be considered not endangered but, on the contrary, supported by the inclusion of administrative cooperation among the EU competences. If administrative cooperation is inherent to the establishment of a governance of compliance, Article 197 enriches the legal bases for developing cooperation among national administrations and European authorities, thus providing further options to the EU political institutions.

Beyond this, the governance of compliance is probably destined to receive new strength from the deep rationale of the new provisions, based on the recognition of the importance of coordination of national administrations for the maturation of the EU. The decisive elements, in our view, may be found in the formalization of the effectiveness of the implementation of EU law by the member states as a 'matter of common interest' and in the acknowledgement that compliance by the addressees of EU law cannot be simply controlled through the traditional coercive means of infringement proceedings and judicial control, but needs to be gradually built through instruments of administrative cooperation managed at the European level. Admittedly, this rationale currently provides the basis only for the support competence laid down by Article 197. And yet, at least in a symbolic plan, it reflects a new 'constitutional' attention to the capacities of national administrations and to their crucial relevance in the implementation of EU law.

[43] This regulatory technique is well-established both at the political and at the legal level. Interestingly enough, the Court of Justice has upheld some particularly incisive applications of this technique. For example, it has held that the EU political institutions may use Treaty provisions laying down material competences in order to establish a European agency providing services to national authorities and to private operators 'which affect the homogenous implementation of harmonising instruments and which are likely to facilitate their application': see Case C-217/04, *United Kingdom of Great Britain and Northern Ireland v European Parliament and Council of the European Union*, [2006] ECR I-3771, Rec 44–5.

3

Article 258/260 TFEU Infringement Procedures: The Commission Perspective in Environmental Cases

*Sibylle Grohs**

1. European Environmental Law

The total number of individual pieces of legislation making up the body of European environmental law is estimated to be around 200, covering a wide range of sectors: nature protection, waste management, air quality, water protection, and industrial pollution control. In addition to this sectoral legislation, horizontal legislation covers environment impact assessment, access to environmental information, access to justice, and public participation. This area of law is dealt with in the European Commission by the Environment Directorate General. Figure 3.1 shows the different areas covered in infringement cases in 2010.

Climate change legislation is dealt with by a separate Directorate General created in 2009. Radiation protection issues fall under the remit of the Energy Directorate General.

Environmental legislation in the European Union covers a large area of subjects and media. The environment chapter of the Treaty on the Functioning of the European Union (TFEU) forms the basis for the adoption of the secondary legislation which makes up most of the body of European environmental law, but it is rarely the legal basis for enforcement action itself. The European Union alongside its member states is also a party to numerous international conventions relevant to environmental protection. These are made operational in European law through the adoption of secondary legislation, often in the form of regulations. Whilst international treaties and conventions are not normally the basis for litigation before the European Court of Justice, enforcement action against a member state can and has included reference to such instruments in the past. In an action brought against France, for instance,

* The opinions contained in this chapter are those of the author and do not represent the formal opinion of the European Commission.

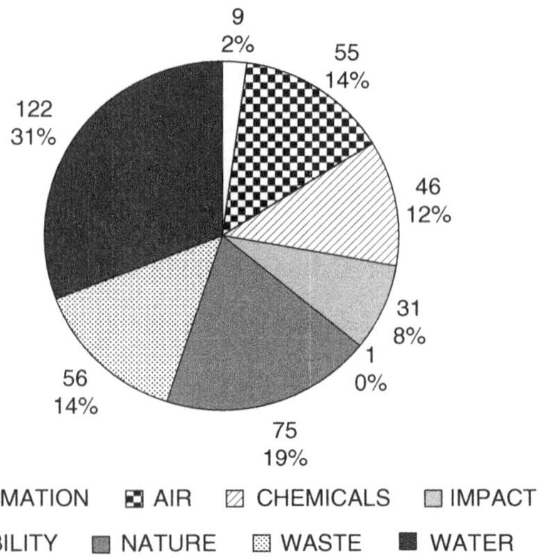

Figure 3.1 Infringements per sector on 31 December 2010

the Commission won a claim under the Barcelona Convention.[1] The Aarhus Convention, which has been ratified by all member states (except Ireland), has also been argued in support of infringement action on the failure to implement and apply Directive 2003/35/EC,[2] which partially implements this Convention within the European Union.

The majority of cases brought by the Commission under Article 258 of the TFEU in the field of the environment, however, concern the implementation and application of directives. As is set out in Article 288 of the TFEU, there are three types of secondary legislation. Regulations, which are often used to implement international obligations from treaties into European Union law, are binding in their entirety and directly applicable within the member states normally without the need for them to adopt additional legislation. Directives are binding on member states as to their result, but leave national authorities the choice of form and methods for their implementation and application. Finally, there are Decisions which are binding only on their addressees, which can also be member states. These are less frequently used in the environment field, but are employed, for example, when adopting individual derogations for member states foreseen in legislation or for the adoption of technical lists such as the list of hazardous waste.[3]

[1] Case C-239/03, *Commission v France*, [2004] ECR I-9325.

[2] Directive 2003/35/EC of the European Parliament and of the Council of 26 May 2003 providing for public participation in respect of the drawing up of certain plans and programmes relating to the environment and amending with regard to public participation and access to justice Council Directives 85/337 and 96/61, OJ 2003 L 156/17.

[3] Council Decision 2001/573/EC of 23 July 2001 amending Commission Decision 2000/532 as regards the list of wastes, OJ 2001 L 203/18.

2. Sources of Infringement Cases

The Environment Directorate General has various sources that it draws on for its work on infringements. It receives large numbers of complaints, many from private individuals or citizen groups, some from environmental non-governmental organizations (NGOs) and a few from industry groups relating to more limited sectoral legislation with direct industry relevance, such as legislation on waste management.

In 2009, the Secretariat General of the European Commission set up a new system whereby complaints and enquiries are all registered in a central registry (CHAP).[4] A large number of complaints are received with regard to the implementation and application of European environmental law and many require additional assessment and investigation. Often this requires that enquiries be made with the member state concerned, which can be done by writing to the member state's Representation Office in Brussels or through so-called package meetings where enquiries and questions are grouped and the Commission seeks clarification at a meeting in the relevant member state capital.

Direct contact with the member state is now also facilitated through the so-called EU pilot system launched by the Commission in April 2008. This allows the Commission to refer correspondence and complaints it receives directly to the member state for comment, hopefully enabling a resolution of the problems raised to be found. Complainants who agree to reveal their identity can be brought into the loop with the member state sending them their observations directly and copying these to the Commission. If the matter is not resolved, the Commission retains the option to take further action and launch formal infringement proceedings. The practice at present is to use the EU pilot mechanism in all cases before launching formal infringement procedures under Article 258 of the TFEU. The Commission issued its first report on the mechanism in March 2010.[5]

Another important source of information for the Commission is the implementation reports it receives from member states, as most directives contain reporting obligations. The Commission also draws on its own implementation reports, in particular to check the conformity of national legislation that has been adopted, but also reports which examine the practical application of directives.

3. The Role of the European Commission

The role of the European Commission in enforcing European environmental legislation is set out in Article 17, paragraph 1 of the TFEU, which states that

[4] <http://ec.europa.eu/community_law/your_rights/your_rights_en.htm#1depot> last accessed 19 October 2011.

[5] <http://ec.europa.eu/community_law/docs/docs_infringements/com_2010_70_en.pdf> last accessed 19 October 2011.

the Commission 'shall ensure the application of the Treaties, and of measures adopted by the institutions pursuant to them'. The article goes on to state that the Commission 'shall oversee the application of Union law under the control of the Court of Justice to the European Union'. The powers of the Commission to take member states to the European Court of Justice are set out in Article 258 and 260 of the TFEU.[6]

The Court of Justice has long recognized that the Commission has full discretion in deciding whether or not to bring enforcement action under Article 258 of the TFEU.[7] However, that discretion is not entirely unfettered, as was recognized by the European Ombudsman in 1998 in the Greek Metro case.[8] Whilst the Ombudsman did not question the discretion of the Commission to close the case, he stated that its decision not to instigate or continue with infringement action where evidence of a breach existed would need to be clearly and openly reasoned and explained to the complainant.

The work on enforcement is spread among different parts of the Commission, with the Secretariat General of the Commission playing the role of coordinator and formal postman for the infringement letters that are agreed by the Commission College. The Commission's Legal Service also plays a lead role in that any infringement step requires its formal approval before it can be formally proposed for decision by the Commission. The substantive work of checking whether legislation has been adopted, has been fully implemented, and is being correctly applied falls to the individual Commission services. For environmental cases, this is the responsibility of the Environment Directorate General.

The Commission has set out its approach to handling complaints and infringements in a number of Communications. There are separate Communications for the rules under which the Commission will propose fines and penalties; these will be discussed below. Furthermore, separate sectoral Communications have been adopted explaining the policy approach to be taken on enforcement. For environmental case work the most recent is the Communication of 2008.[9] Whilst the general rules applicable to the registration and handling of complaints is harmonized across the entire Commission, individual Directorate Generals have their own specific approaches tailored to their area of competence. The differences in approach can sometimes be explained by the fact that some Directorates General have substantial case loads and complaint numbers to handle, whereas others have relatively few. The Environment Directorate General has always received substantial numbers of complaints from citizens, NGOs, and, to a lesser extent, from industry

[6] Formerly Arts 226 and 228 of the EC Treaty respectively.

[7] Case 247/87, *Star Fruit v Commission*, [1989] ECR 00291, and Case C-422/92, *Commission v Germany*, [1995] ECR I-1097.

[8] See European Ombudsman Decision on complaint 995/98/OV concerning the Macedonian Metro Joint Venture, in European Ombudsman's Annual Report 2001, at 116–19, available at <http://www.ombudsman.europa.eu/activities/annualreports.faces;jsessionid=08CE09F46682852 1E90ABA6D0CEFB116> last accessed 19 October 2011.

[9] Commission Communication of 18 November 2008 to the European Parliament, the Council, the European Economic and Social Committee and the Committee of the Regions on implementing European Community Environmental Law, COM/2008/0773 final.

groups. The latest Communication on enforcement of environmental law explains how the Environment Directorate General would seek to prioritize its work in the face of the large number of complaints; this is further discussed below.

4. The Role of the European Parliament

The European Parliament also has a role to play in the implementation process. Members of the public have the right to petition the European Parliament's Petitions Committee under Article 227 of the TFEU. Some complainants make use of both the Commission's complaint procedure and their right of petition to the European Parliament. The European Parliament does not generally have the resources to carry out its own investigations and, after an initial assessment of admissibility, will refer the petition to the European Commission for investigation. The Commission must then investigate the question with the member state against which allegations of bad practice have been made and report back on its finding to the Petitions Committee, either through written communications or at oral hearings where the petitioners and Members of the European Parliament (MEPs) can question the Commission about its findings and interpretations. Curiously, the member states themselves are not called to account before the Committee, although each member state is represented in Brussels through its Permanent Representation which coordinates its representation before the Council.

The Petitions Committee generally takes a more political approach to its assessment of petitions, especially in its oral hearings. The Petitions Committee also has the power to carry out site visits. In some cases, these can achieve results that would not be feasible for the Commission through its more formal infringement powers.

The overall number of petitions to the European Parliament has steadily increased over recent years and the Environment Directorate General of the Commission generally handles about a third of all the petitions deemed admissible.

Other Committees of the European Parliament can also become involved in the debate. The Environment Committee of the European Parliament normally scrutinizes new environmental policies and legislation, but it also tries to keep an overview of the enforcement activities of the Commission by holding sessions on implementation. These have often been used by individual MEPs as a forum for asking about the application of Community environmental law in their local constituencies and have less frequently resulted in strategic debates about how implementation work should be structured in the future. Questions about the application of Community law in individual cases also come to the Commission through written and oral questions from the European Parliament, with oral questions requiring an oral response to the European Parliament's plenary session by the Commissioner responsible for the Environment.

The European Ombudsman is elected by and answerable to the European Parliament under Article 228 of the TFEU. Early on in his work, the first Ombudsman carried out an in-depth assessment of the work of the Commission in assessing and dealing with complaints, concluding his investigation with a negative report. The Commission was criticized for its lack of transparency in its complaint-handling procedures and in particular its failure to keep complainants informed about the handling of their complaints. This resulted in the adoption by the Commission of a Communication in 2002[10] and an agreement with the European Parliament as to how complaints would be handled in future, in particular guaranteeing complainants the right to comment on the Commission's assessment and proposals to close complaints.

5. Categories of Infringement Cases

The Commission generally classifies cases into three categories: non-communication, non-conformity, and bad application. The first is the simplest and concerns the failure by a member state to respect the transposition deadline for a particular directive. Normally, after adoption, directives give member states a year or two to adopt new legislation to import the new European obligations into their national law and then report these measures to the Commission. These cases are started automatically by the Secretariat General of the Commission with a simplified Letter of Formal Notice. In most cases the member state will acknowledge its failure and the case moves through the infringement procedure uncontested. Once the member state communicates its new implementing legislation, and this provides coverage for the whole directive and all the jurisdictions of the member state, the case is closed. In some member states transposition is only required through one piece of legislation adopted by the central government. In more federalized member states or member states with different levels of devolved government, full compliance is only assured when every level has adopted and communicated its implementing legislation. In the United Kingdom, for instance, most legislation is adopted separately for England and Wales, Scotland, Northern Ireland, and Gibraltar, each with its own separate legislative body and compliance timetable.

On occasion, however, these cases have been complex despite their simple origins. In *Commission v Luxembourg*, Case C-32/05, the case turned on Luxembourg's failure to adopt implementing legislation for the Water Framework Directive.[11] Initially, Luxembourg indicated that legislation was still being drafted, but then at a very late stage in the proceedings before the Court of Justice, in its Defence to the Commission's Application, Luxembourg sought to argue for the first time that existing legislation on water pollution ensured its compliance with parts of the Directive. The Court had little sympathy for the Commission's difficulty at this late stage in dealing with these new arguments in the short time scale given for the Reply.

[10] Commission Communication of 10 October 2002 to the European Parliament and the European Ombudsman on relations with the complainant in respect of infringements of community law, COM/2002/0141 final, OJ 2002 C 244/5, at 5–8.

[11] Directive 2000/60/EC of the European Parliament and the Council of 23 October 2000 establishing a framework for Community action in the field of water policy, OJ 2000 L 327/1.

The next group of cases concern non-conformity. These are usually launched once the member state has adopted and communicated implementing legislation and this has undergone a conformity check. The Environment Directorate General has conformity checks for newly implemented directives carried out by consultants and uses these and the information it has available from its own sources, including complaints, to finalize its own analysis and follow up on any gaps or areas of non-conformity that this reveals. These can be complex cases particularly where the directive requires complex new procedures to be put into practice. In recent years, the Environment Directorate General has focused on these cases as a priority, especially for the key directives such as the Habitats and Wild Birds Directives[12] and the Environmental Impact Assessment Directive.[13] These are often in the front line of complaints with regard to new infrastructure developments, which in numerous member states also attract EU funding.

The last category of cases concerns bad application. Most complaints and petitions lodged with the Commission and European Parliament concern this case category. The directive in question has been transposed and the legislation communicated to the Commission, but concerns are raised that the legislation is not being applied correctly or at all. In some cases, the bad application is in part the result of the implementing legislation not having been correctly or fully transposed, but in many it is simply a failure by the relevant member state authorities to act in accordance with the rules laid down. This category of cases is one of the most difficult for the Commission to pursue. In environmental cases, unlike for example in fisheries policy, the Commission does not have its own inspectors that it can send out to verify conflicting claims made by complainants and the national authorities. Unless the complainants are well resourced and informed with the capacity of providing sufficiently clear evidence of a breach, bad application cases rarely get as far as the Court of Justice. However, many are resolved at earlier stages of the infringement procedure or even during the pre-infringement procedure once the attention of the member state is drawn to the infringement. Where the evidence of bad application is less clear or strongly contested by the member state, the Commission has to carefully weigh up the evidence, given that the burden of proof is squarely placed on the Commission to prove that the member state is in breach.

Figure 3.2 shows the distribution of infringement cases among the different case categories in 2010. The Environment Directorate General tends to have a larger percentage of non-conformity cases in part because of its responsibility for such a large number of directives and the regular follow up of transposition checked

[12] Council Directive 92/43/EEC of 21 May 1992 on the conservation of natural habitats and of wild fauna and flora, OJ 1992 L 206/7 (as amended) and Directive 2009/147/EC of the European Parliament and of the Council of 30 November 2009 on the conservation of wild birds (codifying former Directive 79/409/EEC), OJ 2010 L 20/7.

[13] Council Directive 85/337/EEC of 27 June 1985 on the assessment of the effects of certain public and private projects on the environment, OJ 1985 L 175/40 as amended by Directives 97/11/EC, OJ 1997 L 73/5, and Directive 2003/35/EC, OJ 2003 L 156/17.

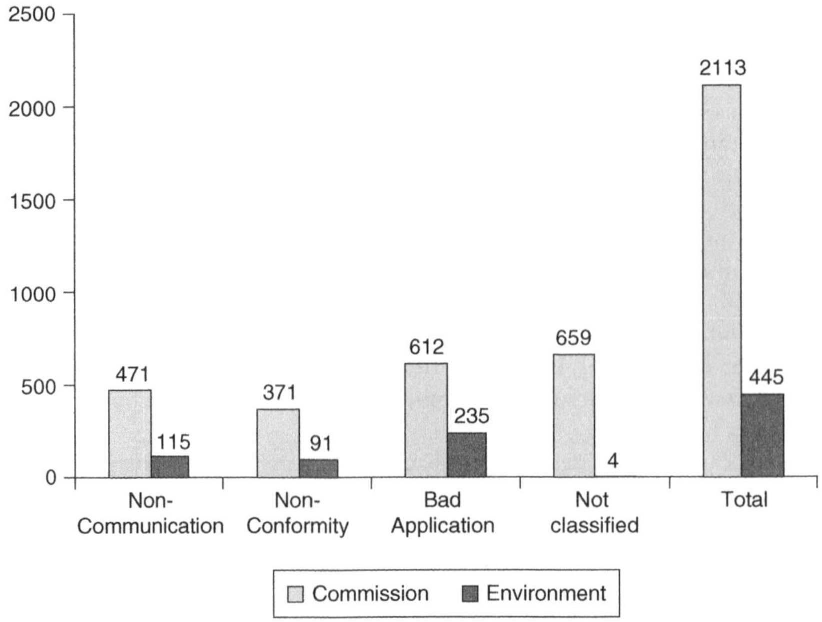

Figure 3.2 Infringements by type as at 31 December 2010

through conformity studies. The slightly higher percentage of bad application cases is likely to be due to the large number of complaints and petitions received by the Environment Directorate General, which relate to the bad application of European environmental rules.

6. The Article 258 TFEU Infringement Procedure

Where the early investigations outlined above show that a breach of European law exists and has not been resolved, the Commission may decide to launch formal infringement procedures under Article 258 of the TFEU. The Commission has discretionary powers in taking this decision, but must give clear explanations to complainants in situations where a breach of Community law is uncovered but a decision is taken to close a case nevertheless. This might be because the member state has undertaken to remedy the breach or because the breach is deemed to be too minor or possibly too old to warrant the launching of infringement proceedings.

Infringement action by the Commission against a member state requires that a number of formal procedural steps be followed. Each formal step, including closure of the case, requires a formal decision of the Commission sitting as a College, ie a decision by all the Commissioners.

The first step is the issuing of the Letter of Formal Notice, a step which is not described in the Treaty, but which has become a formal requirement accepted by the Court of Justice. The Letter of Formal Notice sets the frame for the case beyond which future action cannot stray.[14] If the Commission in later stages discovers new grounds which it wishes to add, a supplementary Letter of Formal Notice is required. The Letter of Formal Notice is drafted by lawyers in the relevant Directorate General responsible for the area of law concerned in consultation with the Legal Service of the Commission. For simple non-communication cases where a member state is late in adopting and communicating to the Commission national legislation transposing a particular directive, simplified Letters of Formal Notice are sent automatically by the Secretariat General of the Commission once the implementation deadline has elapsed. Letters of Formal Notice normally give the member states two months to reply, although this period can be shortened if the case is urgent.

If the Commission is not happy with the reply to the Letter of Formal Notice or receives no reply, the Commission can propose a Reasoned Opinion. This is similar in format to the Letter of Formal Notice and also sets a two-month deadline. However, there is a difference. The Reasoned Opinion is a formal statement by the Commission of the breach that it considers to exist and requires the member state to take action to bring itself into compliance before the two-month deadline. If the Commission is still concerned after this action, it can make a proposal to refer the member state to the European Court of Justice. It should be noted that the deadline for reply to the Reasoned Opinion is also the point in time used by the Court of Justice as the basis for its judgment, so that the Commission can still obtain a judgment against a member state if by this date compliance has not been achieved, even if after this date, but before judgement, the infringement has been resolved.

For each stage of the procedure a decision of the Commission College of Commissioners is required. To this end, a draft Letter of Formal Notice or Reasoned Opinion is prepared for consultation between the relevant services of the Commission. The service proposing the infringement action also fills in what is known as a 'fiche', which is a one-page summary of the case with details of its history held in a centralized database. It is this fiche or summary case sheet that forms the formal basis for the decision of the Commission College.

It is rare for the Commissioners themselves to discuss proposals in detail. The decisions are prepared on their behalf by their Cabinets, who meet first at so-called 'special chefs' for the working-level discussions, then at 'HEBDO' where heads of cabinet discuss cases that their junior staff have not been able to resolve at the previous meeting. The final decision is then taken at the meeting of the Commissioners themselves. Once the decision has been taken, the Letters of Formal Notice and Reasoned Opinions are sent out to the Brussels-based Permanent Representatives of the member states concerned, who will forward

[14] Case C-52/90, *Commission v Denmark*, [1992] ECR I-2187; Case C-337/89, *Commission v United Kingdom*, [1992] ECR I-6103.

these to their capitals. The texts are not made public, but press releases are issued for Reasoned Opinions and decisions to refer a member state to the Court of Justice. The decisions are all logged on the website of the Secretariat General of the Commission.

7. Referring a Case to the Court of Justice under Article 258 TFEU

The aim of the Commission is not to bring cases before the Court of Justice. Most complainants and petitioners find this attitude frustrating and perplexing. The aim of the procedures under Article 258 TFEU and all the recently adopted pre-investigations mechanisms described above, such as the EU pilot system and the raising of cases at package meetings, is to get the member state concerned to bring itself into compliance as soon as possible. The Commission's tactics in the infringements procedures are therefore significantly different from those that might be used by a national prosecution service that may see its success in the number of cases for which it obtains a successful judgment.

The Commission's infringement procedure is different as it aims to give the member state the chance to come into compliance at every stage. However, once a decision to go to the Court of Justice is executed, the process changes and the timing of the procedure is dictated by the Court of Justice, and no longer by the Commission. Once a decision is taken by the Commission College to refer a case to the Court of Justice, the Legal Service of the Commission together with the Service responsible for the file drafts the Application. This is lodged with the Court of Justice and the case is allocated a formal number. The member state then puts in its Defence. The Commission has the right of Reply, which is optional and might not be necessary in a simple non-communication case where the member state concedes the breach in its Defence. If the Commission decides to lodge a Reply, the member state then has the right to put in a Rejoinder.

Another member state not directly concerned by the proceedings might decide to join the case, pleading either for the position of the Commission or the member state or simply adding its own observations on the issues in question. The Commission and the member state may decide to reply to these third-party observations with their own comments. The written pleading stage is then closed. Whilst either party may ask for an oral hearing, the decision whether or not to hold one rests with the Court of Justice. The Court of Justice will also decide whether an Opinion from the Advocate General allocated to the case is required. Given that most cases are decided on the written pleadings, the oral hearing, if one takes place at all, tends to be a relatively short and low-key affair. The Court appoints a Reporting Judge to the case, who will generally write the judgment. Judgments tend to be relatively short and are written by consensus. There is no scope for a judge to give a dissenting judgment. This means that in those cases where a judgment is reached by compromise the conclusions may not always read smoothly. On average, it takes about 18 months from the Application being drafted to the full judgment being received.

8. The Burden of Proof

One factor that must be borne in mind and is often overlooked by complainants when a case is brought before the Court of Justice is that the Commission as the applicant bears the burden of proof. There is no special relationship between the Court of Justice and the Commission whereby this concept is relaxed. In environmental cases concerning allegations of the bad application of the law this is a major factor for the Commission to consider, given that it has no inspectors to reply upon to provide it with evidence. In a case that concerned the Commission claiming that Ireland was systematically failing to apply correctly the Waste Framework Directive,[15] providing evidence to back up this claim in 12 individual cases, the Court of Justice gave the following guidance on the burden of proof at paragraph 41:

> It is the Commission's responsibility to place before the Court the information needed to enable the Court to establish that the obligation has not been fulfilled, and in doing so the Commission may not rely on any presumption.[16]

At paragraph 42 the Court went on:

> However, the Member States are required, under Article 10 EC, to facilitate the achievement of the Commission's task... in ensuring that the provisions of the Treaty and the measures taken by the institutions pursuant thereto are applied.[17]

There is a clear tension between these two parts of the judgment and in *Commission v Ireland* this resulted in substantial evidence being presented and the judgment being unusually long.

The burden of proof can be particularly difficult for the Commission in certain categories of cases where the inspection powers on the ground to verify compliance lie solely with the member state. The Commission has launched a series of cases regarding the failure to correctly apply the Landfill Directive[18] and the Urban Waste Water Treatment Directive,[19] based on findings from independent studies and complaints for the former and on reports from the member states themselves for the latter. The Court of Justice has been particularly tough on the Commission in the latter case group in a series of largely negative judgments delivered at the end of 2009. The judgement in *Commission v United Kingdom,* Case C-390/07 in particular has resulted in the bar for proving that a water body

[15] At the time of Council Directive 75/442/EEC, OJ 1975 L 194 which has now been replaced by Directive 2008/98/EC of the European Parliament and of the Council of 19 November 2008 on waste and repealing certain Directives, OJ 2008 L 312/3.

[16] Case C-494/01, *Commission v Ireland,* [2005] ECR I-3331. [17] Ibid.

[18] Council Directive 1999/31/EC of 26 April 1999 on the landfill of waste, OJ 1999 L 182/1.

[19] Council Directive 91/271/EEC of 21 May 1991 concerning urban waste water treatment, OJ 1991 L 135/40.

is eutrophic becoming so high that future cases may arguably only be contemplated where the water body shows clear evidence of symptoms at the top end of the eutrophication spectrum, namely with fish deaths and dense algal mats. The Urban Waste Water Directive requires member states to meet staged obligations to ensure that urban waste waters are collected and treated before discharge and that the treatment provided is particularly thorough where the waters discharge into sensitive waters. A water body can be deemed sensitive if it is in danger of eutrophication, whereby excessive nutrients (nitrogen and phosphorus) cause an acceleration of plant growth which have detrimental effects; in the extreme, these effects result in the water body choking. Warning signs of less extreme eutrophication are more subtle, for instance the gradual disappearance of nutrient sensitive species such as eelgrass. If the member states do not regularly monitor and report these effects then complainants can only detect the effects once they have become visible as algal mats and fish deaths, effectively deleting the precautionary principle from the Directive.

Given that the Court has emphasized the need for member states to cooperate with the Commission in its investigations of alleged infringements, the Commission will in future need to be more precise and exacting in the information it seeks to show how member states are fulfilling their obligations in practice.

9. Interim Injunctions

If a case is found to be urgent, the Commission or the member state can ask the Court to expedite proceedings. Such requests, however, are rare. In cases where the Commission is concerned that irreversible environmental damage may occur if the infringement process is allowed to proceed according to the usual time scale, which can take two years from the Letter of Formal Notice to judgment even if the case is brought quickly, an application can be made to the Court of Justice, under Article 279 TFEU, asking for interim measures before the judgment is made. This article provides that:

> The Court of Justice may in any cases before it prescribe any necessary interim measures.

The Court of Justice can order the member state in question to stay any damaging activities until final judgment is given. In recent years the Commission has successfully invoked this article in three cases, after an initial failed attempt in *Commission v Germany,* Case C-57/89R, the so-called 'Leybucht case'. In that case, the Commission tried to stop the construction of coastal protection infrastructure on a bird reserve. The Commission lost the case as the Court of Justice found that the action lacked urgency. Planning permission for the work had been applied for in 1985, construction commenced in 1986 and was almost completed when the Commission lodged its application in July 1989.

Commission v Italy, Case C-503/06R was the first successful environmental case in which interim measures were granted. The case concerned bird hunting in

Italy in breach of the Wild Birds Directive 79/409/EEC, now codified as Directive 2009/14/EC.[20] This was followed by *Commission v Malta*, Case C-76/08R, which also concerned a failure to control bird hunting. The Court of Justice set out the test for a successful grant of an interim measures order stating at paragraph 21:

> It is settled case-law that the judge hearing an application for interim measures may order interim relief only if it is established that such an order is justified, prima facie, in fact and in law that it is urgent in so far as, in order to avoid serious and irreparable harm to the applicant's interests, it must be made and produce its effects before a decision is reached in the main action. Where appropriate, the judge hearing such an application must also weigh up the interests involved.

In Malta, the control of bird hunting by Europe was a very political issue and had already formed a difficult part of the Accession debate. The Commission asked for the suspension of spring hunting of quail and turtle doves (migratory birds) in 2008 and 2009. Malta allowed their hunting each year by decision and the Commission's case was intended to stop a decision being taken to authorize hunting in 2008. The Court of Justice assessed the claims from both sides and found that the protection of birds was an interest trumping the rights of hunters to what was effectively a leisure activity. As the Court of Justice pointed out, the aim of the Wild Birds Directive was not to guarantee each hunter a minimum number of birds.

The Commission was again required to apply for interim measures in *Commission v Poland,* Case C-193/07, where the Polish authorities were on the point of building a road through a protected Natura 2000 area, in part with EU funds. The Court granted a short interim order preventing the execution of certain measures purporting to compensate for damage that the main project would cause. The Commission had argued that these so-called 'compensatory measures' would themselves inflict habitat damage. No interim order was granted for the main project as Poland voluntarily suspended works pending the outcome of the proceedings. It later abandoned the controversial road alignment in favour of an alternative.

The option of interim measures has now become a real one for the Commission, but is reserved for extreme cases in which urgency in action can clearly be shown to the Court of Justice. In most cases, the issue in question is controversial and the member state defiant or otherwise unable to stop the illegal activities without considerable external pressure.

10. Following up on a Judgment under Article 260 TFEU

If a member state fails to comply with a judgment of the Court of Justice, the Commission is required to restart the next round of the infringements procedure under Article 260(2) TFEU to ensure compliance. Article 260(2) TFEU provides:

> If the Commission considers that the Member State concerned has not taken the necessary measures to comply with the judgement of the Court, it may bring the case before the

[20] *Supra* note 12.

Court after giving that State the opportunity to submit its observations. It shall specify the amount of the lump sum or penalty payment to be paid by the Member State concerned which it considers appropriate in the circumstances.

If the Court of Justice finds that the Member State concerned has not complied with its judgment it may impose a lump sum or penalty payment.

The procedure followed is similar to that leading to the first judgment under Article 258 TFEU. The Commission issues a pre-260 letter to the member state immediately after a successful or partially successful action, asking what measures have been taken to bring about compliance. If compliance has still not been assured, then the case proceeds to the Letter of Formal Notice stage giving the member state two months to reply. If the member state is still not in compliance, under the amendments to the TFEU brought about by the Lisbon Treaty, the Commission can then apply directly to the Court of Justice without having to issue a Reasoned Opinion. The Commission proposal to refer a member state to the Court of Justice for a second judgment must be accompanied by a proposal for fines. The Commission College therefore decides on the penalty it would like to propose on the basis of a so-called 'penalty fiche' prepared by the Commission services.

Whilst Article 260(2) TFEU would appear to imply that the Commission can ask for either a lump sum or daily penalties in the alternative, the Court of Justice in *Commission v France,* C-304/02 made clear that both could be awarded. As a result, the Commission amended its guidance on penalties in 2005[21] indicating that it would in all cases ask for both. The 2005 Communication, as amended and updated a number of times since adoption,[22] sets out clear guidelines on the calculation of fines by the Commission in a simple mathematical formula. The calculation multiplies the seriousness of the breach (factor 1 to 20) by a set Euro sum by the time since the first judgment, the so-called duration factor (1 to 3), by a factor calculated individually for each member state based on its GDP and voting rights within the Council. The Communication also sets out minimum lump sums that will be requested for each member state, ranging from just over 11 million Euros for Germany to 177,000 Euros for Malta.[23] The key factor for which the Commission has scope for changing the final sum requested is the so-called seriousness factor. In calculating this, the Commission needs to assess the importance of the European Union rules breached and the impact of the infringement on the general and particular interests of the Union. Factors that could be taken into account in environmental cases include whether the breach concerns the whole territory of the member state, whether the member state has been cooperative in trying to resolve the infringement, whether the infringement is a one off

[21] Commission Communication of 9 December 2005 on the Application of Art 228 SEC(2005)1658.

[22] Commission Communication Application of Art 260 TFEU. Updating of data used to calculate lump sum and penalty payments to be proposed by the Commission to the Court of Justice in infringement proceedings SEC (2010) 923.

[23] The amounts were last updated in 2011 by SEC (2011) 1024 Communication from the Commission—updating of data used to calculate lump sum and penalty payments to be proposed by the Commission to the Court of Justice in infringement proceedings.

or part of a series of similar cases, and whether the member state has obtained a financial advantage from the breach. Account is also taken of the legal instrument breached and whether this has resulted in serious or irreparable harm to human health or the environment.

The Environment Directorate General has referred a number of cases to the Court of Justice with a request for fines. Most of these did not reach judgment; three cases did. The first case was *Commission v Greece,* C-387/97, concerning the illegal Kouroupitos landfill in Greece for which the Court of Justice gave judgment in July 2000. The Commission's request for fines was made under the guidance of its first Communication on fines from 1996[24] under which the Commission restricted itself to requesting only daily penalties. In this case, the Commission requested a daily penalty of 24,600 ECU (the currency forerunner to the Euro). The Court of Justice awarded a 20,000 ECU fine. The case concerned the failure to apply the Waste Framework Directive[25] and Hazardous Waste Directive[26] in order to close and clean up an old illegal landfill located at the mouth of a river in Chania, Crete. The complaint originated from 1987, the first Court judgment was given in 1992 and the case was referred for a second judgment under the former Article 228 EC Treaty in 1997. The Commission proposed a seriousness factor of 6 out of 20. The Court of Justice provided guidance for future cases stating that 'the process of compliance must be initiated at once and completed as soon as possible'. The Court of Justice went on to observe that whilst the Commission's guidelines as then set out in its 1996 Communication did not bind the Court, they 'ensured that the Commission acts in a manner which is transparent, foreseeable and consistent with legal certainty and designed to achieve proportionality'.

The next judgment was in November 2003 in *Commission v Spain,* C-278/01 concerning the Bathing Waters Directive[27] and Spain's failure to ensure compliance with the Directive in its inland bathing waters. The first judgment of the Court of Justice under the former Article 226 EC Treaty was in 1998 and the second referral under the former Article 228 was in 2001. The judgment concerned Spain's 302 internal bathing waters of which in 1992 only 54 per cent were compliant with the mandatory standards of the 1976 Directive. By 2001 compliance had improved to 85 per cent compliance. The guidance given by the Court was that the Commission had to have regard to the situation at the elapse of the deadline for reply to the Reasoned Opinion issued under the former Article 228 EC Treaty.[28] An issue of concern for the Commission was that whilst in 2001 the percentage of compliance had improved, this improvement was partly achieved by

[24] See Information from the Commission of 21 August 1996 on applying Art 177 EC Treaty, OJ 1996 C 242, and Information from the Commission of 28 February 1997 on the method of calculating the penalty payments, OJ 1997 C 63.

[25] *Supra* note 15.

[26] At the time of judgment Council Directive 91/689/EEC of 12 December 1991 on hazardous waste, OJ 1991 L 377/20 now replaced by Directive 2008/98/EC as explained in *supra* note 15.

[27] At the time of judgment Council Directive 76/160/EEC of 8 December 1975 concerning the quality of bathing water, OJ 1976 L 31/1.

[28] Under the former Art 228 EC Treaty both a Letter of Formal Notice and Reasoned Opinion were required before the case could be referred to the Court of Justice for a second time. Since the Lisbon Treaty, the Reasoned Opinion stage is not longer required.

the de-designation of 100 bathing waters. The Commission proposed a seriousness factor of 4 out of 20 and asked for a daily penalty to be applied. The Court of Justice however rejected this proposal, preferring instead to set an annual penalty based on the results of the annual bathing water report. The Court of Justice also required the penalty to take into account progress made towards compliance, proposing a more complex solution tailored to the case in such a way that the penalty would be degressive with increased compliance.

Whilst not a case brought by the Environment Directorate General, it is worth mentioning *Commission v France,* Case C-304/02, a case concerning France's long-running failure to apply European Union fishing legislation. The original judgment dated from 1991, with the second judgment given 14 years later in 2005. Seventeen member states intervened in the case before the Court of Justice ruled on the penalties to be applied. The Court of Justice stood previous guidelines on their head, taking a dim view of the lengthy failure by France to comply with its previous judgment. Whilst most of the member states intervening argued that the possibility to award penalties against member states under the former Article 228 EC Treaty should not be punitive, the Court of Justice stated that this function of the provisions was not precluded where the infringement continued to persist over a long period of time and was likely to be repeated. The seriousness factor in this case was 10 out of 20. The Commission requested a daily penalty of 316,000 Euros, which the Court of Justice accepted as a total amount but decided to allocate on a six-monthly basis to allow France time to implement the necessary administrative measures and assess their effectiveness. The Court of Justice then added a 20 million Euro lump sum fine on its own initiative. It was this judgment which forced the Commission to rethink its 1996 Communication on how to calculate fines. This was replaced with the 2005 version, providing that both a lump sum and daily penalty would be requested in all future cases.

The most recent judgment given by the Court of Justice in a case brought by the Environment Directorate General was in December 2008 in *Commission v France,* Case C-121/07 concerning the failure to transpose the Directive on genetically modified organisms (GMOs).[29] This was the first case proposed to the Court of Justice by the Commission under the 2005 Communication, requesting both a lump sum and penalty payment. In practice, the new dual request means that the Commission will no longer withdraw the case from the Court of Justice if compliance is achieved before judgment as was the practice in the past, but will maintain the action until judgment, maintaining at least the lump sum request. In this case, France had transposed the Directive after the close of pleadings and before the date of judgment and the grounds for allocating a daily penalty therefore fell away. The Advocate General was sceptical about the Commission's new policy of always asking for both a lump sum and daily penalty. However, the Court of Justice awarded a lump sum of 10 million Euros, with the apparent aim of deterring member states from waiting until the last minute for compliance. The Court of Justice also took

[29] Directive 2001/18/EC of the European Parliament and of the Council of 12 March 2001 on the deliberate release into the environment of genetically modified organisms and repealing Council Directive 90/220/EEC, OJ 2001 L 106.

into account the fact that France had a history of non-compliance with European legislation on GMOs.

More requests for fines are likely when the Commission applies the new powers introduced by the Lisbon Treaty to request fines already at the first Article 258 TFEU referral for non-communication cases under Article 260(3) TFEU.[30]

11. Conclusion

Future work on enforcement and implementation of European environmental legislation is likely to continue to be considerable. Whilst the number of new pieces of legislation being produced has slowed, implementation challenges remain. In particular, the accession of 12 new member states in recent years, with many of the additional accession deadlines now coming to a close, will continue to occupy attention.

In its 2008 Communication, the Commission set out some of its priorities for future case work on environmental law enforcement. In addition to the swift follow up of non-communication cases and Article 260 TFEU cases, focused attention will continue to be given to non-conformity cases. The Environment Directorate General has also recognized as strategic those cases in which there is evidence of serious systemic breaches. Where, for example, there is evidence that there are multiple illegal landfills in a particular member state or a multiple failure to ensure compliance with the collecting and treatment obligations of the Urban Waste Water Treatment Directive for numerous towns and cities, it is preferable to follow these up in one horizontal case rather than with individual and scattered cases. Particular attention will also continue to be given to following up on cases where there is evidence of a lack of compliance with the fundamental obligations under some of the key directives in the environmental sector, for example, the failure by a member state to designate Natura 2000 sites under the Habitats or Birds Directives. Finally, the focus will be on large infrastructure projects, and particularly where these have been subject to EU funding, attention will be given to ensuring that these are granted consent in compliance with the requirements of European environmental law.

Further developments are likely to show an emphasis on national courts in the member states playing a more active role in ensuring that environmental rules are applied correctly. The national judges are often better placed to weigh up conflicting reports at a level that is closer to the breach. In recent years, the Environment Directorate General has focused on training and information programmes for national judges and is turning its attention to the need for better access to justice rules for environmental cases in certain member states. However, improvements in national enforcement will not replace the Commission in its role as guardian of the Treaties.

[30] See now Communication from the Commission—Implementation of Article 260(3) of the Treaty at OJ C 12, 15.01.2011, p 1.

4

From the Velvet Glove to the Iron Fist: Criminal Sanctions for the Enforcement of Union Law

*Michael Dougan**

1. Introduction

It is a commonplace to observe that, since criminal law found no place whatsoever within the original Treaty of Rome, it was assumed to fall altogether outside the scope or influence of Community law. However, as with so many other fields subject to only weak or non-existent Community regulatory competence, it soon became clear that the Treaty could indeed have an important impact upon the national systems of criminal justice.[1] As the Court of Justice has confirmed many times since, criminal law—whether it be the substantive law on offences, or the regime governing sanctions, or the rules of criminal procedure—is not some 'special' sphere immune from the obligations imposed upon member states pursuant to the Treaty.[2] This chapter is concerned with one distinct category of such obligations: those concerning the enforcement of substantive Union policies by the member states within the national legal systems.[3]

The use of criminal penalties for the enforcement of substantive Union law arises in two main categories of situation. The first (considered in Section 2) can usefully be termed the 'velvet glove': in the absence of Union legislation prescribing precise sanctions for its own enforcement, the member states are free to impose appropriate sanctions within their own legal systems—including penalties of a criminal nature—subject to various obligations imposed under Union law as interpreted by

* I am very grateful to participants at the 2009 session of the Academy of European Law for their insightful questions and comments. I am also indebted to Eleanor Spaventa for her comments on an earlier draft. The law is stated as at 31 January 2010.

[1] Consider, eg, Case 82/71, *SAIL*, [1972] ECR 119; Case 203/80, *Casati*, [1981] ECR 2595.

[2] Eg, Case 299/86, *Drexl*, [1988] ECR 1213; Case 186/87, *Cowan*, [1989] ECR 195; Case C-348/96, *Calfa*, [1999] ECR I-11.

[3] We are not here concerned with other aspects of Union intervention in national criminal law, in particular, through the programme of cross-border police and judicial cooperation (which includes the harmonization of certain domestic penal legislation, especially so as to facilitate mutual recognition between member states).

the Court in the famous *Greek Maize* ruling.[4] In the second situation (dealt with in Section 3), the Union legislature positively requires the member states to criminalize certain infringements of Union law, and may even prescribe the detailed rules governing the imposition of liability and the type/level of sanction. That 'iron fist' can claim a constitutional provenance both more recent and more rumbustious than the *Greek Maize* jurisprudence: pre-Lisbon, bitter institutional disputes about whether criminal sanctions could or should be imposed under the First (or instead the Third) Pillar culminated in the Court's controversial rulings in the *Environmental Crimes* and *Ship-Source Pollution* cases;[5] since 1 December 2009, the revised provisions of the Treaty on the Functioning of the European Union have radically changed the relevant legal framework once again.[6]

The particularly sensitive constitutional structures underpinning the use of penal sanctions for the enforcement of Union policies illustrates that, even if criminal law is not immune from the Treaties, it does to some extent occupy a special place within the Union legal order. That specificity also emerges from an analysis (in Section 4) of the safeguards provided for under Union law before the national courts, so as to protect individuals from the unfair or arbitrary exercise of coercive public power, whenever the member state either seeks or is obliged to impose criminal sanctions for the enforcement of Union law. Our attention will focus on two of the most important safeguards explored in the Court's case law: the principle of non-retroactivity and, more broadly, of legality in criminal law; and the retroactive application of the most lenient criminal rules. Such safeguards act (argues Section 5) as an important unifying force at the frontline of the criminal justice system. Thanks to the patient work of the Court, and some important interventions by the Lisbon Treaty, we can at least feel assured that the Union's obsession with constructing a politically palatable but legally complex framework to deal with the imposition of penal sanctions does not compromise the fundamental imperative of offering adequate and consistent standards of judicial protection to individuals accused of comparable offences.

2. The Velvet Glove: National Criminal Sanctions for the Enforcement of Union Law

Before looking at the *Greek Maize* jurisprudence on national sanctions for the enforcement of Union law, it is necessary to recall the principles governing domestic penalties in situations where the member states are instead derogating from Union law.[7]

[4] Case 68/88, *Commission v Greece*, [1989] ECR 2965.

[5] Case C-176/03, *Commission v Council*, [2005] ECR I-7879 and Case C-440/05, *Commission v Council*, [2007] ECR I-9097, respectively.

[6] The consolidated texts were published in OJ 2008 C 115.

[7] Further, eg, Delmas-Marty, 'The European Union and Penal Law', 4 *European Law Journal* (1998) 87; Baker, 'Taking European Criminal Law Seriously', *Criminal Law Review* (1998) 361.

A. Member State Derogating from the Treaty

Where a national measure is held to be incompatible with a primary Treaty provision, such as the free movement of goods under Article 34 TFEU (ex-Article 28 EC), or the free movement of workers under Article 45 TFEU (ex-Article 39 EC), any sanction intended to enforce that national measure is automatically prohibited by Union law, without the need to conduct an independent assessment of whether the sanction itself complies, for example, with the principle of proportionality.[8] Even where a domestic rule is found to be compatible with the free movement provisions (because it benefits from an express Treaty derogation or pursues a valid imperative requirement), any sanction intended to enforce that domestic rule must itself comply with various requirements imposed by Union law:[9] in particular, there can be no discrimination on grounds of nationality as compared to the penalty imposed upon own nationals for breaching comparable obligations;[10] and the penalty itself must in any event comply also with the principle of proportionality.[11]

In the above situations, national penalties fall within the scope of the Treaties because of the substantive provisions they are intended to enforce. However, it is also possible that certain national sanctions may give rise to an entirely autonomous breach of Union law (regardless of the substantive domestic provisions to which they otherwise relate). In the first place, the administration of criminal justice may give rise to an independent infringement of the principle of non-discrimination, where the relevant situation can be brought within the scope of Union law for the purposes of Article 18 TFEU (ex-Article 12 EC)—hardly a difficult task given the Court's generous approach to triggering the application of the Treaties.[12] In the second place, there is support in the case law for the proposition that certain national penalties—and particularly the decision to impose criminal as opposed to civil or administrative liability—can in themselves, and even in the absence of any discrimination on grounds of nationality, hinder the exercise of a migrant Union citizen's free movement rights. In *Skanavi*, the Court held that it would be incompatible with Article 49 TFEU (ex-Article 43 EC) on the freedom of establishment

[8] Eg, Case 88/77, *Schonenberg*, [1978] ECR 473; Case 179/78, *Rivoira*, [1979] ECR 1147; Case 269/80, *Tymen*, [1981] ECR 3079; Cases C-388 and 429/00, *Radiosistemi*, [2002] ECR I-5845; Case C-13/01, *Safalero*, [2003] ECR I-8679; Case C-167/01, *Inspire Art*, [2003] ECR I-10155; Case C-12/02, *Grilli*, [2003] ECR I-11585. See also, eg, Case 5/83, *Rienks*, [1983] ECR 4233; Cases C-338, 359 and 360/04, *Placanica*, [2007] ECR I-1891; Case C-197/06, *Van Leuken*, [2008] ECR I-2627. Cf Art 1(5) Directive 2006/123 of the European Parliament and of the Council of 12 December 2006 on services in the internal market, OJ 2006 L 376/36.

[9] Note the additional restrictions imposed upon member state competence here, through the other general principles of Union law, especially the obligation to respect fundamental rights, see Section 4.

[10] Eg, Case C-24/97, *Commission v Germany*, [1998] ECR I-2133.

[11] Eg, Case 48/75, *Royer*, [1976] ECR 497; Case 118/75, *Watson and Belmann*, [1976] ECR 1185; Case 8/77, *Sagulo*, [1977] ECR 1495; Case 157/79, *Pieck*, [1980] ECR 2171; Case C-265/88, *Messner*, [1989] ECR 4209; Case C-348/96, *Calfa*, *supra* note 2, Case C-378/97, *Wijsenbeek*, [1999] ECR I-6207.

[12] Eg, Case 186/87, *Cowan*, *supra* note 2; Case C-274/96, *Bickel and Franz*, [1998] ECR I-7637; Case C-224/00, *Commission v Italy*, [2002] ECR I-2965. See also, eg, Case 299/86, *Drexl*, *supra* note 2; C-276/91, *Commission v France*, [1993] ECR I-4413; cf Cases C-155/08 and C-157/08, *Passenheim-van Schoot*, [2009] ECR I-5093.

for Germany to subject foreign nationals to criminal penalties for failing to comply with the (otherwise justified) obligation to exchange their driving licence within one year of taking up residence within the host state. The Court's reasoning was influenced both by the importance of the right to drive a motor vehicle for the practical exercise of a claimant's free movement rights, and by the lasting consequences a criminal conviction could have for the exercise of his/her trade or profession.[13]

However, the latter line of reasoning is capable of giving rise to serious definitional problems concerning the proper scope of application of the Treaties. After all, a wide range of criminal offences—which have nothing in themselves to do with Union law—might nevertheless result in serious practical consequences for the convicted person, capable of adversely affecting his/her exercise of free movement rights across the Union. Drawing the line between which practical consequences should attract the scrutiny of Union law, and those which fall altogether outside the scope of the Treaties, becomes a difficult if not altogether arbitrary task. Following the logic of *Skanavi*, it could be argued that any criminal infraction resulting in a sentence of imprisonment creates such inevitable disruption to the claimant's professional activities as to amount to a breach of the free movement provisions, which requires scrutiny (in particular) for its proportionality. On the one hand, the ruling in *Kremzow* suggests that the Court would be unsympathetic to such arguments on the grounds that the hypothetical possibility of a barrier to movement resulting from one's imprisonment for a crime totally unconnected to Union law falls outside the scope of the free movement provisions.[14] On the other hand, the ruling in *Carpenter*—where the Court seemed happy to scrutinize national rules on the basis of a frankly remote and unconvincing connection to Union law—might support the argument that a deprivation of liberty is indeed capable of acting as a barrier to movement, where the claimant can demonstrate a tangible impact upon his/her rights under the Treaties, which must then be objectively justified and tested for its proportionality.[15] But the manifestly absurd result of such reasoning would be that the national systems of criminal justice are subject almost per se to scrutiny under Union law, based on only a tenuous link to the exercise of free movement rights, in a manner reminiscent of the problems which arose in ascertaining the appropriate boundaries of Article 34 TFEU during the era of the *Sunday Trading* case law.[16]

The ruling in *Skanavi* should therefore be treated with caution. The Court's dictum might be better explained by the fact that the substantive obligation to exchange driving licences at issue in *Skanavi* could have been treated as indirectly discriminatory against foreign migrants; or in any event was itself regulated by Community secondary legislation, thus providing the basis for accepting that

[13] Case C-193/94, *Skanavi*, [1996] ECR I-929. See also, Case C-156/04, *Commission v Greece*, [2007] ECR I-4129.

[14] Case C-299/95, *Kremzow*, [1997] ECR I-2629.

[15] Case C-60/00, *Carpenter*, [2002] ECR I-6279.

[16] In particular, Case 145/88, *Torfaen BC v B&Q*, [1989] ECR 3851. Not that one can say, with the benefit of hindsight, that the ruling in Cases C-267/91 and 268/91, *Keck and Mithouard*, [1993] ECR I-6097 necessarily changed much, see further, eg, Spaventa, 'The Outer Limit of the Treaty Free Movement Provisions', in C. Barnard and O. Odudu (eds), *The Outer Limits of European Union Law* (2009).

Germany was either derogating from or implementing Union law.[17] Reference to the professional difficulties which might be encountered by migrant Union citizens as a result of the imposition of criminal penalties was merely intended to reinforce the need to undertake a careful proportionality assessment—not to justify undertaking such an assessment in the first place. Otherwise, it would be better to restrict any autonomous scrutiny of national criminal sanctions to their compatibility with the principle of non-discrimination within the scope of Union law, avoiding the categorization of domestic criminal law as a non-discriminatory barrier to movement simply through its alleged severity and regardless of the substantive obligations it is actually intended to enforce.

B. Member State Implementing the Treaty

Where national sanctions fall within the scope of Union law because the member state is derogating from the Treaties, the Court's main aim is to restrain the exercise of domestic competence and temper the harshness of the national penalty, to the benefit of the individual defendant, since that best serves the objective of promoting free movement. But when national sanctions fall within the scope of Union law because the member state is implementing the Treaties, the case law pursues additional and potentially competing objectives. On the one hand, application of the duty of loyal cooperation between the Union and the member states obliges the national authorities to penalize breaches of the Treaties through the imposition of effective sanctions for the vindication of the general interest, which means acting counter to the interests of the individual who has transgressed his/her obligations under Union law. On the other hand, the general principles of Union law, controlling the unfair exercise of public power contrary to the rights and interests of the citizen, require the Court to limit the member state's obligation to penalize breaches of Community law, and indeed to constrain if necessary the national authority's discretion to impose sanctions upon wrongdoing individuals.

Which legal principles govern the resolution of these potentially competing policy goals? The early ruling in *Amsterdam Bulb* suggested that the Court was prepared to offer the member states a very wide, if not unlimited, margin of discretion over the choice of sanctions for enforcing Community law.[18] However, the subsequent *Greek Maize* case established the framework for a more intrusive Union scrutiny of national autonomy in this field.[19] Where Union legislation does not specifically provide any penalty for its infringement, or refers for that purpose to national law, Article 4(3) TEU (ex-Article 10 EC) requires the member state to take all measures necessary to guarantee the application and effectiveness of Union law. For that purpose, whilst the choice of penalties remains within its discretion, the member state must ensure that infringements of Union law are penalized under

[17] *In casu,* First Council Directive 80/1263 of 4 December 1980 on the introduction of a Community driving licence, OJ 1980 L 375/1.

[18] Case 50/76, *Amsterdam Bulb,* [1977] ECR 137.

[19] Case 68/88, *Commission v Greece, supra* note 4.

substantive and procedural conditions analogous to those applicable to infringements of national law of a similar nature and importance and which, in any event, make the penalty effective, proportionate, and dissuasive. Moreover, the national authorities must proceed, with respect to infringements of Union law, with the same diligence as that which they bring to bear in implementing corresponding national laws.[20] Those *Greek Maize* principles soon came to be included as a matter of routine in various instruments of Union secondary legislation,[21] and indeed have been partially incorporated into the text of the Treaties themselves,[22] although it is generally agreed that such provisions add nothing of substance to the obligations already imposed upon the member states in any case pursuant to Article 4(3) TEU.[23]

In principle, as the Court asserted in *Sagulo*,

> [i]f a member state has not adapted its legal provisions to the requirements of [Union] law in this sphere, it is the task for the national court to use its judicial discretion to impose a punishment appropriate to the character and objective of the provisions of [Union] law the observance of which the penalty is intended to safeguard.[24]

That may well be true in situations where the principle of proportionality requires the imposition of a more lenient penalty. But it is not necessarily so straightforward when it comes to the obligation of the domestic court to 'create' equivalent and/or effective penalties capable of adversely affecting the defendant's interests. After all, the *Greek Maize* criteria are themselves limited in practice by the other general principles of Union law, especially the obligation to respect fundamental rights as discussed in Section 4, including particular guarantees of judicial protection in situations concerning the aggravation of criminal liability. For now, however, we shall explore in greater detail the various requirements imposed upon member states under the *Greek Maize* ruling itself.

1. *Requirement of Equivalence*

Where the member state is implementing Union law, the principle of equal treatment on grounds of nationality will still apply to its choice of sanctions so as to prohibit both direct and indirect discrimination.[25] But in addition, the principle of equivalence set out in *Greek Maize* requires that any sanctions adopted by the

[20] Ibid, Rec 23–5. Note that, in certain situations, Art 4(3) TEU may be combined with substantive Treaty provisions to create new obligations for member states, also capable of impacting upon national discretion over law enforcement, eg, Case C-265/95, *Commission v France*, [1997] ECR I-6959.

[21] See, in particular, Commission Communication of 3 May 1995 to the Council and the European Parliament on the role of penalties in implementing Community internal market legislation, COM (95) 162 final; Council Resolution of 29 June 1995 on the effective uniform application of Community law and on the penalties applicable for breaches of Community law in the internal market, OJ 1995 C 188/1.

[22] See Art 325 of the Treaty on the Functioning of the European Union (the 'TFEU') (ex-Art 280 EC).

[23] Consider, eg, Case C-186/98, *Nunes and de Matos*, [1999] ECR I-4883.

[24] Case 8/77, *Sagulo, supra* note 11, Rec. 12.

[25] Subject to justification. Consider, eg, Case C-29/95, *Pastoors*, [1997] ECR I-285; Case C-167/01, *Inspire Art, supra* note 8.

member state for the enforcement of Union law must be similar to those applicable for the enforcement of comparable obligations derived from purely national law.[26] As with the analogous principle of equivalence which applies in cases involving domestic remedies and procedural rules under the *Rewe/Comet* jurisprudence concerning the effective judicial protection of individual rights derived from Union law,[27] application of the principle of equivalence under *Greek Maize* can involve difficult questions: for example, about the existence of comparability between Union and national obligations, and whether any discrimination can be objectively justified by factors unrelated to the legal provenance of the relevant sanctions.[28] However, very little case law has developed under *Greek Maize* to shed useful light on the Court's understanding and approach.[29] Certain lessons can, of course, be learned by analogy from the *Rewe/Comet* jurisprudence. For example, it appears safe to assume that the principle of equivalence is concerned only with ensuring that the penalty for enforcing Union law is no more lenient than that applicable to its national comparator; there will be no infringement of *Greek Maize* where the sanction as regards Union law is found to be more severe than that in respect of domestic law. After all, the requirement of effectiveness might well demand a heavier sanction specifically in Union law situations; we know from the *Rewe/Comet* case law that such unequal treatment in favour of the Treaties does not infringe the principle of equivalence.[30] Greater leniency, if at all, must come from the moderating influence of the proportionality assessment.[31] Other open questions nevertheless remain; future *Greek Maize* rulings will have to explore (for example) how far the domestic courts may take into consideration social and cultural factors specific to their own territory which might serve to differentiate a prima facie similar Union duty from its alleged national comparator.[32]

2. *Requirement of Effectiveness*

Even if a national sanction for enforcing Community law complies with the principle of equivalence, it must in any case satisfy the requirement of effectiveness (which, for present purposes, can be taken to embrace the *Greek Maize* demand for both 'effective' and 'dissuasive' penalties).

The main issue here concerns just how prescriptive the Court is prepared to be when it comes to defining and applying the requirement of effectiveness. It is true that the decided case law offers some straightforward examples of national sanctions

[26] And presumably that equivalent sanctions must be provided for the enforcement also of comparable Union obligations inter se: cf Case C-460/06, *Paquay*, [2007] ECR I-8511.

[27] Case 33/76, *Rewe-Zentralfinanz v Landwirtschaftskammer für das Saarland*, [1976] ECR 1989; Case 45/76, *Comet BV v Produktschap voor Siergewassen*, [1976] ECR 2043.

[28] Further, eg, Dougan, 'The Vicissitudes of Life at the Coalface: Remedies and Procedures for Enforcing Union Law before the National Courts', in P. Craig and G. de Búrca (eds), *The Evolution of EU Law* (2010).

[29] One of the few sanctions cases where the ECJ has done anything more than merely recite the principle of equivalence is Case C-326/88, *Hansen*, [1990] ECR I-2911.

[30] Consider eg, Case C-432/05, *Unibet*, [2007] ECR I-2271.

[31] See Section 2.B.3.

[32] Cf Case C-156/04, *Commission v Greece*, *supra* note 13.

which patently failed to satisfy the threshold of effectiveness.[33] But beyond that, the precise threshold of effectiveness that member states are expected to satisfy under *Greek Maize* remains relatively poorly defined. The expectations imposed by Union law are usually phrased in general terms: for example, the member state's obligation to combat agricultural fraud effectively includes a duty to initiate all available proceedings under administrative, fiscal, or civil law for the collection or recovery of duties or levies fraudulently evaded or for damages.[34] If anything, the Court seems to offer the member states a generous margin of discretion in choosing an appropriate system of sanctions and defining the criteria for assessing the latter's effectiveness.[35] For instance, it was held in *Vandevenne* that, for the purposes of penalizing Union road safety regulations concerning maximum driving and minimum rest periods, Article 4(3) TEU neither requires nor precludes a system of sanctions based on the criminal liability of legal persons (a principle which might be unknown to the national legal system) or on strict criminal liability (as opposed to some standard of fault such as an obligation to take best endeavours).[36] Certainly, there is nothing so dramatic in the field of domestic sanctions for enforcing Union law as we witnessed in the field of national remedies for the protection of Union right-holders, where rulings such as *Francovich* and *Marshall II* went much further than criticizing the blatant failure by member states to comply with some generic requirement of effectiveness, so as to forge more detailed standards of effective judicial protection for the benefit of individual claimants under the Treaties.[37]

There are, to be fair, a few isolated dicta from Luxembourg which suggest the possibility of Union law prescribing the precise nature of the penalty required for the effective enforcement of a given Treaty obligation, including even a requirement for the member state to adopt specifically criminal sanctions. In *Zwartveld*, the Court observed that Article 4(3) TEU requires member states to take all the measures necessary to guarantee the application and effectiveness of Union law, if necessary by instituting criminal proceedings.[38] Yet that throwaway remark had little to do with the dispute at hand, which concerned the Commission's obligations to cooperate with the competent national judicial authorities when the latter were investigating alleged criminal activities within

[33] Eg, Case C-383/92, *Commission v United Kingdom*, [1994] ECR I-2479; Case C-382/92, *Commission v United Kingdom*, [1994] ECR I-2435. Consider also eg, Case C-429/07, *Inspecteur van de Belastingdienst v X*, [2009] ECR I-04833.

[34] Eg, Case C-352/92, *Milchwerke Köln*, [1994] ECR I-3385; Case C-230/01, *Penycoed Framing Partnership*, [2004] ECR I-937. Note that a considerable jurisprudence has built up concerning the member state's duty to recover wrongly paid (as opposed to fraudulently obtained) Union monies, eg, Cases 205–215/82, *Deutsche Milchkontor*, [1983] ECR 2633; Case C-366/95, *Steff-Houlberg*, [1998] ECR I-2661; Case C-298/96, *Oelmühle Hamburg*, [1998] ECR I-4767; Case C-336/00, *Huber*, [2002] ECR I-7699. Further, Dougan, 'Cutting Your Losses in the Enforcement Deficit: A Community Right to the Recovery of Unlawfully Levied Charges?', 1 *Cambridge Yearbook of European Legal Studies* (1998) 233.

[35] See recently, Case C-45/08, *Spector Photo Group*, [2009] ECR I-12073.

[36] Case C-7/90, *Vandevenne*, [1991] ECR I-4371. See also, eg, Case C-326/88, *Hansen*, *supra* note 29; Case C-177/95, *Ebony Maritime*, [1997] ECR I-1111. Consider also, eg, Case C-315/05, *Lidl Italia*, [2006] ECR I-11181.

[37] Cases C-6/90 and 9/90, *Francovich*, [1991] ECR I-5357; Case C-271/91, *Marshall II*, [1993] ECR I-4367.

[38] Case C-2/88 IMM, *Zwartveld*, [1990] ECR I-3365.

the member state. In *Österreichische Unilever*, the Court stated that member states are obliged by the Union rules governing cosmetic products to ensure that labels or adverts implying that such products have characteristics they do not in fact possess constitute a breach of the law and, in particular, a criminal offence punishable by penalties having a deterrent effect.[39] Again, however, this dictum should be placed in its true context: the ruling actually concerned a civil action between rival undertakings about the lawfulness of national rules which were stricter than the standards contained in Union law itself. Any evidence for the proposition that the duty of loyal cooperation under Article 4(3) TEU may directly oblige the member states to enforce Union obligations specifically through the imposition of criminal offences and sanctions is thus at best scant and unconvincing.

3. *Principle of Proportionality*

Regardless of whether the national sanction for enforcing Union law complies with the requirements of equivalence and effectiveness, it must in any event satisfy the principle of proportionality. That is particularly true when the member state chooses to enforce Union law through a system of criminal sanctions: Article 49(3) of the Charter of Fundamental Rights specifically provides that the severity of penalties must not be disproportionate to the criminal offence.[40]

Nevertheless, the Court's case law on the proportionality of national sanctions is again generally characterized by the recognition of a wide margin of discretion for member states to adopt an appropriate system of penalties for enforcing Union law; having regard to factors such as the fundamental principles of the national legal system, the objectives of prevention and deterrence, the difficulties of penalizing infringements by alternative means, and the importance of the public interest which the relevant Union legislation seeks to protect or advance.[41] Furthermore, the Court stresses that choices about the means of coercive state enforcement will depend on social and cultural factors specific to each individual territory. For example, it was held in *Commission v Greece* (2007) that 'criminal punishment for particular behaviour, which is intended by the national legislature, is linked to the economic and social situation of the relevant member state'.[42] The fact that car registration fees in Greece were particularly high, tempting residents into fraudulently driving vehicles registered in other member states purely so as to evade the applicable Greek taxation, therefore justified the use of criminal sanctions which potentially included imprisonment of the accused and seizure of the vehicle. This strong territorial element to the proportionality assessment implies that the choices made by one member state should not be considered excessive simply because other member states have reached a different assessment of the type and severity of sanctions required to enforce any given Union obligation.[43] Certainly, the

[39] Case C-77/97, *Österreichische Unilever*, [1999] ECR I-431.

[40] 2000 version, OJ 2000 C 364. 2007 version, OJ 2007 C 303.

[41] Eg, Case C-326/88, *Hansen*, *supra* note 29; Case C-177/95, *Ebony Maritime*, *supra* note 36.

[42] Case C-156/04, *Commission v Greece*, *supra* note 13, Rec 71.

[43] Cf case law on moral/cultural choices in free movement law, eg, Case C-275/92, *Schindler*, [1994] ECR I-1039; Case C-36/02, *Omega*, [2004] ECR I-9609.

Court is unsympathetic to the argument that differences in the nature or severity of the penalties chosen by each member state give rise to unlawful discrimination between undertakings, or unacceptable distortions of competition, within the internal market.[44]

4. From Legislative Schemes to Administrative Practices Right Down into Individual Disputes

Clearly, both the member state's prima facie autonomy and the various tools for Union scrutiny as recognized in *Greek Maize* apply to every aspect of the enforcement of Union law: not only the nature of the sanction, but also the conditions for its imposition, and even the actual character and level of the penalty imposed. In a similar vein, the Court's supervision is not limited to the formal legislative framework established by the member state, but also extends to scrutinizing whether the actual practices of the national administration fulfil the requirements of equivalence, effectiveness, and proportionality.[45] Indeed, the obligations imposed upon member states under *Greek Maize* are to be considered dynamic in character, implying an obligation upon member states to keep their existing systems of sanctions under active review to ensure that they remain equivalent, effective, and proportionate (for example, taking into account the effects of inflation on the real value of financial penalties).[46]

Critical analysis under *Greek Maize* can also reach right down into individual disputes, particularly in the context of preliminary references under Article 267 TFEU (ex-Article 234 EC). Indeed, it is at this point that the Court's standard of review, particularly on grounds of proportionality, can assume a more intrusive character—sometimes exerting a direct influence on the relevant factors which the competent authorities and national courts should take into account for the purposes of setting the actual level of any fine or other punishment imposed for the purposes of enforcing Union obligations.[47] For example, *Louloudakis* concerned proceedings against an individual accused of evading the payment of the Greek vehicle tax by driving a vehicle registered in another member state. The Court held that, just as the choice over whether to impose a criminal penalty falls to national law, so too does the decision about whether account should be taken of the accused person's good faith: Union law does not preclude the application of a general principle contained in the national criminal justice system to the effect that everyone is presumed to know the law. However, for the purposes of determining the actual penalty imposed upon the offender, the domestic court must take into account

[44] Eg, Case C-326/88, *Hansen*, *supra* note 29; Case C-273/90, *Meico-Fell*, [1991] ECR I-5569. Cf case law on the principle of equal treatment not prohibiting disparities of treatment that arise from mere differences in national law as between member states, eg, Case C-137/00, *Milk Marque*, [2003] ECR I-7975; Case C-92/02, *Kristiansen*, [2003] ECR I-14597.

[45] Eg, Case C-140/00, *Commission v United Kingdom*, [2002] ECR I-10379; Case C-454/99, *Commission v United Kingdom*, [2002] ECR I-10323. Consider also, eg, Case C-8/88, *Germany v Commission*, [1990] ECR I-2321; Case C-54/95, *Germany v Commission*, [1999] ECR I-35; Case C-277/98, *France v Commission*, [2001] ECR I-8453.

[46] Eg, C-354/99, *Commission v Ireland*, [2001] ECR I-7657.

[47] Cf, Case C-210/91, *Commission v Greece*, [1992] ECR I-6735.

his/her good faith, at least where the determination of the applicable tax liabilities has given rise to difficulties, and particularly having regard to the relevant Union legislation's objective of promoting free movement.[48] Similarly, the Court held in *Lindqvist* that, although member states must impose effective sanctions against individuals who process personal data in contravention of Directive 95/46,[49] such sanctions must nevertheless comply with the principle of proportionality. Especially given that the scope of the Directive is very wide, and the obligations imposed upon those who process personal data are diverse and potentially significant, the national court is obliged to take into account all the circumstances of each case before it, including the duration of the relevant breach of Union law, the importance of protecting the data which has been disclosed, and the need to respect the accused person's fundamental rights (such as the freedom of expression).[50]

C. Ascertaining the Boundaries of the *Greek Maize* Case Law

The *Greek Maize* case law therefore imposes duties upon the member state which are relatively clear in the abstract yet often vague in their specifics. Further problems arise when one considers another issue: What exactly is the scope of application of the *Greek Maize* case law, ie, to precisely which national sanctions will its requirements of equivalent, effective, and proportionate penalties actually apply? Uncertainties arise at two separate frontiers: the difficulty of clearly distinguishing situations of derogation from those of implementation; and the overlap between the imposition of public sanctions and the provision of private remedies.

1. Distinguishing Derogations from Implementations

As we have seen, for the purposes of bringing national sanctions within the scope of the Treaties, Union law distinguishes between two main categories of situation: where the member state is derogating from its Treaty obligations (so that the system of national sanctions is scrutinized under the free movement and non-discrimination provisions); and where the member state is implementing Union law (such that the relevant domestic penalties are subject to the requirements established in *Greek Maize*).

Confusion derives from the fact that it is not always obvious whether a given dispute should be categorized as a derogation or rather as an implementation. Consider, for example, the provisions of Directive 2004/38 whereby member states may require migrant Union citizens to report their presence within the territory and (for longer stays) to register and obtain a residence certificate.[51]

[48] Case C-262/99, *Louloudakis*, [2001] ECR I-5547. See also, Case C-156/04, *Commission v Greece*, *supra* note 13.

[49] Directive 95/46 of the European Parliament and of the Council of 24 October 1995 on the protection of individuals with regard to the processing of personal data and on the free movement of such data, OJ 1995 L 281/31.

[50] Case C-101/01, *Lindqvist*, [2003] ECR I-12971.

[51] Directive 2004/38 of the European Parliament and of the Council of 29 April 2004 on the right of citizens of the Union and their family members to move and reside freely within the territory of the member states, OJ 2004 L 158/77, especially Arts 5 and 8.

It is open to discussion whether a member state is thereby taking advantage of a derogation permitted by Union law, or instead implementing a requirement (albeit an optional one) imposed pursuant to Union law.[52] Similarly, consider the obligation to exchange one's driving licence after residing for a certain period of time within another member state as once provided for under Directive 80/1263.[53] Again, one could have disputed whether a host country which penalized an individual for breaching that obligation was exercising its own competences, which happened to be recognized as such under Union secondary legislation, but nevertheless gave rise to a breach of the Treaty that had to be objectively justified; or instead whether the national authorities were implementing regulatory standards imposed by or directly authorized under Union law, the enforcement of which triggered the duty of loyal cooperation under *Greek Maize*.[54]

In many cases, such uncertainties about the correct classification of a given dispute as one involving either a derogation or an implementation carry little practical relevance: in both situations, the national sanctions must comply with the principle of proportionality.[55] But in other cases, the dividing line between derogation and implementation will indeed prove more important. In the first place, the member state is only obliged to impose an effective penalty if it is implementing Union law; effectiveness is not a criterion relevant to situations of derogation.[56] From that perspective, correct classification of the dispute will obviously affect the degree and indeed the nature of judicial scrutiny over the member state's choice of sanctions.[57] In the second place, if the situation is classed as derogation, not implementation, then the individual's protection from disproportionate penalties derives from the primary Treaty provisions on free movement and equal treatment (not from the duty of loyal cooperation under Article 4(3) TEU). In that regard, protection from disproportionate penalties will be restricted to those individuals who can claim to fall within the personal scope of the primary Treaty provisions in the first place. That will preclude (for example) third country nationals from invoking Union law to challenge the proportionality of national sanctions where they do not otherwise fall within the scope of the Treaties.[58]

[52] Certain rulings suggest the obligation to report constitutes a derogation, eg, Case 118/75, *Watson and Belmann*, [1976] ECR 1185; Case C-265/88, *Messner*, [1989] ECR 4209. In others, the obligation to obtain a residence document seems to be treated as an implementation, eg, Case 8/77, *Sagulo*, *supra* note 11; Case 157/79, *Pieck*, *supra* note 11.

[53] Directive 80/1263, *supra* note 17, repealed by Council Directive 91/439 of 29 July 1991 on driving licences, OJ 1991 L 237/1.

[54] Consider Case C-193/94, *Skanavi*, *supra* note 13.

[55] Though consider the 'double standards' critique, as regards the proportionality assessment, discussed in Section 5.

[56] Note that, insofar as the proportionality assessment requires investigation of how far national rules are not only necessary for but also appropriate to their objective, some element of 'effectiveness review' is implicit even in derogation situations. But such review is of a purely negative character, in the sense that the lack of a truly suitable sanction suggests a disproportionate exercise of public power; by contrast, the criterion of appropriateness within the proportionality assessment does not contain any positive obligation upon the member state to impose an effective sanction per se.

[57] Providing the basis for another 'double standards' critique, as between derogations and implementations, again discussed in Section 5.

[58] Consider, eg, Case C-230/97, *Awoyemi*, [1998] ECR I-6781.

2. Distinguishing Public Sanctions from Private Remedies

The *Greek Maize* case law governing the member state's obligations when it comes to imposing sanctions for the enforcement of Union law is closely intertwined with the *Rewe/Comet* jurisprudence concerning the member state's duty to ensure the effective judicial protection of individuals whose rights derive from the Union legal order. One reason for that close relationship is a shared historical experience: the ruling in *Amsterdam Bulb* surely reflected the Court's equally restrained approach throughout the 1970s to scrutinizing whatever remedies and procedural rules the member state offered to individual right-holders;[59] for its part, *Greek Maize* can also be viewed as part of a wider trend in the case law, gathering pace throughout the 1980s, whereby the Court became much more willing to interfere in the domestic legal systems so as to enhance the effective protection of Community law rights.[60]

But besides their historical kinship, the relationship between *Greek Maize* and *Rewe/Comet* raises a whole host of difficult legal and conceptual problems. After all, the imposition of an obligation on one party will often involve the creation of an individual right for another, such that the duty to impose an equivalent, effective, and proportionate public sanction under *Greek Maize* begins to overlap with, and indeed often becomes difficult to separate out from, the duty to provide an equivalent and effective private remedy under *Rewe/Comet*. Indeed, in certain situations, the Court seems to treat the two bodies of case law as virtually interchangeable.[61] Such habits risk creating significant problems—not least because the proportionality assessment over member state sanctions is a well-established part of the *Greek Maize* test, whereas proportionality is not used as a yardstick for reining-in the judicial protection of individual right-holders: there is no evidence that the Court would scrutinize the remedies provided against a respondent on the grounds that they render the relevant Union norms *too* effective.[62]

It therefore seems preferable to keep the *Greek Maize* case law on member state sanctions conceptually as well as doctrinally distinct from the *Rewe/Comet* case law on individual remedies. The real question concerns the manner in which those two different perspectives on decentralized enforcement—the public sanction and the private remedy—interact with each other and thereby mutually fulfil or even exhaust the member state's obligations under *Greek Maize* and/or *Rewe/Comet*. For example, how far can the member state discharge its own *Greek Maize* obligation to provide a system of sanctions, by entrusting the enforcement of Union law instead to the resources of private

[59] Eg, Case 60/75, *Russo*, [1976] ECR 45; Case 26/74, *Roquette Frères*, [1976] ECR 677; Case 158/80, *Rewe-Handelsgesellschaft Nord v Hauptzollamt Kiel*, [1981] ECR 1805.

[60] Eg, Case 199/82, *San Giorgio*, [1983] ECR 3595; Case C-213/89, *Factortame*, [1990] ECR I-2433; Case C-208/90, *Emmott*, [1991] ECR I-4269.

[61] Eg, Case 14/83, *von Colson*, [1984] ECR 1891. Also, eg, Case C-212/04, *Adeneler*, [2006] ECR I-6057; Cases C-378/07 and C-380/07, *Angelidaki*, [2009] ECR I-3071.

[62] Contrast, eg, Case C-271/91, *Marshall II*, *supra* note 37 on effectiveness with Case C-55/07, *Michaeler*, [2008] ECR I-3135 on proportionality.

actors?[63] Conversely, how far can the member state seek to exclude the possibility of independent individual action by reserving the power to pursue and punish infringements of Union law to the competent public authorities?[64] In any case, when might the accumulation of different public sanctions and private remedies in respect of one and the same Treaty obligation become so oppressive as to amount in itself to a disproportionate system of penalties under Union law?[65] Such difficult questions have scarcely been addressed as such in the case law or scholarship.[66]

3. The Iron Fist: Union Criminal Sanctions for the Enforcement of Union Law

Greek Maize covers the situation where, in the absence of Union provisions, each member state must provide sanctions (which may include the possibility of adopting criminal penalties) for the enforcement of Union law. In certain situations, however, Union law does indeed supply a system of 'own sanctions' for the enforcement of substantive Treaty policies. Some such own sanctions are direct in nature, whereby a Union institution is itself empowered to impose penalties upon a given individual/s: that is true, for example, as regards the enforcement by the Commission of Union competition law under Articles 101 and 102 TFEU (ex-Articles 81 and 82 EC); and also of financial restrictions imposed upon named individuals or groups suspected of involvement with terrorism, based on lists adopted and maintained by the Union institutions.[67] In other situations, Union own sanctions are instead indirect in character, whereby the competent Union institutions legislate for harmonized systems of penalties, which will then be applied to individuals in an executive sense by the relevant national authorities. That is the case, for example, with the longstanding and diverse system of financial sanctions provided for under various instruments of the Common Agricultural Policy (CAP); and with Regulation 2988/95 on the protection of the Union's financial interests.[68] More importantly for present purposes, the model of indirect own sanctions is also that employed by the Union when imposing criminal penalties for the infringement of substantive Union law.

[63] In which regard, consider, eg, Case C-132/05, *Commission v Germany*, [2008] ECR I-957.

[64] In which regard, consider, eg, Case C-253/00, *Muñoz*, [2002] ECR I-7289.

[65] In which regard, consider, eg, Case 14/68, *Walt Wilhelm*, [1969] ECR 1; Case 137/85, *Maizena Gesellschaft*, [1987] ECR 4587; Case C-45/08, *Spector Photo Group*, *supra* note 35.

[66] Dougan, 'Who Exactly Benefits from the Treaties? The Murky Interaction Between Union and National Competence Over the Capacity to Enforce EU Law', *Cambridge Yearbook of European Legal Studies*, 12 (2009–2010) 73.

[67] Though the Council would surely consider such restrictions as precautionary measures rather than penalties *stricto sensu*.

[68] Council Regulation 2988/95 of 18 December 1995 on the protection of the European Communities financial interests, OJ 1995 L 312/1.

A. Competence Questions and the Distinction between Administrative and Criminal Sanctions

The possibility of adopting Union own sanctions, whether direct or indirect in character, is governed in the first instance by the usual principle of attributed powers now contained in Article 5 TEU (ex-Article 5 EC). In fact, the Court recognized relatively early in its case law that the Union institutions must demonstrate a clear legal basis under the Treaties before they can provide for the imposition of own sanctions.[69] Sometimes the necessary competence is clear and undisputed,[70] but in other situations, the necessary legal basis under the Treaties has proved less clear and more contested: recall, for example, the complex competence debates surrounding the use of what were then Articles 60, 301, and 308 EC in order to impose financial restrictions upon individuals or groups suspected of involvement in terrorism but unconnected to third countries.[71] Such competence disputes are nothing new: the Community's competence to provide for the imposition of various types of sanctions and penalties in the field of the CAP, pursuant to what are now Articles 40 and 43 TFEU (ex-Articles 34 and 37 EC), was challenged before and upheld by the ECJ on many occasions.[72]

For present purposes, perhaps the most important part of the debates concerning the existence of Treaty competence to provide for the imposition of own sanctions has been the latter's potential classification as either administrative or criminal in nature. In particular, before the entry into force of the Lisbon Treaty, the member states long objected to the proposition that the Community institutions enjoyed any power to provide for criminal sanctions for the enforcement of substantive Community policies. Until recently, therefore, such Community own sanctions as were adopted were invariably categorized as purely administrative in nature.[73] It is true that political choices about the classification of a given sanction/penalty are not decisive as to their substantive nature as civil, administrative, or criminal in character. After all, the European Court of Human Rights (ECtHR) has held that the concept of a criminal offence or penalty has an autonomous meaning under the European Convention on Human Rights (ECHR): while classification of an offence or penalty as 'criminal' is decisive in that regard, even offences or penalties formally described as purely civil or administrative in nature

[69] Eg, Case 117/83, *Könecke*, [1984] ECR 3291. More recently, eg, Case C-210/00, *Käserei Champignon Hofmeister*, [2002] ECR I-6453; Case C-94/05, *Emsland-Stärke*, [2006] ECR I-2619; Case C-274/04, *ED & F Man Sugar*, [2006] ECR I-3269. Consider also, eg, C-356/97, *Molkereigenossenschaft Wiedergeltingen*, [2000] ECR I-5461; Case C-143/07, *AOB Reuter*, [2008] ECR I-3171.

[70] Eg, Art 103 and 105 TFEU (ex-Art 83 and 85 EC) and Council Regulation 1/2003 of 16 December 2002 on the implementation of the rules on competition, OJ 2003 L 1/1.

[71] In particular: Case T-315/01, *Kadi*, [2005] ECR II-3649; Case T-306/01, *Yusuf and Al Barakaat*, [2005] ECR II-3533; Cases C-402 and 415/05, *Kadi and Al Barakaat*, [2008] ECR I-6351. See now Art 75, 215 and 275 TFEU.

[72] Eg, Case 11/70, *Internationale Handelsgesellschaft*, [1970] ECR 1125; Case 25/70, *Köster*, [1970] ECR 1161; Case 288/85, *Plange Kraftfutterwerke*, [1987] ECR 611; Case 137/85, *Maizena Gesellschaft*, *supra* note 65; Case C-199/90, *Italtrade*, [1990] ECR I-5545; Case C-240/90, *Germany v Commission*, [1992] ECR I-5383.

[73] Eg, Art 23(5) Regulation 1/2003, *supra* note 70.

can still be found to be criminal in substance, having regard to factors such as the nature of the offence and the character and severity of the penalty.[74] Nevertheless, although member state sanctions adopted pursuant to *Greek Maize* have occasionally been reclassified as criminal in character for the purposes of Union law, in accordance with the criteria embodied in the ECHR,[75] the Community courts traditionally proved loathe to overturn any decision by the political institutions that direct or indirect own sanctions should be treated as purely administrative in nature—even if that classification sometimes proved controversial in the scholarship—in fields ranging from competition law,[76] to financial restrictions upon individuals,[77] CAP sanctions and penalties,[78] and the operation of the European Social Fund.[79]

Some commentators have sought to explain this reluctance on the part of the Court to recognize that Community own sanctions might be administrative in label but criminal in nature by reference to doctrinal considerations relating to the specific constitutional principles and higher standards of judicial protection applicable to criminal sanctions and penalties. In particular, the principle of legality demands (in a formal sense) that criminal penalties should be provided for only by the legislature, not through action of the executive and (in a substantive sense) that the defendant in criminal proceedings benefit from additional safeguards, for example, as regards his/her rights of defence and to a fair hearing.[80] Particularly in the context of direct own sanctions, where responsibility for judicial scrutiny lies entirely with the Union (not national) courts,[81] it has been argued that the reclassification as 'criminal' rather than 'administrative' in nature, either of the competition fines and penalties adopted by the Commission, or of the financial restrictions imposed on persons suspected of involvement in terrorism, would imply a much higher standard of judicial review, so as to comply with the requirements of a fair

[74] Eg, *Engel v The Netherlands*, ECHR (1976) Series A, No 22; *Öztürk v Germany*, ECHR (1984) Series A, No 73; *Demicoli v Malta*, ECHR (1991) Series A, No 210; *Schmautzer v Austria*, ECHR (1995) Series A, No 328-A. See further, eg, S. Trechsel, *Human Rights in Criminal Proceedings* (2005), chapter 2.

[75] Eg, Case C-45/08, *Spector Photo Group*, *supra* note 65.

[76] The Union courts do not categorize competition proceedings as criminal in nature, but are prepared to extend certain equivalent standards of protection thereto: consider, eg, Case T-67/00, *JFE v Commission*, [2004] ECR II-2501; Case C-3/06, *Groupe Danone*, [2007] ECR I-1331. Cf European Commission of Human Rights in *Stenuit v France* (Report of 30 May 1991).

[77] Eg, Case T-306/01, *Yusuf and Al Barakaat* and Case T-315/01, *Kadi v Council and Commission*, *supra* note 71; Case T-47/03, *Jose Maria Sison v Council*, [2007] ECR II-73.

[78] Eg, Case 11/70, *Internationale Handelsgesellschaft*, *supra* note 72; Case 25/70, *Köster*, *supra* note 72; Case 137/85, *Maizena Gesellschaft*, *supra* note 65; Case C-240/90, *Germany v Commission*, *supra* note 72; Case C-210/00, *Käserei Champignon Hofmeister*, *supra* note 69; Case C-143/07, *AOB Reuter*, *supra* note 69.

[79] Eg, Case C-186/98, *Nunes and de Matos*, *supra* note 23. See further, eg, Harding, 'Exploring the Intersection of European Law and National Criminal Law', 25 *European Law Review* (2000) 374.

[80] Further, eg, Albrecht and Braum, 'Deficiencies in the Development of European Criminal Law', 5 *European Law Journal* (1999) 293; Van den Wyngaert, 'Eurojust and the European Public Prosecutor in the *Corpus Juris* Model: Water and Fire?', in N. Walker (ed), *Europe's Area of Freedom, Security and Justice* (2004); Vogel, 'The European Integrated Criminal Justice System and Its Constitutional Framework', 12 *Maastricht Journal of European and Comparative Law* (2005) 125; Weyembergh, 'Approximation of Criminal Laws, the Constitutional Treaty and the Hague Programme', 42 *Common Market Law Review* (2005) 1567.

[81] Cf, Case 314/85, *Firma Foto-Frost*, [1987] ECR 4199.

trial and the exercise of full jurisdiction, than has traditionally been practised in the case law.[82]

Be that as it may, there was surely another—perhaps more important—explanation for the Court's longstanding reluctance to reclassify Community own sanctions as criminal rather than merely administrative in nature. Particularly as regards indirect own sanctions in fields such as the CAP, the Court was surely acutely aware that the member states themselves remained implacably hostile to the proposition that, without any clear mandate from the EC Treaty itself, the Community institutions might nevertheless enjoy the power to legislate for the imposition of criminal sanctions so as to enhance the effective enforcement of substantive Community policies. Indeed, as we shall now see, the prospect of a Community competence to adopt measures providing for the harmonization of criminal offences and sanctions provoked profound discord.

B. Debate over the Existence of a Community Criminal Competence

That debate over the existence of a Community competence to harmonize criminal offences and sanctions must be considered in its changing historical context.

1. Divining the Intentions Enshrined in the Original Treaty of Rome

As is usually the case, a mere textual analysis of the original Treaty of Rome yielded no decisive results: it was true that there were no explicit provisions authorizing Community intervention in the national systems of criminal justice; but the essentially functional nature of the Community's competences kept open the possibility of harmonizing aspects of national criminal law in accordance with existing Treaty legal bases.[83] In such circumstances, the debate tended inevitably to mix together questions not only about the formal existence of Community regulatory competence, but also the political desirability and practical feasibility of harmonizing national criminal rules. In other words, horns were locked over the *very principle* of whether there should be any involvement by the supranational legislature in the criminal justice system. Even if (as we shall see) the question of principle has now been answered decisively in the affirmative,[84] many of the broader issues about the construction of a 'European criminal law' first explored in these early debates remain highly resonant today.

On the one side, the prospect of Community competence over certain criminal matters was championed on the basis of familiar arguments about securing the effective and uniform application of the EC Treaty: if the enforcement of

[82] See further, eg, A. Andreangeli, *EU Competition Enforcement and Human Rights* (2008); Spaventa, 'Fundamental What? The Difficult Relationship Between Foreign Policy and Fundamental Rights', in M. Cremona and B. de Witte (eds), *EU Foreign Relations Law: Constitutional Fundamentals* (2008).

[83] Further, eg, Wasmeier and Thwaites, 'The "Battle of the Pillars": Does the European Community have the power to approximate national criminal laws?', 29 *European Law Review* (2004) 613; V. Mitsilegas, *EU Criminal Law* (2009), chapter 2.

[84] See Sections 3.B.2 and 3.E.2.

Community law required criminal rather than merely civil/administrative sanctions, it should fall within the competence of the Community institutions to enact the necessary legislation; similarly, the uniform application of the EC Treaty might well justify the harmonization of certain criminal sanctions, particularly in situations related to the internal market, where differences between each member state's own choice of penalties pursuant to *Greek Maize* could lead to distortions of competition.[85] On the other side, arguments based on effectiveness and uniformity were open to question on the grounds that they were often unpersuasive and unrealistic. One could query the assumption that criminalizing a given activity is necessarily the most effective way of suppressing such conduct; ill-considered criminalization can actually tend to exacerbate problems rather than solve them (for example, by driving the anti-social behaviour further underground or into the arms of organized gangs).[86] One might also doubt whether the harmonization of national criminal rules would really contribute anything to greater uniformity: after all, there would remain significant differences between the member states as regards important matters such as inchoate and ancillary offences (such as attempts, conspiracies, aiding and abetting, the liability of legal persons); the calculation and enforcement of penalties (including taking into account previous convictions, mitigating circumstances, eligibility for parole); and the role of prosecutorial and/or judicial discretion (for example, in deciding whether to bring or terminate prosecution).[87]

More fundamentally, however, the debate about the possible existence of a Community criminal competence was linked to notions of sovereignty and identity. Surely no one doubts the political sensitivity of supranational involvement in criminal law issues—a sensitivity which reflects the close relationship between coercive powers, state sovereignty, popular democracy, and individual rights.[88] And equally, no one would deny the existence of enormous differences between the national systems of criminal justice, reflecting the intimate link between criminal law and the specific political, social, cultural, and economic situation in each member state.[89] Against that background, the prospect of a supranational criminal competence necessarily implied a demos-style debate about whether there could ever exist a 'European public interest'; if so, what might be its scope, nature, and

[85] Further, eg, Sevenster, 'Criminal Law and EC Law', 29 *Common Market Law Review* (1992) 29. On effectiveness and uniformity as normative concepts justifying Union intervention in the domestic enforcement of the Treaties, see further, eg, M. Dougan, *National Remedies Before the Court of Justice: Issues of Harmonisation and Differentiation* (2004).

[86] For discussion, eg, D. Husak, *Overcriminalisation* (2007). For more EU-specific studies, eg, Faure, 'European Environmental Criminal Law: Do we really need it?', 13 *European Environmental Law Review* (2004) 18; K. Cseres, M. Schinkel and F. Vogelaar (eds), *Criminalisation of Competition Law Enforcement: Economic and Legal Implications for the EU Member States* (2006).

[87] For numerous examples, see Green Paper of the Commission on the Approximation, Mutual Recognition and Enforcement of Criminal Sanctions in the European Union, COM (2004) 334 final. Further, eg, Harding, 'Member State Enforcement of European Community Measures: The Chimera of "Effective" Enforcement', 4 *Maastricht Journal of European and Comparative Law* (1997) 5.

[88] Further, eg, Albrecht and Braum, 'Deficiencies in the Development of European Criminal Law', 5 *European Law Journal* (1999) 293; S. Peers, *EU Justice and Home Affairs Law* (2006), especially chapter 8.

[89] As the Court itself acknowledged in Case C-156/04, *Commission v Greece, supra* note 13.

content; and furthermore, which institutions and processes allowed it to be identified, defined, and controlled.[90] It is true that some actors have understood those challenges as a positive reason for recognizing a supranational criminal competence: the very process of formulating and articulating a common understanding of which activities should be considered as criminal, could encourage the fostering of a pan-European consciousness about the appropriate role of criminal justice, and thereby contribute to the gradual construction of a European political identity.[91] But other actors have viewed such aspirations as at best artificially programmatic and at worst entirely misplaced. By and large, considerations relating to the social context of criminal law, and its link to the exercise of popular sovereignty, seemed to caution against any premature recognition of some ambitious and/or ill-defined supranational criminal competence—certainly against smuggling Community powers to harmonize national criminal rules into the EC Treaty by process of mere implication, when a whole host of fundamental issues had not yet been the subject of full and proper scrutiny by the member states themselves.

Indeed, absent such full and proper scrutiny, the prospect of a supranational criminal competence actually seemed to pose certain dangers. The Court's *Greek Maize* case law at least operated from a presumption of equivalence between the enforcement of comparable national and Community obligations, so that Community law would be absorbed into the domestic legal orders in a way that respected the latter's specificity and diversity. By contrast, the mandatory categorization of a given activity as criminal by the Community seemed to risk rupturing the pre-existing state of equivalence between comparable national and Community obligations, and giving rise to serious incoherence within the domestic criminal justice system (whereby one activity would be considered criminal, and another purely civil or administrative, depending solely on whether its legal origin happened to be national or supranational).[92] Of course, such incoherence could be solved by process of spill-over, whereby the member state voluntarily extends the Community's criminal principles into wholly internal situations.[93] But the costs of such spill-over were to be measured not only in the ability of Community law to impact yet more profoundly upon fundamental aspects of national criminal justice, but also in the risk that Community law could thereby exert a momentum (however unintended) towards ever extending the reach of the criminal law. For many, such a prospect would fly in the face of countervailing concerns about

[90] Consider, eg, Baker, 'Criminal Jurisdiction, the Public Dimension to "Effective Protection" and the Construction of Community-Citizen Relations', 4 *Cambridge Yearbook of European Legal Studies* (2001) 25.

[91] Consider, eg, Green Paper on the Approximation, Mutual Recognition and Enforcement of Criminal Sanctions in the European Union, *supra* note 87. Cf, Weyembergh, 'The Functions of Approximation of Penal Legislation Within the European Union', 12 *Maastricht Journal of European and Comparative Law* (2005) 149.

[92] Cf, Biondi, 'The European Court of Justice and Certain National Procedural Limitations: Not Such a Tough Relationship', 36 *Common Market Law Review* (1999) 1271; Harlow, 'Voices of Difference in a Pluralist Community', in P. Beaumont, C. Lyons and N. Walker (eds), *Convergence and Divergence in European Public Law* (2002).

[93] Cf, Caranta, 'Judicial Protection Against Member States: A New *Jus Commune* Takes Shape', 32 *Common Market Law Review* (1995) 703 and 'Learning from our Neighbours: Public Law Remedies, Homogenisation from Bottom Up', 4 *Maastricht Journal of European and Comparative Law* (1997) 220.

controlling the excessive exercise of state coercion and curbing the urge towards retributive justice.[94]

2. *Divining the Intentions Enshrined in the Treaty on European Union*

Against that complex and essentially political background, it is perhaps unsurprising that the Court in *Germany v Commission* (1992) expressly left open the question of whether the Community enjoyed any competence in principle to provide for criminal sanctions in the enforcement of substantive Treaty policies.[95] Such judicial restraint proved well-judged, since the entry into force of the Maastricht Treaty (and the subsequent amendments contained in the Treaties of Amsterdam and Nice) radically changed the terms of the entire debate.[96] In particular, the underlying question of principle was finally settled: there would indeed be a supranational competence over various aspects of criminal law and policy. The focus shifted instead to determining the proper constitutional channels through which such competence—and especially the power to harmonize criminal offences and sanctions for the enforcement of substantive Treaty norms—should be exercised in practice: by continuing to press for a generous interpretation of the Community's existing competences under the Treaty of Rome; or by relying instead on the express powers concerning cross-border criminal cooperation contained in Title VI of the (pre-Lisbon) Treaty on European Union.

That choice was particularly important because the legal regime of the Third Pillar differed markedly from the 'Community method' familiar from the First Pillar. First, the system of decision-making was skewed towards the intergovernmental: the Council adopted (almost) all Third Pillar measures by unanimity; the Commission shared its right of legislate initiative with every member state; the European Parliament performed only a consultative role.[97] Secondly, instead of employing the usual First Pillar instruments (regulations, directives, and decisions), the Third Pillar had its own specific legal acts (common positions, framework decisions, decisions, and conventions) capable of having only truncated effects within the national legal orders.[98] Thirdly, the Court had only limited jurisdiction over matters falling within the scope of the Third Pillar, as compared to its usual powers under Community law.[99] Finally, special rules governed the possibility of engaging in enhanced cooperation in the field of cross-border criminal cooperation, as compared to the system of flexibility applicable to those policies falling within the Community's competences.[100]

[94] For a critique of the extensive and unprincipled expansion of the criminal law, consider Ashworth, 'Is the Criminal Law a Lost Cause?', 116 *LQR* (2000) 225.

[95] Case C-240/90, *Germany v Commission*, *supra* note 72, Rec 24.

[96] We need not dwell on the introduction of amendments to more marginal Treaty provisions such as Art 280 EC or Art 135 EC (now Art 325 and 33 TFEU respectively).

[97] Ex-Arts 34, 36, and 39 TEU. Further, eg, Dashwood, 'Issues of Decision-Making in the European Union after Nice', in A. Arnull and D. Wincott (eds), *Accountability and Legitimacy in the European Union* (2003).

[98] Ex-Art 34 TEU. [99] Ex-Art 35 TEU. [100] Ex-Arts 40–40b TEU.

On the one side, it could be argued that the introduction of the Third Pillar had provided an explicit legal basis under the Treaties for the pursuit of common action in the field of criminal law. As such, supranational criminal policies should be pursued (if at all) only under the auspices of ex-Title VI TEU, not through the medium of the First Pillar. After all, the fact that the Third Pillar was based on such different constitutional principles from the 'Community method' was obviously intended to reflect the member states' collective wish to reconcile the development of a 'European criminal law' with the peculiarly sensitive nature of criminal justice.[101] On the other side, however, even the introduction of dedicated provisions under the Third Pillar did not affect the possible existence of certain Community criminal competences under the First Pillar. In particular, ex-Article 29 TEU specifically stated that criminal cooperation under the TEU should be '[w]ithout prejudice to the powers of the European Community'. Similarly, ex-Article 47 TEU made clear that 'nothing in this Treaty shall affect the Treaties establishing the European Communities or the subsequent Treaties and Acts modifying or supplementing them'.[102] If the First Pillar did indeed include certain criminal law competences, then they should automatically take priority over any Third Pillar powers; the introduction of the Third Pillar was, therefore, at most of neutral relevance to the pre-existing debate on the harmonization of criminal law for the purposes of enforcing substantive Community policies.[103]

Indeed, if anything, many commentators argued that the constitutional specificities of the Third Pillar gave serious cause for concern as regards criminal law-making at the Union level.[104] One need only briefly recall the main criticisms: that the scope of Union competence to harmonize national criminal law under ex-Title VI TEU was unclear and open to challenge;[105] that the Union's institutional balance entrenched executive dominance over the legislative process in a manner difficult to reconcile with the formal principle of legality in the sphere of criminal law;[106] that the exclusion of direct effect for framework decisions and decisions undermined the effective enforcement of Union law, and raised difficult questions about how far other Community principles concerned with safeguarding judicial protection before the national courts might extend into the Third Pillar;[107] and

[101] Further, eg, Dawes and Lynskey, 'The Ever-Longer Arm of EC Law: The Extension of Community Competence into the Field of Criminal Law', 45 *Common Market Law Review* (2008) 131.

[102] Cf, Case C-170/96, *Commission v Council*, [1998] ECR I-2763 on the justiciability of ex-Art 47 TEU pre-Nice.

[103] Further, eg, Wasmeier and Thwaites, 'The "Battle of the Pillars": Does the European Community have the power to approximate national criminal laws?', 29 *European Law Review* (2004) 613.

[104] Further, eg, N. Walker (ed), *Europe's Area of Freedom, Security and Justice* (2004); S. Peers, *EU Justice and Home Affairs Law* (2006); V. Mitsilegas, *EU Criminal Law* (2009).

[105] Eg, Vogel, *supra* note 80; Weyembergh, *supra* note 80.

[106] Eg, Douglas-Scott, 'The rule of law in the European Union: Putting the security into the area of freedom, security and justice', 29 *European Law Review* (2004) 219.

[107] Eg, Fletcher, 'Extending "Indirect Effect" to the Third Pillar: The Significance of *Pupino*', 30 *European Law Review* (2005) 862; Spaventa, 'Opening Pandora's Box: Some Reflections on the Constitutional Effects of the Decision in *Pupino*', 3 *EuConst* (2006) 5; Peers, 'Salvation Outside the Church: Judicial Protection in the Third Pillar After the *Pupino* and *Segi* Judgments', 44 *Common Market Law Review* (2007) 883; Hinarejos, 'On the Legal Effects of Framework Decisions and Decisions: Directly Applicable, Directly Effective, Self-Executing, Supreme?', 14 *European Law Journal* (2008)

that the limitations imposed upon the jurisdiction of the Union courts—especially the lack of direct actions open to natural and legal persons, combined with the voluntary character of the jurisdiction to deliver preliminary references—created serious lacunae in the Union's system of legal remedies.[108] The cumulative effect of those problems was to render the Third Pillar an unappetizing prospect. For the Commission and the European Parliament, the preferred solution was for the Council to exercise its power under ex-Article 42 TEU to transfer cross-border criminal cooperation into the First Pillar and 'normalize' its constitutional framework in accordance with the ordinary 'Community method'.[109] In the meantime, according to this line of argument, if the harmonization of criminal law was to be pursued at all, it seemed best done, as far as possible, through the medium of the First Pillar; as a minimum, that should include legislation relating to the enforcement of substantive Community law.

C. From Institutional Squabbling to Judicial Intervention

1. *Jostling between the Commission and the Council*

Before the entry into force of the Maastricht Treaty, the Commission attempted on several occasions to include specific 'criminal sanctions' provisions in Community legislative proposals, but such efforts invariably foundered in the face of member state opposition within the Council.[110]

Post-Maastricht, and especially post-Amsterdam, the Tampere European Council conclusions from 1999,[111] and the adoption of the Hague Programme in 2004,[112] signalled a gathering political momentum in favour of greater harmonization of national criminal law. That momentum translated into the adoption by the Council, using its powers under ex-Title VI TEU, of a significant number of Union measures aimed at the approximation of criminal offences and/or sanctions in fields clearly falling within the ambit of the Third Pillar.[113] Such measures have

620. Consider also, Borgers, 'Implementing Framework Decisions', 44 *Common Market Law Review* (2007) 1361.

[108] Eg, Claes, 'Judicial Protection in the Area of Freedom, Security and Justice: Passing the Hot Potato?', in H. Schneider (eds), *Migration, Integration and Citizenship: A Challenge for Europe's Future: Volume II* (2005); Davies, '*Segi* and the Future of Judicial Rights Protection in the Third Pillar of the EU', 14 *European Public Law* (2008) 311.

[109] Eg, Communication from the Commission of 28 June 2006 to the Council and the European Parliament on Implementing the Hague Programme: The Way Forward, COM (2006) 331 final; European Parliament Resolution of 14 June 2006 on the consequences of the judgment of the Court of 13 September 2005, OJ 2006 C 300E.

[110] Eg, Commission Proposal of 23 March 1990 for a Council Directive on prevention of the financial system for the purpose of money laundering, COM (90) 106 final, OJ 1990 C 106; Council Directive 91/308 of 10 June 1991 on prevention of the use of the financial system for the purpose of money laundering, OJ 1991 L 166/77.

[111] Tampere European Council Conclusions (15–16 October 1999).

[112] Brussels European Council Conclusions (4–5 November 2004).

[113] Eg, Council Framework Decision 2002/475 of 13 June 2002 on combating terrorism, OJ 2002 L 164/3; Council Framework Decision 2002/629 of 19 July 2002 on trafficking in human beings, OJ 2002 L 203/1; Council Framework Decision 2004/68 of 22 December 2003 on combating the sexual exploitation of children and child pornography, OJ 2004 L 13/44; Council Framework

been heavily criticized on various grounds: for example, the breadth of application and relative vagueness with which various offences are defined; an obsession with custodial penalties to the neglect of other forms of punishment, and especially of alternative and innovative forms of criminal justice; and the pursuit of 'minimum maximum' penalties which encourages even moderate member states to buy into a culture of repression. Overall, the Union has been accused of the excessive pursuit of criminalization, motivated either by the simplistic notion that the abolition of barriers to movement must be accompanied by stronger measures to suppress the criminals who might also take advantage of the greater freedoms offered by a borderless Europe; or by the equally one-dimensional securitization agenda prompted by the terrorist attacks in cities such as New York, Madrid, and London, which risks harnessing the Union's decision-making powers to the service of executive coercion in a way which trumps countervailing concerns about respect for civil liberties.[114]

In addition to those criticisms aimed at the content of European criminal legislation, the Commission also began to press the competence point more forcefully: the Third Pillar was being used for the adoption of harmonizing measures that could and (thanks to ex-Article 47 TEU) should have been adopted by the Community institutions under the First Pillar. In fact, certain Commission attempts to include 'criminal sanctions' provisions in First Pillar measures were again simply rejected by the Council.[115] Other Commission proposals for 'criminal sanctions' provisions under the First Pillar were eventually adopted by the Council as Third Pillar measures on the basis of a separate member state initiative.[116] Yet another set of Commission proposals under the First Pillar gave rise to the so-called 'dual text' approach: the substantive policy measures would indeed be enacted as Community measures, but the criminal enforcement provisions would be adopted separately by the Council under ex-Title VI TEU.[117]

Decision 2004/757 of 25 October 2004 laying down minimum provisions on the constituent elements of criminal acts and penalties in the field of illicit drug trafficking, OJ 2004 L 335/8; Council Framework Decision 2008/841 of 24 October 2008 on the fight against organized crime, OJ 2008 L 300/42; Council Framework Decision 2008/913 of 28 November 2008 on combating certain forms and expressions of racism and xenophobia by means of criminal law, OJ 2008 L 328/55.

[114] Further, eg, Asp, 'Harmonisation and Cooperation within the Third Pillar: Built-In Risks', 4 *Cambridge Yearbook of European Legal Studies* (2001) 15; Weyembergh, *supra* note 80; Lavenex and Wagner, 'Which European Public Order? Sources of Imbalance in the European Area of Freedom, Security and Justice', 16 *European Security* (2007) 225.

[115] Eg, Commission Proposal for a Directive on the criminal law protection of the Community's financial interests, COM (2001) 272 final, OJ 2001 C 240E/19. Also, eg, Commission Proposal for a Directive on insider dealing and market manipulation, COM (2001) 281 final, OJ 2001 C 240E/32; Directive 2003/6 of the European Parliament and of the Council of 28 January 2003 on insider dealing market manipulation (market abuse), OJ 2003 L 96/16.

[116] Eg, Commission Proposal for a Directive of the European Parliament and of the Council on the protection of the environment through criminal law, COM (2001) 139 final, OJ 2001 C180E; Council Framework Decision 2003/80 of 27 January 2003 on the protection of the environment through criminal law, OJ 2003 L 29/55.

[117] Eg, Commission Proposal for a Directive of the European Parliament and of the Council on ship-source pollution and on the introduction of sanctions, including criminal sanctions, for pollution offences, COM (2003) 92 final; Directive 2005/35 of the European Parliament and of the Council of 7 September 2005 on ship-source pollution and on the introduction

2. *The* Environmental Crimes *Ruling*

That period of inter-institutional wrangling came to a head when the Commission decided to challenge the legality of the Environmental Crimes Framework Decision before the European Court of Justice (ECJ).[118]

In 2001, the Commission made a proposal to the Council, on the basis of Article 175 EC (now Article 192 TFEU), for a directive on the protection of the environment through criminal law, defining the conduct which member states should establish as criminal offences under domestic law, including a list of the Community environmental measures which should become subject to those criminal offences.[119] In the end, however, the Council, acting on a Danish proposal under ex-Title VI TEU, adopted Framework Decision 2003/80 on the protection of the environment through criminal law (which nevertheless incorporated certain aspects of the Commission's draft directive).[120] The Commission sought annulment of the Framework Decision on the grounds that it infringed ex-Article 47 TEU, since the Community itself enjoyed the competence to require member states to prescribe criminal penalties for infringement of First Pillar legislation, where that was necessary to ensure such legislation was effective.

The ECJ began by ascertaining whether the relevant provisions of the Framework Decision could indeed have been adopted under Article 175 EC. It noted that protection of the environment constitutes one of the Community's fundamental objectives and must be incorporated into the full range of Community policies and activities, though Articles 174–176 EC provide the specific framework and legal basis for conducting the Community's environmental policy. Although, as a general rule, criminal law and criminal procedure fall outside the Community's competence, this does not prevent the Community legislature from adopting measures relating to national criminal law, which it considers necessary to ensure that the rules it lays down on environmental protection are fully effective, in particular, where the application of effective and dissuasive criminal penalties by the competent domestic authorities is essential for combating serious environmental offences. Having regard to the aim and content of Framework Decision 2003/80, the contested provisions had as their main purpose the protection of the environment and could properly have been adopted on the basis of Article 175 EC. By thus encroaching upon the powers reserved to the Community under the EC Treaty, the Framework Decision infringed ex-Article 47 TEU and was annulled in its entirety.

of penalties for infringements, OJ 2005 L 255/11; Council Framework Decision 2005/667 of 12 July 2005 on strengthening the criminal law framework for the enforcement of the law against ship-source pollution, OJ 2005 L 255/164. Also, eg, Council Directive 2002/90 of 28 November 2002 defining the facilitation of unauthorized entry, transit and residence, OJ 2002 L 328/17; Council Framework Decision 2002/946 of 28 November 2002 on the strengthening of the penal framework to prevent the facilitation of unauthorized entry, transit, and residence, OJ 2002 L 328/1.

118 Case C-176/03, *Commission v Council*, *supra* note 5.

119 Commission Proposal COM (2001) 139 final, *supra note* 116.

120 Council Framework Decision 2003/80, *supra* note 116.

3. *The* Ship-Source Pollution *Ruling*

Environmental Crimes was the first case in which the Court confirmed unequivocally that the Community did enjoy certain legislative competences of its own in the field of criminal law and that, pursuant to ex-Article 47 TEU, such Community competence was protected against encroachment by the Union taking action pursuant to its Third Pillar powers. Unsurprisingly, reactions to the ruling were very mixed. The Commission warmly welcomed the ruling and advocated a far-reaching interpretation of its scope and effects.[121] The European Parliament was generally supportive of the ruling, but urged the Commission to exercise greater caution in its understanding of the implications.[122] The member states, unsurprisingly, were less enthusiastic: Eleven had intervened in support of the Council in *Environmental Crimes* itself, and 19 were about to intervene in support of the Council in the next (*Ship-Source Pollution*) dispute.

In fact, much of the initial reaction to *Environmental Crimes* resulted from and focused on the vagueness of the Court's guidance concerning the Community's newfound criminal competences. In doctrinal terms, three main questions seemed to cry out for clarification. First, were the Community's powers limited to the field of environmental law, or could they extend to other internal policies such as agriculture, internal market, and social protection? Secondly, what threshold had to be crossed before the effectiveness of any given Community policy could justify not only the adoption of ordinary civil or administrative sanctions, but also the imposition of criminal law liabilities? Thirdly, what degree of detail could the Community legitimately prescribe when harmonizing national criminal legislation under its First Pillar powers? In particular, was Community competence limited to establishing the principle of criminalization and defining the constituent elements of offences; or did it extend also to prescribing the form and degree of severity of the consequent penalties themselves? In practical terms, there was also the urgent question of which other measures already adopted under the Third Pillar were affected by the ruling; and indeed, which pending/future proposals for the adoption of criminal sanctions to enforce substantive Community policies would have to be pursued under the First rather than the Third Pillar.

The ruling in *Ship-Source Pollution* gave the Court an opportunity to clarify these issues.[123] The Council adopted Framework Decision 2005/667 on strengthening the criminal law framework for the enforcement of the law against ship-source pollution under ex-Title VI TEU.[124] Its aim was to supplement the Ship-Source Pollution Directive 2005/35,[125] a First Pillar act, by requiring the member states to adopt various criminal law measures with a view to ensuring

[121] Communication from the Commission to the European Parliament and the Council of 23 November 2005 on the implications of the Court's judgment of 13 September 2005, COM (2005) 583 final.

[122] European Parliament Resolution, *supra* note 109.

[123] Case C-440/05, *Commission v Council*, *supra* note 5.

[124] Council Framework Decision 2005/667, *supra* note 117.

[125] Directive 2005/35, *supra* note 117.

a high level of safety and environmental protection in relation to maritime transport. To that end, Articles 2, 3, and 5 of the Framework Decision established a basic obligation to ensure that certain infringements of the Directive, whether committed by natural or legal persons, were regarded as criminal offences under national law, punishable by effective, proportionate, and dissuasive penalties. Moreover, Articles 4 and 6 of the Framework Decision set out detailed rules on the types and levels of criminal sanctions to be imposed under national law, according to factors such as the defendant's state of mind and degree of culpability and the severity of the damage inflicted on the marine environment. The Commission considered that all of the provisions contained in Framework Decision 2005/667 could have been enacted by the Community under Article 80(2) EC (now Article 100(2) TFEU), which provides for the adoption of specific measures concerning sea transport within the context of the common transport policy, including measures aimed at improving maritime transport safety and (in accordance with Article 6 EC (now Article 11 TFEU)) promoting environmental protection. Arguing that the Council had therefore infringed ex-Article 47 TEU by adopting those provisions under the Third Pillar, the Commission sought annulment of the Framework Decision.

The ECJ reiterated its finding in *Environmental Crimes* that, although criminal law generally falls outside the Community's competence, when the application of effective, proportionate and dissuasive criminal penalties is an essential measure for combating serious environmental offences, the Community legislature may require member states to introduce such penalties, in order to ensure that the relevant Community rules are fully effective. Here, the provisions laid down in Framework Decision 2005/667 related to conduct likely to cause particularly serious environmental damage as a result of the infringement of Community rules on maritime safety. Furthermore, the Council had clearly taken the view that criminal penalties were indeed necessary to ensure compliance with those Community rules. Accordingly, Articles 2, 3, and 5 of the Framework Decision, requiring member states to apply criminal penalties to certain forms of conduct, could have been validly adopted under Article 80(2) EC; to that extent, the Council had infringed ex-Article 47 TEU. By contrast, determination of the type and level of the criminal penalties to be applied did not fall within the Community's sphere of competence. Thus, Articles 4 and 6 of the Framework Decision could not have been adopted by the Community legislature; to that extent, the Council had not infringed ex-Article 47 TEU. Nevertheless, since all of the Framework Decision's provisions were inextricably linked together, such that it was impossible to sever good from bad, the measure was annulled in its entirety.

D. Assessing the Legal Framework After *Environmental Crimes* and *Ship-Source Pollution*

Given the reforms contained in the Lisbon Treaty, it is perhaps unnecessary to offer an exhaustive analysis of the rulings in *Environmental Crimes* and *Ship-Source Pollution* (despite their fundamental constitutional significance in the eyes of contemporary observers).[126] Nevertheless, some discussion is surely called for: not only so as to understand the background to and significance of the post-Lisbon provisions, but also because (as we saw also in another context) the debates surrounding *Environmental Crimes* and *Ship-Source Pollution* addressed broader issues of principle which retain important resonances even today,[127] and indeed (as we shall explore further below) it is not yet entirely certain that the specific criminal law competences recognized by the ECJ in its rulings have finally been retired from active service within the Union legal order.[128]

1. Effectiveness as the Basis of Community Criminal Competence

A useful starting point is to clarify the precise nature of the Community criminal competence recognized in *Environmental Crimes* and *Ship Source Pollution.*

It seems safe to assume that the Community's criminal competence was not conceived as an 'implied power' in the sense of *Germany v Commission* (1987).[129] The latter ruling established that, where a Treaty provision confers responsibility for carrying out a specific task but does not create any explicit competence to adopt the acts necessary to fulfil that responsibility, the relevant Treaty provision must be regarded as impliedly conferring those powers which are indispensable in order to carry out that task. That simply does not describe the situation under present consideration: the harmonization of criminal offences for the purposes of enforcing a given Community policy was nowhere set out as a specific task or responsibility in the sense of *Germany v Commission*; furthermore, as it turned out, appropriate legal bases for such harmonization of national criminal rules were not in fact lacking under the EC Treaty.

Nor does it seem appropriate to conceptualize *Environmental Crimes* and *Ship-Source Pollution* as the transformation of negative Community control over member state sanctions under *Greek Maize*, into a positive Community competence to harmonize criminal legislation on the basis of the duty of loyal cooperation. Besides the fact that Article 10 EC (now Article 4(3) TEU) is not in itself a legal basis for legislating, and was not referred to by the ECJ in *Environmental Crimes* or *Ship-Source Pollution* to explain the constitutional origin of the Community's criminal competence, there is no persuasive reason why the member state's obligation to cooperate in achieving the tasks of the Treaties under Article 4(3) TEU should provide the basis for vesting a legislative power in the Union to harmonize the subject-matter of that cooperation. Indeed, given the extensive ways in which the Court has interpreted Article 4(3) TEU as a source of obligations for the member states, such a proposition could seriously undermine the principle of attributed powers.[130]

[126] On the Lisbon reforms, see Section 3.E. [127] See Section 3.B.1.

[128] See Section 3.E.2.

[129] Cases 281, 283–5 and 287/85, *Germany v Commission*, [1987] ECR 3203.

[130] Further, eg, Temple Lang, 'The Duties of National Courts under Community Constitutional Law', 22 *European Law Review* (1997) 3, and 'The Duties of National Authorities under Community Constitutional Law', 23 *European Law Review* (1998) 109.

The preferred interpretation of *Environmental Crimes* and *Ship-Source Pollution* is that the Court treated the Community's criminal competence as inherent in the relevant legal basis, albeit in a second-order manner, to be triggered whenever criminal sanctions were necessary for the enforcement of substantive secondary legislation already enacted under that same Treaty provision. The powers recognized in *Environmental Crimes* were thus of a derived nature: they presupposed the existence of a substantive policy initiative, and sought merely to reinforce the latter's effectiveness, as regards its enforcement within the domestic legal systems, in accordance with the same legal basis. For those purposes, the Court in *Environmental Crimes* described the threshold for exercising the Community's derived criminal competences in quite stringent terms: criminal sanctions must be 'essential' in the case of 'serious' offences, and their use 'necessary' to ensure that Community rules are 'fully effective'. Nevertheless, questions still arise about how far that idea of 'effectiveness'—which (as we shall see)[131] has certainly survived into the post-Lisbon era—is really a suitable criterion for establishing the existence of, and indeed identifying the conditions for exercising, a derived supranational competence to harmonize criminal offences.

In particular, some commentators have seen *Environmental Crimes* as problematic from the viewpoint of the principles of attributed powers and subsidiarity. Such problems are attributed to the Court's purely functional approach to the existence/exercise of the Community's criminal competence, whereby attention seems fixed entirely on securing the more effective enforcement of substantive Treaty policies. After all, effectiveness is not the only criterion upon which society decides to criminalize a given anti-social behaviour; such choices involve a whole series of other political, social, cultural, and moral judgments as well.[132] Conversely, the Court seemed to endorse the assumption that criminal sanctions are per se the most effective form of enforcement tool, whereas (as we have seen) many would challenge the tendency towards over-criminalization as undesirable and often counter-productive.[133] Furthermore, the criterion of effectiveness as described in *Environmental Crimes*, and especially the requirement of necessity, seemed to be judged in the abstract, not in its broader context, ie without taking into account any other sanctions and enforcement mechanisms provided for under Community law and/or available within the national legal systems.[134] A proper analysis of effectiveness and necessity should be able to provide a detailed and convincing answer to the question: Why should supranational criminal law measures really be considered 'essential', when the member states are already obliged to provide 'effective and dissuasive sanctions'—which may include the possibility

[131] See Section 3.E.2.

[132] For general discussion, eg, A. Simester and G.R. Sullivan, *Criminal Law: Theory and Doctrine* (2007), chapter 16; A. Ashworth, *Principles of Criminal Law* (2009), chapter 2.

[133] Further, eg, White, 'Harmonisation of Criminal Law under the First Pillar', 31 *European Law Review* (2006) 81; Herlin-Karnell, '*Commission v. Council:* Some Reflections on Criminal Law in the First Pillar', 13 *European Public Law* (2007) 69 Mitsilegas, 'The Third Wave of Third Pillar Law: Which Direction for EU Criminal Justice?', 34 *European Law Review* (2009) 523.

[134] Cf, Tobler, Casenote on *Commission v Council (Environmental Crimes)*, 43 *CMLRev* (2006) 835; Herlin-Karnell, Casenote on *Commission v Council (Ship-Source Pollution)*, 14 *EPL* (2008) 533.

of criminal penalties—under the *Greek Maize* case law? In short: from the perspective of attributed powers and subsidiarity, the Court's effectiveness test under *Environmental Crimes* seemed to lack any specifically criminal dimension, and emerged instead as a highly abstract and artificial concept that fails to offer any real check on the existence and/or exercise of Community criminal competence.[135]

If one accepts that critique, the solution would have been for the Court to define the criteria governing the Community's derived criminal law competences both with much greater precision, and in a more multi-dimensional manner, which acknowledges the competing factors relevant to the issue of criminalization.[136] However, it is arguable that the force of such criticisms is undermined—at least in part—by their failure to take into account the institutional dimension to the rulings in *Environmental Crimes* and *Ship-Source Pollution*. In particular, the Court in both cases referred to the fact that the Council considered criminal penalties to be necessary to ensure compliance with the relevant Community rules.[137] That seems to imply that the choice to impose criminal sanctions is essentially a complex political one, to be applied in the first instance by the responsible political institutions. It is at that stage, and in that forum, that consideration should be given (for example) to whether existing national or supranational sanctions are sufficient to ensure the effectiveness of substantive Treaty norms; whether harmonized criminal sanctions would actually enhance effectiveness at all; and whether various cultural or moral concerns act as a counter-weight to considerations of effectiveness alone. Such basic political choices about the appropriate role and scope of the criminal justice system are not (and should not) be open to second-guessing by the courts.[138] The judicial function is better discharged by a careful scrutiny of whether the legislature's more detailed choices about offences and sanctions, as well as their actual application and enforcement within the member states, complies with the principle of proportionality and other fundamental rights guarantees.[139]

2. Scope and Strength of Community Criminal Competence

Much attention after *Environmental Crimes* focused on the scope and strength of the Community's derived criminal competence.

Consider first the scope of the ruling. *Environmental Crimes* was phrased in relatively cautious terms: the existence of a derived criminal competence was intimately connected to the pursuit of the EC Treaty's environmental policy objectives. However, as a matter of principle, there seemed no reason to restrict the

[135] Further, eg, Herlin-Karnell, 'An Exercise in Effectiveness?', *European Business Law Review* (2007) 1181 and 'Subsidiarity in the Area of EU Justice and Home Affairs Law: A Lost Cause?', 15 *European Law Journal* (2009) 351.

[136] Cf, European Parliament Resolution, *supra* note 109, especially para 15.

[137] Case C-176/03, *Commission v Council*, *supra* note 5, Rec 48; Case C-440/05, *Commission v Council*, *supra* note 5, Rec 68.

[138] Cf case law on judicial deference to broad political discretion in other contexts, eg, Case C-84/94, *United Kingdom v Council*, [1996] ECR I-5755; Case C-233/94, *Germany v Parliament and Council*, [1997] ECR I-2405; Case C-189/01, *Jippes*, [2001] ECR I-5689; Case C-434/02, *Arnold André*, [2004] ECR I-11825; Case C-210/03, *Swedish Match*, [2004] ECR I-11893.

[139] See Section 5.

judgment to the field of environmental policy rather than also extending to fields such as the internal market, non-discrimination, consumer protection, and agricultural policy (assuming the same threshold of effectiveness was traversed).[140] After all, Articles 2 and 3 EC did not establish any hierarchy between the Treaty's various aims and objectives. Moreover, the EC Treaty contained 'integration clauses' for other important policy fields analogous to that concerning environmental protection under Article 6 EC.[141] Finally, the Court has referred to the fundamental nature of other policy goals under the EC Treaty besides environmental protection.[142]

The Commission certainly supported that broad interpretation of *Environmental Crimes*. Indeed, its 2005 communication specifically identified a whole series of other Third Pillar framework decisions deemed to have infringed the Community's criminal competences (even if the limitation period for seeking their annulment had already expired).[143] The European Parliament was less aggressive in its interpretation than the Commission, urging that the ruling should only apply in practice to those fields which were among the Community's 'main principles, objectives and competences'.[144] The Council's views on this issue became clear in the *Ship-Source Pollution* dispute, where it was argued that the scope of *Environmental Crimes* should be restricted to objectives that were 'essential, transversal and fundamental'—a test that the Council believed was not satisfied in the case of transport policy, even if it could apply to environmental policy.[145]

The ruling in *Ship-Source Pollution* itself failed to offer much illumination as to the potential scope of the Community's criminal competences. Even though the case involved maritime transport and safety, the Court's reasoning was still closely tied to the objective of environmental protection, which formed an integral part of the Framework Directive's provisions. The Court neither endorsed nor rejected explicitly either the Commission or the Council's interpretation of *Environmental Crimes*. However, subsequent institutional practice did tend to support a more generous approach to the scope of Community criminal competence: for example, Directive 2009/52, providing for sanctions against employers of illegal migrants,

[140] Though subject to the express exclusion of criminal competence under Art 135 and 280 EC.

[141] Eg, Art 152(1) EC on public health and Art 153(2) EC on consumer protection (see now Arts 9 and 12 TFEU).

[142] Eg, Case C-126/97, *Eco Swiss v Benetton*, [1999] ECR I-3055 (competition law); Case C-243/08, *Pannon*, [2009] ECR I-4713 (consumer protection).

[143] Communication from the Commission COM (2005) 583 final, *supra* note 121, eg, Council Framework Decision 2000/383 of 29 May 2000 on increasing protection by criminal penalties and other sanctions against counterfeiting in connection with the introduction of the euro, OJ 2000 L 140/1; Council Framework Decision 2001/413 of 28 May 2001 on combating fraud and counterfeiting of non-cash means of payment, OJ 2001 L 149/1; Council Framework Decision 2001/500 of 26 June 2001 on money laundering, the identification, tracing, freezing, seizing, and confiscation of instrumentalities and the proceeds of crime, OJ 2001 L 182/1; Council Framework Decision 2002/946 of 28 November 2002 on the strengthening of the penal framework to prevent the facilitation of unauthorized entry, transit, and residence, OJ 2002 L 328/1; Council Framework Decision 2003/568 of 22 July 2003 on combating corruption in the private sector, OJ 2003 L 192/54; Council Framework Decision 2005/222 of 24 February 2005 on attacks on information systems, OJ 2005 L 69/67.

[144] European Parliament Resolution, *supra* note 109, especially para 10.

[145] Case C-440/05, *Commission v Council*, *supra* note 5, Rec 44.

including the harmonization of certain criminal offences, was adopted under Article 63 EC (now Article 79 TFEU).[146]

Consider second the strength of the Community's criminal competences. Advocate General Colomer in *Environmental Crimes* suggested that those powers should be limited to establishing the principle of criminalization, and defining the constituent elements of the offences, but should not extend to determining the nature and severity of any penalty to be imposed. The latter should be left to the member states or dealt with (if necessary) through the adoption of Third Pillar measures. That approach was justified on the grounds that, having regard to the legal and sociological particularities of each member state, the national legislatures were best placed to determine exactly which criminal sanctions would be most appropriate for fulfilling the EC Treaty's objectives.[147] The Court itself in *Environmental Crimes* did not address this issue directly. But there seemed no logical reason to limit the Community's criminal competences to establishing the principle of criminalization and defining the relevant offences. After all, if such regulatory powers were to be judged according to the criterion of effectiveness, it seemed difficult to rule out a priori the possibility that the enforcement of substantive Treaty norms might well necessitate harmonization of the penalties as well. That was the view taken by the Commission in its 2005 communication,[148] this time fully supported by the European Parliament.[149]

When the issue returned in *Ship-Source Pollution*, Advocate General Mazák again recommended that the Community's criminal competences should be limited to the principle of criminalization and the definition of offences. Any more intrusive powers over the nature and level of sanctions, he argued, could upset the internal coherence of each national penal system. In accordance with the principle of subsidiarity, the member states were as a rule better placed to translate the concept of effective, proportionate, and dissuasive criminal penalties into their own legal systems and societal contexts.[150] Once more, closer inspection suggests that the Advocate General's arguments were not necessarily convincing. After all, for the Community to insist that a given form of conduct must be criminalized can be just as or even more intrusive of national sovereignty, local preferences, and the internal coherence of the domestic criminal justice system than provisions concerning the nature and level of penalties.[151] The fact that supranational harmonization of actual penalties remained possible, albeit under the Third Pillar, also

[146] Directive 2009/52 of the European Parliament and of the Council of 18 June 2009 providing for minimum standards on sanctions and measures against employers of illegally staying third-country nationals, OJ 2009 L 168/24.

[147] Case C-176/03, *Commission v Council, supra* note 5, paras 84–7 of the Opinion.

[148] Consider also, eg, Amended Proposal of the Commission of 26 April 2006 for a Directive of the European Parliament and the Council on criminal measures aimed at ensuring the enforcement of intellectual property rights, COM (2006) 168 final; Commission Proposal of 9 February 2007 for a Directive of the European Parliament and of the Council on the protection of the environment through criminal law, COM (2007) 51 final.

[149] European Parliament Resolution, *supra* note 109, especially para 16.

[150] Case C-440/05, *Commission v Council, supra* note 5, paras 103–10 of the Opinion.

[151] Cf Peers, 'The European Community's Criminal Law Competence: The Plot Thickens', 33 *European Law Review* (2008) 399.

undermined the proposition that that was an issue which belonged inherently to the member states themselves.

Nevertheless, on this issue at least, *Ship-Source Pollution* did provide a clear steer: albeit without any real reasoning, the Court held that determination of the type and level of criminal penalties does not fall within the Community's sphere of competence. First Pillar measures were therefore limited to imposing upon member states a basic obligation to ensure that effective, proportionate, and dissuasive criminal sanctions existed under national law; if the need arose for more detailed rules concerning the actual type and/or level of penalties, it should be fulfilled (if at all) through approximation measures adopted pursuant to ex-Title VI TEU. That approach was subsequently followed (for example) in the new directives concerning environmental crimes[152] and ship-source pollution;[153] and also as regards criminal sanctions against employers of illegal third country nationals.[154]

3. *Further Implications of the Community's Criminal Competence*

Assuming that the Community's criminal competences were capable of extending beyond the field of environmental protection, but did not apply to determining the nature/level of actual penalties, two further consequences deserve brief mention.

First, the fact that the Community's criminal law powers were derived in nature necessarily implied that they were subject to all the same conditions imposed under the relevant Treaty legal basis as the underlying substantive norms the harmonized criminal offences were intended to help enforce. Those conditions embraced not only the applicable decision-making procedures, but also the available range of legal instruments, and indeed the permissible degree of pre-emption (such as whether the measures should be limited to minimum harmonization only, or were capable of having more exhaustive legal effects to the exclusion of national regulatory power). Perhaps less obvious was the question of how far any Treaty conditions required to trigger the Community's primary substantive competences should apply also to the exercise of its derived criminal law powers. For example, if the relevant legal basis was Article 95 EC (now Article 114 TFEU), would it be necessary to demonstrate that differences in national sanctions for the enforcement of substantive internal market rules created *their own* barriers to trade or distortions of competition;[155] or would it be sufficient to establish that, differences in national law as regards the relevant substantive rules having triggered the exercise of inter-

[152] Directive 2008/99 of the European Parliament and of the Council of 19 November 2008 on the protection of the environment through criminal law, OJ 2008 L 328/28. Cf, Commission Proposal COM (2007) 51 final, *supra* note 148.

[153] Directive 2009/123 of the European Parliament and of the Council of 21 October 2009 amending Directive 2005/35 on ship-source pollution and on the introduction of penalties for infringements, OJ 2009 L 280/52. Cf, Commission Proposal of 11 March 2008 for a Directive amending Directive 2005/35 on ship-source pollution and on the introduction of penalties for infringements, COM (2008) 134 final.

[154] Directive 2009/52, *supra* note 146. Cf Commission Proposal of 16 May 2007 for a Directive providing for sanctions against employers of illegally staying third-country nationals, COM (2007) 249 final.

[155] In accordance with Case C-376/98, *Germany v Parliament and Council*, [2000] ECR I-8419.

nal market competence in the first place, the Community's derived power to adopt criminal enforcement measures was *simply necessary* to secure the effectiveness of the harmonized regulatory standards? Given that the overriding criterion for triggering the Community's derived criminal powers related to effective enforcement, the latter interpretation was surely more appropriate.[156]

Secondly, *Environmental Crimes* and *Ship-Source Pollution* inevitably had important implications for the constitutional relationship between the First and Third Pillars. The effect of ex-Article 47 TEU was indeed to create a hierarchy in favour of the EC Treaty, so that Third Pillar powers could be exercised only in default of Community competence.[157] Establishing the principle of criminalization and defining the relevant offences, where required for the effective enforcement of substantive Community policies, had to be completed under the First Pillar. Ex-Title IV TEU could then be used (if necessary) to determine the nature and level of the actual penalty imposed, consequent upon such First Pillar criminal measures.[158] Otherwise, the focus of the Third Pillar became fixed very firmly on the adoption of measures concerning cross-border police and judicial criminal cooperation, unrelated to the enforcement of substantive Community policies per se—though such cooperation could still include the approximation of national criminal law, whether concerning those offences (such as organized crime, terrorism, and illicit drug trafficking) identified in ex-Title VI TEU as a policy end in itself, or for the purposes of facilitating the mutual recognition of criminal judgments across the member states within the area of freedom, security, and justice.[159]

E. Harmonization of Criminal Offences and Sanctions after the Lisbon Treaty

With effect from 1 December 2009, the revised provisions of the Treaty on the Functioning of the European Union have once more radically altered the legal

[156] An interpretation not contradicted by the 'cross-pillar' dispute in Case C-301/06, *Ireland v Council and Parliament*, [2009] ECR I-593, since the disputed measure in that case did not concern the second-order harmonization of criminal sanctions, but the first-order harmonization of substantive rules on data retention. Further, eg, Konstadinides, 'Wavering between centres of gravity: Comment on *Ireland v. Parliament and Council*', 34 *European Law Review* (2010) 88.

[157] Cf, Case C-91/05, *Commission v Council (Small Arms and Light Weapons)*, [2008] ECR I-3651 on ex-Art 47 TEU as a dividing line between First and Second Pillar competences. See further, eg, Heliskoski, 'Small arms and light weapons within the Union's pillar structure: An analysis of Art 47 of the EU Treaty', 33 *European Law Review* (2008) 898; Hillion and Wessel, 'Competence Distribution in EU External Relations after *ECOWAS*: Clarification or Continued Fuzziness?', 46 *Common Market Law Review* (2009) 551.

[158] In default of which, Union scrutiny over the member state's choice of criminal sanctions would presumably continue under a modified version of the *Greek Maize* jurisprudence—modified in the sense that the requirements of equivalence, effectiveness, and proportionality would thenceforth be directed only towards the type and level of penalties.

[159] Which has produced an extensive body of critical academic analysis in its own right: see, eg, Peers, 'Mutual Recognition and Criminal Law in the European Union: Has the Council Got it Wrong?', 41 *Common Market Law Review* (2004) 5; Weyembergh, 'The Functions of Approximation of Penal Legislation Within the European Union', 12 *Maastricht Jorunal of European and Comparative Law* (2005) 149; Mitsilegas, 'The Constitutional Implications of Mutual Recognition in Criminal Matters in the EU', 43 *Common Market Law Review* (2006) 1277; Bantekas, 'The Principle of Mutual Recognition in EU Criminal Law', 32 *European Law Review* (2007) 365.

framework governing European criminal law: in the first place, by abolishing the Third Pillar as a distinct constitutional regime and absorbing cross-border criminal cooperation (with certain exceptions) into the mainstream techniques of Union governance; in the second place, by introducing a dedicated legal basis for the harmonization of criminal offences and penalties in the enforcement of substantive Treaty norms.

1. *The New Provisions on Cross-Border Criminal Cooperation*

Under Lisbon, the old Title VI TEU on cross-border criminal cooperation has been amalgamated with the old Title IV, Part Three EC on border checks, asylum, immigration, and judicial cooperation in civil matters so as to create a new Title V, Part Three TFEU on the Area of Freedom, Security and Justice (AFSJ). Most of the distinct constitutional features of the previous Third Pillar—which had made it so objectionable to many commentators—have now been suppressed.[160] Thus, the specific legal instruments previously used under the Third Pillar have been replaced by ordinary regulations, directives, and decisions (all capable in principle of having direct effect within the national legal systems).[161] There is a significant enhancement in the powers of the European Parliament, and the use of qualified majority voting (QMV) within the Council of Ministers: the 'ordinary legislative procedure' has become the standard decision-making process across the entire AFSJ. Almost all of the previous restrictions on the jurisdiction of the Union courts as regards cross-border criminal cooperation have been removed.[162] Finally, the distinct provisions governing enhanced cooperation in the field of criminal law have also been abolished.[163]

That said, Title V still manifests certain specific characteristics as compared to other fields of internal Union action, particularly as regards cross-border criminal cooperation, thus reflecting the political sensitivities which continue to surround the Union's involvement in the field of criminal law.[164] First, the Commission shares its prerogative of legislative initiative in this field; proposals may also be brought forward by one-quarter of member states.[165] Secondly, certain Union competences remain subject to a 'special legislative procedure' based on the Council acting unanimously, either after consulting the European Parliament,[166] or with the latter's consent.[167] In those situations, however, failure to secure the required

[160] See further, eg, Dougan, 'The Treaty of Lisbon 2007: Winning Minds, Not Hearts', 45 *Common Market Law Review* (2008) 617; Ladenburger, 'Police and Criminal Law in the Treaty of Lisbon: A New Dimension for the Community Method', 4 *European Constitutional Law Review* (2008) 20; Mitsilegas, *supra* note 83. Consider also, eg, Baker and Harding, 'From Past Imperfect to Future Perfect? A Longitudinal Study of the Third Pillar', 34 *European Law Review* (2009) 25; Hinarejos, 'The Lisbon Treaty Versus Standing Still: A View from the Third Pillar', 5 *European Constitutional Law Review* (2009) 99.

[161] Subject to the transitional provisions contained in Art 9 Protocol 36, OJ 2008 C 115/322.

[162] Only Art 276 TFEU (ex-Art 35(5) TEU) remains. However, see the transitional provisions contained in Art 10 Protocol 36, *supra* note 161.

[163] See now Art 20 TEU and Arts 326–334 TFEU.

[164] See further, eg, Herlin-Karnell, 'The Lisbon Treaty and the Area of Criminal Law and Justice', *European Policy Analysis* (2008) 3; Peers, 'EU Criminal Law and the Treaty of Lisbon', 33 *European Law Review* (2008) 507.

[165] Art 76 TFEU.

[166] See Art 87(3) TFEU on operational cooperation between national law enforcement services.

[167] See Art 86(1) TFEU on establishing a European Public Prosecutor's Office.

unanimity in the Council may lead to a group of at least nine member states being exceptionally authorized to proceed with an enhanced cooperation on the basis of the draft act.[168] Thirdly, even as regards certain legal bases governed by the 'ordinary legislative procedure', the revised Treaties provide for a special 'emergency brake' mechanism, offering each member state an effective right of veto where it considers that draft legislation would affect fundamental aspects of its criminal justice system.[169] In such situations, a group of at least nine member states may again be automatically authorized to pursue an enhanced cooperation on the basis of the relevant proposal. Fourthly, the threshold for national parliaments to show a 'yellow card' to a Union legislative proposal in the field of cross-border criminal cooperation, on the grounds that it breaches the principle of subsidiarity, is lowered from one-third to one-quarter.[170] Indeed, Lisbon facilitates the greater involvement of national parliaments in the Union's criminal law activities more generally.[171]

Left at that, one could have said that Lisbon removed many of the problems that previously required us to distinguish the First from the Third Pillar, and therefore much of the incentive for engaging in disputes such as *Environmental Crimes* and *Ship-Source Pollution*. But Lisbon went further than mere depillarization, since it also created a new legal basis specifically for the adoption of criminal sanctions required for the enforcement of substantive Union policies—and this new provision brings with it both the promise of greater clarity and the danger of new complications.

2. Express Power to Harmonize Criminal Law for Enforcing Substantive Policies

Article 83(2) TFEU provides as follows:

> If the approximation of criminal laws and regulations of the member states proves essential to ensure the effective implementation of a Union policy in an area which has been subject to harmonisation measures, directives may establish minimum rules with regard to the definition of criminal offences and sanctions in the area concerned. Such directives shall be adopted by the same ordinary or special legislative procedure as was followed for the adoption of the harmonisation measures in question, without prejudice to Article 76 [TFEU on the special power of groups of Member States to make their own legislative proposals].[172]

[168] However, this 'emergency brake' does not apply to Art 89 TFEU (special legislative procedure based on consultation of European Parliament concerning operational activities in the territory of another member state).

[169] Ie, judicial cooperation in criminal matters, and the definition of criminal offences and sanctions, under Arts 82(2)–(3) and 83 TFEU (respectively).

[170] Art 69 TFEU and Art 7(2) of the Protocol on the application of the principles of subsidiarity and proportionality.

[171] Eg, Art 70 TFEU on evaluation of the AFSJ; Arts 85 and 88 TFEU on Eurojust and Europol (respectively).

[172] Note that the express exclusion of criminal sanctions as regards combating fraud against the Community's financial interests under old Art 280 EC and as regards customs cooperation between member states under old Art 135 EC are suppressed: see Art 325 TFEU and Art 33 TFEU (respectively).

On its face, the introduction of Article 83(2) TFEU might really appear to render redundant the old debate about Community/Union competence to harmonize criminal sanctions for the enforcement of substantive Treaty norms. After all, we seem here to have a provision which not only affirms the underlying point of principle (that such harmonization falls squarely within the Union's competence) but also expresses a clear will on the part of member states, to replace the previous era of institutional wrangling and judicial fumbling with a carefully defined legal basis to govern future Union action in this field.[173] In particular, Article 83(2) TFEU confirms that 'effectiveness' (here defined by reference to a threshold of 'essential' criminalization) still provides the primary trigger for Union competence over the adoption of criminal sanctions. Moreover, that competence can potentially extend to all fields of Union policy susceptible to the prior adoption of substantive harmonization measures—not just environmental protection—though for that reason, Article 83(2) TFEU does appear implicitly to rule out any centralized regulation of criminal sanctions in the field of the Common Foreign Security Policy,[174] or areas governed by merely complementary Union competence.[175] Article 83(2) TFEU seems also to assume that the substantive measures whose effective enforcement now requires the imposition of criminal sanctions were themselves adopted in the form of a legislative (as opposed to non-legislative) instrument—an assumption that may prove (perhaps inadvertently) problematic for fields such as competition law, where the relevant rules are contained in primary Treaty provisions rather than legislative acts per se,[176] and such secondary measures as are adopted by the Union institutions have been designated as non-legislative in character.[177] In any case, Article 83(2) TFEU explicitly refers to the Union's power both to establish the constituent elements of the relevant criminal offence and to prescribe the accompanying penalties.

However, it is hopefully no mere lawyer's sophistry to argue that matters may not be so clear-cut as the Treaty drafters seem to have intended. From a doctrinal point of view, this is where the distinction between the *Environmental Crimes* competence as an instance of implied powers or instead of derived powers becomes particularly relevant.[178] If *Environmental Crimes* had been treated as an instance of implied powers in the sense of *Germany v Commission* (1987),[179] then the introduction of Article 83(2) TFEU—an explicit legal basis for discharging the task of

[173] Though note that the provisions now contained in Art 83(2) TFEU were originally conceived by the Convention on the Future of Europe well before the *Environmental Crimes* ruling was delivered by the ECJ (see Final Report of Working Group X on Freedom, Security and Justice, CONV 426/02 and Art III-172(2) Draft Treaty establishing a Constitution for Europe, OJ 2003 C 169). The Convention's proposals were adopted with certain amendments (particularly the introduction of an 'emergency break') by the subsequent Intergovernmental Conference (see Art III-271(2) Treaty establishing a Constitution for Europe, OJ 2004 C 310); then retained subject to various revisions in the mandate drawn up by the European Council for the drafting of the Lisbon Treaty (see Presidency Conclusions of 23 June 2007).

[174] Where the adoption of legislative acts is expressly precluded, see Art 24 TEU.

[175] See Arts 2(5) and 6 TFEU.

[176] In particular, Arts 101 and 102 TFEU.

[177] In particular, Arts 103 and 105 TFEU.

[178] See Section 3.D.1.

[179] Cases 281, 283–5 and 287/85, *Germany v Commission*, *supra* note 129.

harmonizing criminal sanctions—would have had the automatic effect of extinguishing altogether the constitutional justification for recognizing those implied powers. Article 83(2) TFEU would have assumed the role of sole possible legal basis within the Treaties. But since *Environmental Crimes* is properly understood as a manifestation of derived powers—inherent in every legal basis under the Treaties, and dependent only upon the existence of first-order substantive provisions, together with the need for greater effectiveness in the latter's domestic enforcement—then the introduction of Article 83(2) TFEU cannot in itself have had the effect of simply extirpating such powers altogether from across the Treaties.

If the derived criminal competences recognized in *Environmental Crimes* remain alive as a matter of legal principle, then the revised Treaties offer a range of incentives for various political actors to seek to continue exercising those competences in practice. After all, even despite the largely thorough process of depillarization conducted under Lisbon, there remain situations when recourse to the express powers contained in Article 83(2) TFEU would be appreciably different from the exercise of the Union's derived criminal competence under each substantive legal basis. Some such differences are admittedly relatively marginal in nature and seem unlikely to stir any deep-felt institutional emotions. For example, left to its own devices, Article 83(2) TFEU surely has the effect of altering the relationship between the power to approximate criminal sanctions and the legal basis under which the relevant substantive norms were originally adopted. In particular, as regards both the available legal instruments and the degree of pre-emption over national competence, Article 83(2) TFEU is significantly more prescriptive than the approach under *Environmental Crimes*: in the former case, the Union must always use directives (even if regulations are available under the relevant substantive legal basis); such directives can only ever establish minimum standards (even if fully pre-emptive effects are possible under the Treaty provision whose enforcement demands criminal enforcement measures). But certain other differences between the two categories of Union criminal competence are surely to be considered more politically significant. For example, as we have seen, legislation under Article 83(2) TFEU can be initiated by the member states as well as by the Commission; while the threshold for national parliaments to object on grounds of subsidiarity is lower under Article 83(2) TFEU than in other internal policy fields.[180] Furthermore, the United Kingdom, Ireland, and Denmark all enjoy an automatic right of opt-out from measures adopted under Article 83(2) TFEU, whereas they would be automatically and fully bound by criminal measures adopted under other internal policy legal bases.[181] Finally, in situations where recourse to Article 83(2) TFEU involves the ordinary legislative procedure, every member state has the right to apply an 'emergency brake' within the Council, which might in turn trigger an

[180] See Section 3.E.1.

[181] For detailed analysis, eg, Peers, 'In a World of Their Own? Justice and Home Affairs Opt-Outs and the Treaty of Lisbon', 10 *Cambridge Yearbook of European Legal Studies* (2007/8) 383; Fletcher, 'Schengen, the European Court of Justice and Flexibility under the Lisbon Treaty: Balancing the United Kingdom's Ins and Outs', 5 *European Constitutional Law Review* (2009) 71.

extraordinary authorization for other member states to engage in enhanced cooperation.[182]

For any or all of those reasons, one might therefore find it expedient to either support or contest the proposition that—far from being expunged by Lisbon's entry into force—the competences recognized in *Environmental Crimes* remain potentially operational even under the revised TFEU. The real task is to identify the relationship between the Union's derived criminal powers and the dedicated legal basis now contained in Article 83(2) TFEU. For these purposes, the old Article 47 TEU and its 'Community preference' principle have effectively disappeared.[183] In their place, two main alternative models might be identified. First, it is arguable that Article 83(2) TFEU should be employed only where the Union wishes to set out detailed rules concerning the level and/or type of criminal penalties, effectively assuming the role previously performed under the Third Pillar, and continuing to leave the derived criminal competences recognized in *Environmental Crimes* to the task of establishing the principle of criminalization and harmonizing the relevant offences. However, that interpretation is difficult to reconcile with the express wording of Article 83(2) TFEU, which specifically envisages a power to harmonize *both* the definition of offences *and* the accompanying sanctions. Moreover, to recognize such far-reaching powers to harmonize penal sanctions for the enforcement of substantive Treaty policies other than through Article 83(2) TFEU might seem effectively to undermine Lisbon's desire to increase the Union's democratic legitimacy by offering national parliaments enhanced powers of scrutiny, on subsidiarity grounds, specifically as regards criminal matters.[184]

The second and more likely approach would be to accept that, even if Article 83(2) TFEU has not altogether abrogated the pre-existing *Environmental Crimes* competences, it has nevertheless assumed the role of *lex specialis* in the field of harmonizing criminal sanctions for the enforcement of substantive Union policies.[185] The practical outcome would therefore be that Article 83(2) TFEU should indeed be presumed to provide the legal basis for adopting all post-harmonization criminal measures; while the derived criminal competences recognized in *Environmental Crimes* are to be treated as not only inherent but in fact dormant within their respective substantive Treaty provisions. The only exception might be those Union policies—such as competition law—where (as we have seen) the restrictive wording of Article 83(2) TFEU appears implicitly to rule out the latter's use for the sectoral adoption of criminal sanctions. However, insofar as such an apparent absence of any *lex specialis* might thus leave open the (limited) possibility of the Union's derived criminal competences remaining active under and in accordance with the relevant primary Treaty provisions, that potential exception to the primacy of Article 83(2) TFEU could still run into opposition based on the principle of legality, ie insofar as it would seem to contemplate the harmonization

182 Art 83(3) TFEU.

183 Note Art 40 TEU on relations between the CFSP and other Union policies.

184 Ie as expressed in the lower threshold applicable, within the 'yellow card' system, to proposals made under Chapters 4 and 5, Title V, Part Three TFEU.

185 An approach also supported, eg, by Peers, *supra* note 164.

of criminal sanctions—precisely in fields such as competition law—by means of an explicitly non-legislative competence/decision-making procedure.

In short, Article 83(2) TFEU may well have changed the nature of the debate about the Union's competence to harmonize criminal offences and sanctions, but that debate cannot yet be considered settled, and the rulings in *Environmental Crimes* and *Ship-Source Pollution* should not be too quickly consigned to the realm of pure legal history.

In any case, regardless of whether the future harmonization of criminal sanctions is pursued entirely through the medium of Article 83(2) TFEU or partly also on the basis of the Union's pre-existing derived competences, the changed politico-legal landscape post-Lisbon may well exert a considerable influence on when and how those powers are actually exercised in practice. Certain national courts had already expressed reservations in recent years about the interaction between Union criminal law and domestic constitutional law, particularly as regards the operation of the European Arrest Warrant.[186] It has been argued that the tortured ratification process which engulfed the Constitutional Treaty, and then almost derailed Lisbon itself, might embolden the national judges to police with greater confidence the legal limits governing Union power and, in particular, those separating Union from member state competences.[187] That prospect has arguably been borne out with the German Federal Constitutional Court's 2009 ruling on the compatibility of the Lisbon Treaty with the German Basic Law.[188] The German Federal Constitutional Court (FCC) stressed that, even after Lisbon, the Union remains an association of sovereign states founded upon international law; member states continue to provide the primary focus of democratic expression for their own citizens. The FCC also sends a clear warning that this 'union of nation states' must be taken seriously in practice as well as on paper. Ultimately, the FCC reserves to itself the right to ensure that the Union neither abuses the limits of its own competences, nor exercises those powers in a manner that compromises the fundamental constitutional identity of the German state, which must retain sufficient room for the political formation of the economic, social, and cultural destiny of its own population. In particular, the FCC signalled that it expects a strict interpretation to be given to Union powers in various policy fields—including those concerning criminal law.[189] It remains to be seen whether the FCC's ruling acts as the portent of a chastened political culture across the Union institutions in the post-Lisbon era, urging greater self-restraint in their collective approach to criminal law

[186] See further, eg, Hinarejos, Casenote on German European Arrest Warrant Ruling, 43 *Common Market Law Review* (2006) 583; Leczykiewicz, Casenote on Polish European Arrest Warrant Ruling, 43 *Common Market Law Review* (2006) 1181; Komárek, 'European Constitutionalism and the European Arrest Warrant: In Search of the Limits of Contrapunctual Principles', 44 *Common Market Law Review* (2007) 9.

[187] Eg, Dougan, *supra* note 160.

[188] See *Lisbon Judgment*, German Constitutional Court, Case 2 BvE 2/08, 5/08, 2 BvR 1010/08, 1022/08, 1259/08, 182/09 (2009).

[189] See further, eg, Thym, 'In the Name of Sovereign Statehood: A Critical Introduction to the Lisbon Judgment of the German Constitutional Court', 46 *Common Market Law Review* (2009) 1795; Doukas, 'The Verdict of the German Federal Constitutional Court on the Lisbon Treaty: Not Guilty, But Don't Do It Again!', 34 *European Law Review* (2009) 866.

harmonization; or rather signals the birth of a more fragmented approach between the member states, regarding their willingness to participate in closer integration as regards criminal law harmonization.[190] In either event, the introduction of Article 83(2) TFEU may prove to have not only redefined the legal framework governing Union competence over penal sanctions but also coincided with a reinvigorated debate about the political desirability of Union involvement in criminal matters.

4. Enough Slap—What About The Tickle? Judicial Protection As Regards Criminal Sanctions for Enforcing Union Law

The complex legal and political debates leading up to and following the *Environmental Crimes* and *Ship-Source Pollution* rulings illustrate how, while criminal law is far from immune from the Treaties, it nevertheless occupies a special place within the Union legal order. That specificity also provides the focus for our final main topic: judicial protection before the national courts against the unfair or arbitrary exercise of coercive public power for the benefit of individuals facing criminal liability on account of Union law, specifically, the prospect of penal sanctions for the enforcement of substantive Treaty policies, either as imposed by the member state in the exercise of its discretion under *Greek Maize,* or as required by harmonizing legislation adopted by the Union's political institutions under their pre-/post-Lisbon competences. Such safeguards act as an essential counter-balance for the benefit of accused persons within a system of Union criminal law that might otherwise appear obsessed with promoting its own effectiveness. Indeed, one might argue that, given the relatively weak popular legitimacy of Union criminal law, the existence of high standards of judicial protection for individual citizens becomes all the more compelling.

The relevant legal safeguards have been developed, for the most part, under the tutelage of the Court of Justice as part of the general principles of Community and then Union law. Those general principles are, of course, binding upon the Union institutions in the exercise of their competences under the Treaties. For example, the Court confirmed in rulings such as *Advocaten voor de Wereld* and *Intertanko* that the validity of Third Pillar legislation was dependent upon respect for the general principles of Union law;[191] and in cases such as *Pupino* and *Katz* that Third Pillar legislation must in any event be interpreted in conformity with the fundamental rights recognized under Union law.[192] More importantly, for our purposes, the general principles of Union law bind the member states whenever they act within the scope of the Treaties—which includes national courts dealing with issues of criminal liability based on the implementation of Union law.[193]

[190] Eg, making use of the new emergency brake/special enhanced cooperation provisions; and also taking into account the British, Irish, and Danish opt-outs.

[191] Case C-303/05, *Advocaten voor de Wereld,* [2007] ECR I-3633; Case C-308/06, *Intertanko,* [2008] ECR I-4057.

[192] Case C-105/03, *Pupino,* [2005] ECR I-5285; Case C-404/07, *Katz,* [2008] ECR I-7607.

[193] Further, eg, A. Arnull et al, *Wyatt and Dashwood's European Union Law* (2006), chapters 7 and 8.

Many of the relevant legal safeguards already recognized by the Court in its case law, as well as others deemed by its drafters to constitute essential tenets of the Union's legal values, were codified in the Charter of Fundamental Rights 2000.[194] Within Title VI concerning 'Justice', Article 47 includes the right to a fair trial; Article 48 covers the presumption of innocence and the rights of the defence; Article 49 deals with the principle of non-retroactivity and, more generally, of legality in criminal law, as well as the retroactive application of more lenient criminal rules, and the proportionality of criminal penalties; finally, Article 50 enshrines the principle of *ne bis in idem*. The Charter of Fundamental Rights is now legally binding in its revised 2007 version,[195] though its detailed application is conditioned by the controversial 'horizontal provisions' contained in Title VII, as well as the obtuse protocol agreed at Lisbon dealing with the Charter's legal effects within Poland and the United Kingdom.[196]

This is not the place for a detailed discussion of the constitutional relationship between the general principles of Union law and the Charter,[197] while space obviously precludes examination of all the various substantive fundamental rights that might be relevant in the criminal law context.[198] We will instead focus on the two most important general principles explored by the Court in its case law concerning criminal sanctions in the domestic enforcement of Union law: the principles of non-retroactivity and legality; and the retroactive application of the most lenient criminal rules.

A. Principles of Non-retroactivity and Legality

Article 49(1) of the Charter is based directly on Article 7(1) ECHR:

> No one shall be held guilty of any criminal offence on account of any act or omission which did not constitute a criminal offence under national law or international law at the time when it was committed. Nor shall a heavier penalty be imposed than that which was applicable at the time the criminal offence was committed...

The most obvious right derived from Article 7(1) ECHR, the non-retroactive application of criminal liabilities and sanctions, has long been recognized by the ECJ in respect of Union law.[199] However, Article 7(1) ECHR is not limited to

[194] Charter of Fundamental Rights, OJ 2000 C 364.

[195] Charter of Fundamental Rights of the European Union, OJ 2007 C 303.

[196] Protocol No 30 on the application of the Charter of Fundamental Rights of the European Union to Poland and to the United Kingdom, OJ 2008 C 115/313. This protocol will in due course be extended also to the Czech Republic, see European Council Presidency Conclusions of 29–30 October 2009.

[197] See further, eg, Dougan, *supra* note 160.

[198] Consider recent rulings on respect for fundamental rights in the context of sanctions in general/criminal penalties in particular, eg, Case C-161/08, *Internationaal Verhuis- en Transportbedrijf Jan de Lely*, [2009] ECR I- 4075; Case C-344/08 *Rubach*, [2009] ECR I-7033; Case C-45/08, *Spector Photo Group*, *supra* note 35.

[199] Eg, Case 63/83, *Kent Kirk*, [1984] ECR 2689; Case C-331/88, *ex parte Fedesa*, [1990] ECR I-4023; Case C-459/02, *Gerekens*, [2004] ECR I-7315; Case C-3/06, *Groupe Danone*, *supra* note 76. Contrast with the non-retroactivity of civil/administrative sanctions, eg, Case 234/83, *Duisburg*, [1985] ECR 327; Case C-331/88, *ex parte Fedesa*, [1990] ECR I-4023; Case C-459/02, *Gerekens*, [2004] ECR I-7315.

enforcing the principle of non-retroactivity in that narrow sense. More generally, it requires that the criminal law must be clearly defined.[200] As the ECtHR held in *S.W v United Kingdom*, the guarantee enshrined in Article 7(1) ECHR, which is an essential element of the rule of law, occupies a prominent place in the Convention system of protection. That provision should be construed and applied, as follows from its object and purpose, in such a way as to provide effective safeguards against arbitrary prosecution, conviction and punishment.[201]

On that basis, the ECtHR has developed an extensive body of case law on the standards expected under Article 7(1) ECHR as regards the definition and interpretation of criminal obligations.[202] It emerges from that jurisprudence that Article 7(1) covers the principle that criminal rules and penalties must be clear and accessible, as well as the requirement that the criminal law should not be interpreted extensively against the defendant (for example, by analogy). In this context, the concept of 'law' consists of both statute and case law. There will inevitably be a need to clarify doubts about the interpretation of criminal legislation, and to adapt the criminal law to different and changing circumstances. The ECHR does not preclude, therefore, the judicial interpretation of criminal legislation, so long as its development is consistent with the essence of the offence and could reasonably have been foreseen. For those purposes, it is appropriate to take into account (for example) whether it was reasonable to expect the defendant to seek legal advice in the circumstances; his/her professional responsibilities; and the importance of the public interest being protected. Against that background, the application of Article 7(1) ECHR will usually involve detailed case-by-case assessments.

How has this broader ECHR principle of legality in the definition and application of the criminal law been translated into Union law? The principle of legal certainty is well established as a general principle of Union law.[203] However, most of the cases concerning the principle of legal certainty specifically in the field of criminal law have concerned directives—moreover, directives which do not expressly require the imposition of penal liabilities, so that the disputed sanctions derive from the member state's *Greek Maize* competence. The peculiar legal nature of such measures might well imply particular considerations not easily transposed to other contexts.

1. Case Law on Non-criminal Directives

From that case law, two main principles emerge. First, as the Court confirmed in *Pretore di Salò*, a directive cannot of itself provide the basis for a criminal

[200] *Kokkinakis v Greece*, ECHR (1993) Series A, No 260-A.

[201] *S.W v United Kingdom*, ECHR (1995) Series A, No 335-B.

[202] See, eg, *S.W v United Kingdom*, *supra* note 201; *C.R. v United Kingdom*, ECHR (1995) Series A, No 335-C; *Cantoni v France*, ECHR (1996); *Başkaya and Okçuoğlu v Turkey*, ECHR (1999); *Coëme v Belgium*, ECHR (2000); *Streletz, Kessler and Krenz v Germany*, ECHR (2001); *Veeber v Estonia (No 2)*, ECHR (2003); *Achour v France*, ECHR (2006); *Kafkaris v Cyprus*, ECHR (2008); *Scoppola v Italy (No 2)*, ECHR (2009).

[203] Consider, eg, rulings where the lack of adequate publication for Union legislation rendered obligations for individuals unenforceable before the national courts, eg, Case C-108/01, *Asda Stores*, [2003] ECR I-5121; Case C-161/06, *Skoma-Lux*, [2007] ECR I-10841; Case C-345/06, *Heinrich*, [2009] I-1659.

prosecution under national law.[204] That simply reflects the broader principle that directives are incapable in themselves of imposing obligations upon private individuals—a principle not confined to the criminal law sphere, but also applicable (for example) as regards disputes between two private parties.[205]

The second principle is more complex. National courts are required to construe domestic law so far as possible in a manner consistent with the aims and content of an unimplemented directive.[206] Unlike direct effect, the duty of consistent interpretation can apply to the detriment of private individuals, whether in their relations inter se,[207] or in civil/administrative actions brought by the member state against a private party.[208] However, the duty of consistent interpretation is limited by the general principles of Union law and, in particular, that of legal certainty: thus, for example, national courts are not required to reach a *contra legem* interpretation of their domestic legislation.[209] In particular, as regards criminal sanctions, the Court has held in rulings such as *Kolpinghuis Nijmegen* and *Luciano Arcaro* that the national court's obligation to refer to the content of a directive when interpreting its own domestic law reaches a limit where such an interpretation has the effect of determining or aggravating, on the basis of the directive and in the absence of a law enacted for its implementation, the liability in criminal law of persons who act in contravention of that directive's provisions.[210]

At first sight, the Court's limitation on the scope of the duty of consistent interpretation in cases involving criminal liabilities seems phrased in absolute or at least rather stringent terms.[211] On that basis, it is tempting to assume that, as soon as a case is found to involve criminal law, any possibility of relying on the duty of consistent interpretation to the potential detriment of the defendant is simply ruled out.[212] Perhaps for that reason, the scholarship has tended to show little more than a passing interest in the duty of consistent interpretation as it applies specifically in the penal context.[213] If correct, that understanding of the *Kolpinghuis Nijmegen* case law would go further than the standard of protection embodied in Article 7(1)

[204] Case 14/86, *Pretore di Salò*, [1987] ECR 2545.

[205] Eg, Case 152/84, *Marshall*, [1986] ECR 723; Case C-91/92, *Faccini Dori*, [1994] ECR I-3325.

[206] Case 14/83, *Von Colson*, *supra* note 61; Case C-106/89, *Marleasing*, [1990] ECR I-4135.

[207] Eg, Case C-2/97, *Società Italiana Petroli v Borsana*, [1998] ECR I-8597; Case C-343/98, *Collino v Telecom Italia*, [2000] ECR I-6659; Cases C-397/01 to C-403/01, *Pfeiffer*, [2004] ECR I-8835; Case C-350/03, *Schulte*, [2005] ECR I-9215.

[208] Eg, Case C-142/04, *Aslanidou*, [2005] ECR I-7181; Case C-321/05, *Kofoed*, [2007] ECR I-5795.

[209] Eg, Case C-105/03, *Pupino*, *supra* note 192; Case C-212/04, *Adeneler*, *supra* note 61.

[210] Case 80/86, *Kolpinghuis Nijmegen*, [1987] ECR 3969; Case C-168/95, *Luciano Arcaro*, [1996] ECR I-4705.

[211] More recently, eg, Case C-457/02, *Niselli*, [2004] ECR I-10853; Joined Cases C-387/02, C-391/02 and C-403/02, *Berlusconi*, [2005] ECR I-3565; Case C-105/03, *Pupino*, *supra* note 192; Case C-384/02, *Grøngaard*, [2005] ECR I-9939.

[212] Cf Dine, 'European Community Criminal Law?', *Criminal Law Review* (1993) 246.

[213] Consider recent analyses, eg, Betlem, 'The Doctrine of Consistent Interpretation: Managing Legal Uncertainty', 22 *OJLS* (2002) 397; Drake, 'Twenty Years After *von Colson*: The Impact of "Indirect Effect" on the Protection of the Individual's Community Rights', 30 *European Law Review* (2005) 329. But see S. Prechal, *Directives in EC Law* (2005), chapter 8 for a more general discussion of how the general principles of Union law act as a limit to the duty of consistent interpretation.

ECHR as construed by the ECtHR. In itself, of course, there is nothing objectionable in the proposition that Union law should offer more stringent protection for the individual, specifically in the case of criminal disputes, than is actually required under the minimum standards embodied in the ECHR. But closer analysis suggests that that interpretation is mistaken: the *Kolpinghuis Nijmegen* case law does not act as an absolute bar to taking into account unimplemented directives for the purposes of interpreting existing national criminal legislation; it merely calls upon the domestic judges to respect the ECHR's basic safeguards against arbitrary prosecution, conviction, and punishment.

In the first place, it seems clear that national courts may and must indeed refer to the content of a directive where the latter is intended merely to act as a point of reference for the purposes of interpreting any relevant national implementing measures, even where the latter involves liabilities of a criminal nature. For example, in *Lindqvist*, the Court provided detailed guidance on the interpretation of the Data Protection Directive,[214] for the purposes of determining the criminal liability of a Swedish defendant, pursuant to the relevant national implementing legislation.[215] Similarly, in *Damgaard*, the Court offered its interpretation of Directive 2001/83 on medicinal products for human use,[216] fully conscious that its interpretation could lead directly to the defendant being found guilty of a criminal offence under the relevant Danish implementing legislation.[217] Union law thus draws a distinction—necessarily based on a sliding scale—between situations where (on the one hand) the role of the relevant directive is merely to shed light on the correct interpretation of the national implementing legislation, and disputes where (on the other hand) reliance upon the relevant directive would tend rather to aggravate the defendant's criminal liabilities beyond the ordinary interpretation to be attributed to the applicable national criminal law.

In the second place, that distinction is reinforced by certain rulings, delivered within the *Kolpinghuis Nijmegen* case law itself, which explore the limits of the duty of consistent interpretation in criminal law situations in greater detail than the Court is usually prepared to offer. Consider *Criminal Proceedings Against X* (1996).[218] The case concerned certain differences between the definition of protected workers under a directive on health and safety, and that contained in the relevant Italian implementing measures imposing criminal sanctions upon the employer. When the national court queried how far it was obliged to take into account the provisions of the directive, the Court clarified its ruling in *Kolpinghuis Nijmegen* by stating that, as regards the extent of criminal liability arising under national legislation adopted for the specific purpose of implementing a directive, the principle that a provision of the criminal law may not be applied extensively to the detriment of the defendant (recognized as a general principle of Union law based on Article 7(1) ECHR) precludes bringing criminal proceedings in respect of

214 Directive 95/46, *supra* note 49.

215 Case C-101/01, *Lindqvist*, *supra* note 50.

216 Directive 2001/83 of the European Parliament and of the Council of 6 November 2001 on the Community code relating to medicinal products for human use, OJ 2001 L 311/67.

217 Case C-421/07, *Damgaard*, [2009] ECR I-2629.

218 Cases C-74/95 and C-129/95, *Criminal Proceedings Against X*, [1996] ECR I-6609.

conduct not clearly defined as culpable by law. 'The national court must therefore ensure that that principle is observed when interpreting, in the light of the wording and purpose of the Directive, the national legislation adopted in order to implement it'.[219] Similarly, consider *Dansk Rørindustri,* which concerned an alleged breach by the Commission of the general principle of Union law prohibiting the retroactive imposition of penalties in the context of competition law.[220] The Court cited in detail the ECtHR's case law concerning the scope of protection conferred by the principle of legality in the definition and application of criminal offences and penalties, including the guidelines to be taken into account during the judicial interpretation of existing legislative provisions based on the test of 'reasonable foreseeability'. 'Those principles', the Court concluded, 'are also consistently reflected in the [*Kolpinghuis Nijmegen*] case-law'.[221]

It thus seems that Union law merely reflects the general standards of protection enshrined in Article 7(1) ECHR. In discharging their duty of consistent interpretation between domestic criminal legislation and a relevant directive, the national courts should therefore undertake a 'reasonable foreseeability' assessment. For those purposes, the particular nature of directives implies taking into account various factors: for example, whether the facts of the dispute arose before or after the entry into force of the directive, or the expiry of the deadline for its implementation;[222] drawing a distinction between national law which was specifically intended to implement the directive, and domestic legislation which merely happens to cover a similar field to the directive;[223] whether national law expressly or implicitly cross-refers to concepts contained or defined in the directive;[224] how far specific provisions of national law actually deviate from those of Union law;[225] as well as the usual ECHR considerations relating to the professional capacity in which the defendant was acting, and the nature/importance of the public interest at stake.[226]

2. *Other Non-criminal Instruments*

Since most of the case law has arisen in the peculiar context of non-criminal directives, we should also consider how far the above principles might extend to other Union legal instruments which the member state has chosen to implement (under *Greek Maize*) through the medium of its national criminal law.

In particular, can such a Union regulation or primary Treaty provision ever provide the direct basis for a criminal prosecution under national law? On one view, the case law on directives is coloured by the inherent need for their transposition into the national legal system, in the absence of which they cannot of themselves impose obligations upon individuals. By contrast, regulations are directly applicable

[219] Ibid, Rec 25–6.

[220] Cases C-189/02, C-202/02, C-205–C-208/02 and C-213/02, *Dansk Rørindustri v Commission*, [2005] ECR I-5425.

[221] Ibid, Rec 220.

[222] Cf, Case C-212/04, *Adeneler, supra* note 61.

[223] Cases C-74/95 and C-129/95, *Criminal Proceedings Against X, supra* note 218.

[224] Case C-101/01, *Lindqvist, supra* note 50; Case C-421/07, *Damgaard, supra* note 217.

[225] Cf, Case C-58/02, *Commission v Spain*, [2004] ECR I-621.

[226] See Section 4.A.

within the national legal order;[227] both regulations and Treaty provisions may have direct effect, even where this would indeed reshape the rights and obligations of purely private parties.[228] It is therefore arguable that many of the limits applicable to directives are simply irrelevant. On another view, however, the direct effect of regulations and Treaty provisions is really beside the point. Specific provisions for the enforcement of regulations and Treaty provisions must still be adopted by each member state in the exercise of its autonomy to choose the appropriate sanctions for penalizing infringements of Union law within its domestic legal system. That process of transposition, albeit subject to the conditions laid down in *Greek Maize*, still involves a wide margin of discretion concerning the nature and level of penalties for enforcing Union law. When it comes to the potential for imposing criminal liability, the same considerations should therefore apply to regulations and Treaty provisions as arise with directives: non-criminal Union measures, whatever their legal form, are incapable in themselves of providing an independent basis for determining or aggravating an individual's criminal liability.

The latter approach is supported by the Court's ruling in *Criminal Proceedings Against X* (2004).[229] Austrian legislation prohibiting the importation or sale of counterfeit goods on pain of criminal penalties failed to fully implement the relevant Community regulation, which also obliged the member states to adopt appropriate sanctions in cases concerning the mere transit of counterfeit goods across the national territory. Asked whether a defendant could be prosecuted on the basis of the regulation itself, or the existing Austrian criminal legislation construed so as to comply with that regulation, the Court confirmed that, in principle, the regulation precluded the application of domestic rules which failed to prohibit mere transit; and that, in principle, national courts are bound by their duty of consistent interpretation under Union law. However, particular problems arise with criminal as opposed to civil law. Even though the case involved a directly applicable regulation, the latter specifically required member states to adopt penalties for its infringement, on which basis the same case law as that governing directives must be applied here by analogy: insofar as national law did not prohibit the mere transit of counterfeit goods, the general principles of Union law based on Article 7(1) ECHR prohibited the imposition of criminal penalties (even if the national rule was in fact contrary to Union law). Advocate General Colomer was even more explicit on this point: the member state's failure to comply with the regulation could well provide the basis for an enforcement action under Article 258 TFEU (ex-Article 226 EC); but it does not allow citizens to be prosecuted for acts which, although unlawful under Union law, are not punishable as such under national law.[230]

Although the Court in *Criminal Proceedings against X* (2004) made play of the fact that the relevant regulation included an express provision requiring the member state to impose appropriate sanctions for its enforcement, that is surely

227 Art 288 TFEU (ex-Art 249 EC).

228 Eg, Case C-253/00, *Muñoz, supra* note 64 (regulations); Case C-281/98, *Angonese*, [2000] ECR I-4131 (Treaty provisions).

229 Case C-60/02, *Criminal Proceedings Against X*, [2004] ECR I-651.

230 Ibid, para 46 of the Opinion.

incidental. After all, such provisions do no more than recall the general obligation to adopt equivalent, effective, and proportionate sanctions, derived from Article 4(3) TEU as interpreted in *Greek Maize*, which are automatically applicable to the enforcement of *all* Union law.[231] On that basis, *Criminal Proceedings against X* (2004) suggests that, directly effective or not, regulations and Treaty provisions can never in themselves provide a direct basis for imposing criminal liability within the national legal system. However, the duty of consistent interpretation does still apply, subject to an assessment under Article 7(1) ECHR to ensure that national criminal legislation, read in the light of Union law, does not provide the basis for arbitrary prosecution, conviction, or punishment. For those purposes, and especially when it comes to conducting the 'reasonable foreseeability' assessment, the Court again seems to stress the fact that transposition at the discretion of the member state is essential before *any* non-penal Union provision is capable of having effects specifically within the national criminal justice system.

3. Criminal Instruments

All of that naturally leads on to the question: How far might these principles require modification, when extended to supranational instruments which *are* specifically intended to harmonize the imposition of criminal liabilities and/or sanctions within the national legal systems (be they pre-Lisbon First Pillar instruments adopted pursuant to *Environmental Crimes*, pre-Lisbon framework decisions based on the Third Pillar, or post-Lisbon measures adopted under Article 83(2) TFEU)?

When it comes to the possibility of a Union criminal measure in itself providing the direct basis for a criminal prosecution within the member state, there is in fact no reason to believe that the Court's approach would be any different from that developed in respect of non-criminal instruments. In the case of a pre-Lisbon criminal directive adopted under the First Pillar in the wake of *Environmental Crimes*, the ruling in *Pretore di Salò* would remain fully applicable: directives cannot of themselves be enforced against individuals, including where the dispute arises in the criminal context. The same would have been true of a (purely hypothetical) First Pillar criminal regulation: given that *Ship-Source Pollution* ruled out any Community competence over the exact nature and level of criminal penalties, the continued existence of member state discretion in this regard would have engaged the analogous principle in *Criminal Proceedings against X* (2004). As regards Third Pillar measures, the position is equally straightforward: ex-Article 34 TEU specifically ruled out the possibility of framework decisions having direct effect, and therefore also the possibility of such measures providing a direct basis for criminal prosecution within the national legal system. Post-Lisbon, Article 82(3) TFEU permits the harmonization of criminal offences and sanctions for the enforcement of substantive Union policies only by means of directives—so *Pretore di Salò* will continue to limit the decentralized enforcement of such Union criminal measures well into the foreseeable future.

[231] See Section 2.B.

Nevertheless, when it comes to the scope and limits of the duty of consistent interpretation, it is possible that the explicitly criminal law nature of certain old Community instruments, surely of all surviving Third Pillar framework decisions, and of any future directives adopted under Article 83(2) TFEU, should be treated as a relevant factor in the national court's assessment of whether an interpretation of existing domestic criminal law in conformity with the relevant supranational legislation would amount to 'determining or aggravating' criminal liability in a manner contrary to the accused person's fundamental rights. After all, for the purposes of the 'reasonable foreseeability' assessment, a defendant—particularly one conducting professional activities, and/or who could reasonably be expected to have sought legal advice about the relevant statutory framework—can claim less cause for complaint about taking into account the provisions of Community/Union instruments which are expressly intended to provide the basis for determining or aggravating criminal liabilities under domestic law (especially where the relevant domestic rules were adopted specifically so as to implement the member state's Treaty obligations).

4. Distinction between Substantive and Procedural Criminal Law

To this discussion on the principles of non-retroactivity and legality in the field of criminal law, as recognized by the ECHR and protected under Union law, there is an important qualification.

Pupino concerned an alleged incompatibility between (on the one hand) Italian rules permitting the cross-examination, during the adversarial stage of criminal proceedings, of evidence given by the child victims of non-sexual abuse and (on the other hand) the obligation under Framework Decision 2001/220, on the standing of victims in criminal proceedings,[232] to ensure that particularly vulnerable victims benefit from specific treatment best suited to their circumstances.[233] The judgment is best known for having recognized that the duty of loyal cooperation applied to member states also within the legal order established under the Third Pillar; despite the lack of direct effect for framework decisions, the national courts were therefore bound by the duty of consistent interpretation. Having made clear that that duty was limited in accordance with the standards developed under the *Kolpinghuis Nijmegen* case law, the Court nevertheless went on to find that 'the provisions which form the subject-matter of this [preliminary reference] do not concern the extent of the criminal liability of the person concerned but the conduct of the proceedings and the means of taking evidence'.[234] In such cases, the duty of consistent interpretation is qualified not by reference to the principle of legality as derived from Article 7(1) ECHR, but rather by the national court's duty to respect the defendant's other fundamental rights under Union law, in particular, the need to ensure that the relevant criminal proceedings (considered as a whole) were not rendered incompatible with the right to a fair trial in the sense of Article 6

[232] Council Framework Decision 2001/220 of 15 March 2001 on the standing of victims in criminal proceedings, OJ 2001 L 82/1.

[233] Case C-105/03, *Pupino*, *supra* note 192.

[234] Ibid, Rec 46.

ECHR. Presumably the duty of consistent interpretation, as regards the rules of criminal procedure and evidence, would also remain subject to the requirement that national courts should not in any event adopt a *contra legem* interpretation of domestic legislation. After all, that requirement derives from the general principle of legal certainty, more broadly understood, and applies under Union law even in civil/administrative proceedings.[235] In any case, a *contra legem* interpretation of the rules of criminal procedure and evidence would surely be highly relevant to any assessment of the defendant's right to a fair trial for the purposes of Article 6 ECHR.

The distinction drawn in *Pupino* between the relevance of the principle of legality for substantive rules of criminal liability, as compared to the rules of criminal procedure and evidence, has since been reinforced in subsequent rulings (also concerning the legal effects under national law of Framework Decision 2001/220).[236] The Court went further in *Dell'Orto*, holding that procedural rules are generally held to be applicable to all proceedings pending at the time they enter into force. As such, the national court was obliged to take into account the provisions of Framework Decision 2001/220 when interpreting Italian legislation concerning the return to the victim of property seized during criminal proceedings, even though the facts of the dispute arose before that measure was even adopted by the Union, let alone the expiry of the deadline for its transposition.[237] In other words, even the narrow principle of non-retroactivity does not apply to procedural as opposed to substantive criminal law rules.

Although the position under Union law does not appear to be incompatible with the standards contained in Article 7(1) ECHR as construed by the ECtHR itself,[238] the Court's approach has nevertheless attracted considerable academic criticism: not only because it will often be difficult to distinguish between substantive and procedural rules (and such distinctions in any case are drawn very differently across the member states); but also on the grounds that changes in the rules of procedure and evidence can still have significant detrimental effects for the defendant, amounting in practice to determining or aggravating his/her criminal liabilities, in a manner which undermines the spirit even if not the letter of the safeguards developed in the *Kolpinghuis Nijmegen* case law.[239]

B. Retroactivity of More Lenient Sanctions

If the Court offers protection on the basis of the principle of legality which does not exceed the standards enshrined in Article 7(1) ECHR, yet tailors them to the specificities of the interaction between the Union and national legal orders, the Union has proved more adventurous in its approach to the converse issue: the degree to which member states might or must enforce retroactively the most lenient criminal

[235] Eg, Case C-212/04, *Adeneler, supra* note 61.
[236] Eg, Case C-404/07 *Katz, supra* note 192.
[237] Case C-467/05, *Dell'Orto*, [2007] ECR I-5557.
[238] Eg, *Coëme v Belgium, supra* note 202; *Scoppola v Italy (No 2), supra* note 202.
[239] Spaventa, *supra* note 107.

law or sanctions against an individual who has breached certain obligations derived from the Treaties.

1. Recognition as a General Principle of Union Law

The Court's earlier case law was unclear about whether the principle of applying the most lenient sanction constituted a general principle of Union law: certain rulings seemed implicitly to rule out any such general principle;[240] at most, the Court seemed prepared to leave this issue to the discretion of each member state.[241] However, the political institutions signalled that a more generous approach could well be justified under Union law itself: the principle of retroactively applying a more lenient administrative 'own sanction' was expressly included in Regulation 2988/95 concerning the protection of the Union's financial interests;[242] more broadly, Article 49(1) of the Charter of Fundamental Rights as adopted in 2000 stated that if, subsequent to the commission of a criminal offence, the law provides for a lighter penalty, that penalty shall be applicable.[243]

Those developments laid the basis for the Court's ruling in *Berlusconi*.[244] During the course of a criminal prosecution for false corporate accounting, in accordance with the Italian rules applicable at the time of the alleged offences, the national parliament adopted more lenient legislation which, under the Italian criminal code, should have been applied retroactively for the benefit of the defendant. However, false corporate accounting fell within a regulatory field occupied by various company law directives: whereas the original Italian rules were assumed adequately to have implemented those Union provisions, the more recent legislation failed to provide any effective sanctions against those who infringed the directives. The question arose: Were the national courts obliged to set aside the more recent but non-compliant legislation, and permit the defendant's criminal prosecution to proceed in accordance with the original Italian rules? The Court began by accepting that the principle of the retroactive application of a more lenient criminal penalty represents a general principle of Union law which national courts must respect when applying domestic legislation adopted for the purpose of implementing the EC Treaty. However, difficulties arise in a situation (such as the present dispute) where the more lenient penalty is itself alleged to be incompatible with Union law. But it was not here necessary to address that difficulty as a matter of principle: directives cannot of themselves impose obligations on an individual, nor have the effect of determining or aggravating criminal liability; reliance on the relevant Union directives so as to set aside the more recent Italian legislation

[240] Eg, Case C-304/94, *Tombesi*, [1997] ECR I-3561; Case C-457/02, *Niselli*, [2004] ECR I-10853.

[241] Eg, Cases C-358/93 and C-416/93, *Bordessa*, [1995] ECR I-361; Cases C-163/94, C-165/94 and C-250/94, *Sanz de Lera*, [1995] ECR I-4821; Case C-341/94, *André Allain and Steel Trading France*, [1996] ECR I-4631; Case C-230/97, *Awoyemi*, *supra* note 58.

[242] Regulation 2988/95, *supra* note 68 (see Art 2(2)). See, eg, Case C-295/02, *Gerken*, [2004] ECR I-6369; Case C-45/06, *Campina*, [2007] ECR I-2089; Case C-420/06, *Jager*, [2008] ECR I-1315.

[243] Charter of Fundamental Rights (2000), *supra* note 194.

[244] Joined Cases C-387/02, C-391/02 and C-403/02, *Berlusconi*, *supra* note 211.

would have the unacceptable effect of rendering applicable to the defendant the manifestly more severe regime contained in the original national rules.

2. Criticism of the Court's Methodology

In theory, the Court could have decided *Berlusconi* without expressing any view on Union law's approach to the retroactive application of more lenient criminal rules, or at least have simply recognized (as in previous rulings) that the member state may offer such protection at its own discretion. The Court's decision instead to elevate the retroactive application of more lenient criminal rules to the status of a general principle of Union law—thus imposing positive obligations upon the Union institutions and member states when acting within the scope of the Treaties—has been criticized on the grounds that the Court failed to offer any clear legal support for its conclusions, either through a thorough analysis of the constitutional traditions common to the member states, or by reference to an equivalent level of protection contained in an international agreement binding upon the member states.[245] After all, if anything, the limited jurisprudence available from Strasbourg suggested that the retroactive application of more lenient criminal rules was not required under the ECHR.[246] As with the similarly controversial ruling in *Mangold*, the ECJ could have countered such methodological criticisms by referring instead to the relevant provisions of the Charter, which were after all meant to represent a convenient summary of the various rights recognized under Union law.[247] At the time of the *Berlusconi* ruling, however, the Charter had not yet publicly entered the Court's fundamental rights lexicon.[248] Nevertheless, the conferral of binding legal force upon the Charter after the entry into force of the Lisbon Treaty has, with hindsight, provided a more solid constitutional basis for the ruling in *Berlusconi*.[249] In the meantime, the ruling of the ECtHR in *Scoppola* had already vindicated the ECJ's admittedly rather lazy reasoning.[250] The ECtHR affirmed that Article 7(1) ECHR does indeed guarantee the retrospectiveness of the more lenient criminal law, in the sense that, where there are differences between the criminal law in force at the time of the commission of the offence and subsequent criminal laws enacted before a final judgment is rendered, the courts must apply those provisions which are most favourable to the defendant.[251] Not only that: the ruling in *Scoppola* was clearly influenced by the fact that such protection was already afforded by Union law, both according to the Charter and through the *Berlusconi* judgment.[252]

[245] Eg, Biondi and Mastroianni, Casenote on *Berlusconi*, 43 *CMLRev* (2006) 553.

[246] In particular, European Commission on Human Rights in *X v Germany* (Report of 6 March 1978). More recently, eg, *Le Petit v United Kingdom*, ECHR (Decision of 5 December 2000); *Zaprianov v Bulgaria*, ECHR (Decision of 6 March 2003).

[247] Case C-144/04, *Mangold*, [2005] ECR I-9981.

[248] See Case C-540/03, *Parliament v Council*, [2006] ECR I-5769. See further, eg, Drywood, 'Giving with One Hand, Taking with the Other: Fundamental Rights, Children and the Family Reunification Decision', 32 *ELRev* (2007) 396.

[249] Art 6(1) TEU. Cf, Case C-555/07, *Kücükdeveci*, [2010] ECR I-00365, reinforcing the constitutional basis of the *Mangold* ruling by reference to the post-Lisbon Charter provisions.

[250] *Scoppola v Italy (No 2)*, *supra* note 202.

[251] Ibid, para 109.

[252] Ibid, eg, para 105.

3. *Scope of Application of the Relevant General Principle*

Criticism of the Court's methodology having been neutralized, the main outstanding issue raised by *Berlusconi* concerns the scope of application of the general principle of Union law requiring the retroactive application of more lenient criminal rules. For present purposes, at least, it is possible to distinguish three distinct situations.[253] First, where any more lenient sanction provided for under national law for the enforcement of substantive Treaty norms still complies with the standards imposed by Union law, in accordance with the *Greek Maize* criteria or (as the case may be) harmonizing legislation on criminal offences and penalties, the general principles of Union law will require the member state to enforce that more lenient sanction retroactively for the benefit of a defendant.[254] Secondly, where the more lenient domestic sanction does not in fact comply with Union standards (under either *Greek Maize* or harmonizing legislation), but that sanction is intended to enforce a Union directive, the Court in *Berlusconi* found that the general principle of retroactive application of the most lenient criminal rules should nevertheless still apply: the relevant directive could not in any case be enforced directly against an individual, and the national court should not follow the duty of consistent interpretation where this would determine or aggravate the defendant's criminal liabilities.

The third and most difficult situation is that expressly left open by the Court in *Berlusconi*: whether to apply the general principle of Union law requiring the retroactive application of more lenient criminal rules, when the relevant national sanction again fails to meet the requirements imposed by Union law (under either *Greek Maize* or harmonizing legislation), but this time is intended to enforce a regulation or Treaty provision, ie measures capable in principle of having direct effect against individuals, and therefore with the potential directly to preclude application of the disputed sanction.[255] As with the implications of the principle of legality for non-criminal Union instruments other than directives,[256] identifying the solution to this conundrum cannot be treated as a self-executing doctrinal task. In this context, it supposes a subjective judgment in answer to the question of which set of Union principles should take priority: the direct effect and supremacy of the relevant Union provisions, or the general principle of Union law advancing the defendant's interests? Or perhaps the question is better expressed in terms of which set of Union values we would prefer to take priority: should the Court maximize the judicial protection provided to individuals faced with criminal liability

[253] There are others, eg, where the relevant national criminal law falls within the scope of the Treaties because the member state is derogating from (rather than implementing) its Union law obligations, eg, Case C-142/05, *Åklagaren v Mickelsson and Roos*, [2009] ECR I-4273.

[254] Cf, Case C-142/05, *Åklagaren v Mickelsson and Roos*, ibid.

[255] It is arguable that that was actually the case even in *Berlusconi* itself: since the relevant provisions of the directive did no more than codify the member state's existing *Greek Maize* obligations, the real incompatibility in *Berlusconi* was actually between the more recent Italian rules and Art 4(3) TEU: eg, Dougan, 'Legal Developments', in U. Sedelmeier and A. Young (eds), *Journal of Common Market Studies: The European Union Annual Review 2005/2006* (2006); Biondi and Mastroianni, *supra* note 245.

[256] See Section 4.A.2.

on account of Union law, even where this would tolerate the member state's failure to comply with its Union obligations, and thereby jeopardize the full effectiveness and uniform application of the Treaties?

On the one hand, the opinion of Advocate General Kokott in *Berlusconi* argues powerfully for the view that, in such situations of conflict, the values of effectiveness and uniformity should take priority; in other words, that the Union's hierarchically superior regulation or Treaty provision requires any incompatible national criminal rules to be set aside, so that there is no 'more lenient penalty' from which the defendant could even claim to benefit in the first place.[257] On the other hand, it must be said that there is nothing logically compelling or legally irresistible about such an analysis. If one adopts the alternative policy viewpoint—that the values of effectiveness and uniformity, however important to the Union legal order, should nevertheless give way to providing high standards of judicial protection to Union citizens faced with the prospect of criminal liabilities on account of Union law itself—then it is perfectly possible to advance a very different legal framework. From that perspective, the principles of direct effect and supremacy are capable of being deferred to other fundamental values as enshrined in the general principles of Union law, including the principle that defendants should benefit retroactively from the most lenient criminal rules, even where this effectively tolerates a member state's failure to comply with its Treaty obligations.[258]

The latter understanding might already be seen reflected in case law, particularly concerning the general principle of legal certainty, where the Court refuses to sanction the enforcement against individuals of (perfectly valid) Union legislation which has not been adequately published;[259] recognizes that Union law does not in principle require national decisions which have acquired the force of *res judicata* to be reopened merely because they are incompatible with the Treaties;[260] and respects the integrity of national decisions which have become final through the expiry of reasonable limitation periods, again, even if those decisions do not fulfil the member state's Treaty obligations.[261] In this context, moreover, the ruling in *Criminal Proceedings Against X* (2004) again seems highly pertinent.[262] It will be recalled that the Court there affirmed the possibility that national law which was clearly incompatible with a Union regulation, and would ordinarily have had to be set aside by virtue of the principles of direct effect and supremacy, should nevertheless remain untouched by the Treaties where the effect would otherwise be to determine or aggravate the criminal liabilities of the individual

[257] Joined Cases C-387/02, C-391/02 and C-403/02, *Berlusconi*, *supra* note 211, especially paras 161–7 of the Opinion. See also, Biondi and Mastroianni, *supra* note 245.

[258] Cf, van der Wilt, Casenote on *Berlusconi*, 2 *European Constitutional Law Review* (2006) 303.

[259] Eg, Case C-108/01, *Asda Stores*, *supra* note 203; Case C-161/06, *Skoma-Lux*, *supra* note 203; Case C-345/06, *Heinrich*, *supra* note 203.

[260] Eg, Case C-453/00, *Kühne & Heitz*, [2004] ECR I-837; Case C-234/04, *Kapferer*, [2006] ECR I-2585; Cases C-392 and 422/04, *i-21 Germany*, [2006] ECR I-8559.

[261] Eg, Case 33/76, *Rewe-Zentralfinanz*, *supra* note 27; Case C-188/95, *Fantask*, [1997] ECR I-6783.

[262] Case C-60/02, *Criminal Proceedings Against X*, *supra* note 229.

citizen.[263] If that is true for the initial step of criminalization, surely the same approach should apply also to subsequent disputes about the retroactivity of more lenient criminal rules.

5. Concluding Assessment: On the Coherence of Judicial Protection

This chapter has explored three prima facie distinct but in fact closely inter-related facets of the legal regime governing criminal sanctions for the enforcement of substantive Union policies: member state discretion over penalties under *Greek Maize*; the Union's harmonizing powers pre- and post-Lisbon; and judicial protection before the national courts for defendants facing liability pursuant to the exercise of either national or Union criminal competences.

Across all three issues, the special place accorded to criminal sanctions within the Union legal order emerges strongly. But it seems appropriate to conclude this study with a discussion of whether those specificities—on the one side, as regards constitutional competence; on the other side, as regards judicial protection—risk pulling Union law in contradictory or even irreconcilable directions. At first glance, one might indeed expect to encounter certain tensions. In particular, there is an obvious risk that the Union's obsession with constructing a politically palatable framework for the adoption/imposition of criminal sanctions will distract attention from the imperative of offering adequate and consistent standards of judicial protection for accused persons. What looks like a workable institutional template for criminal law-making when viewed 'from above' risks emerging as an excessively complex and ultimately incoherent system of criminal justice when viewed 'from below'—whereby citizens accused of comparable criminal offences might be offered rather different standards of judicial protection depending on frankly irrelevant factors such as whether the member state is derogating from or implementing Union law, whether the Union institutions have or have not legislated for the imposition of criminal sanctions, whether that legislation was adopted under the First or Third Pillar or in the wake of the Lisbon Treaty...

Further reflection, however, suggests that the Court of Justice has (by and large) succeeded in transforming its principles of judicial protection into a powerful unifying force which is capable of overreaching the underlying constitutional complexities, so as to shield individuals faced in any case with the exercise of coercive state power from significant and unjustified differences in the levels of judicial protection guaranteed to them under Union law. The combined effect of the case law is that Union law cannot per se adversely affect the criminal liabilities of an accused person without the intervention of the national legislature (either so as to adopt equivalent, effective, and proportionate penalties of its own choosing under *Greek Maize*; or so as to implement into national law those sanctions determined by the Union legislature pre-/post-Lisbon). So, whatever the differences that might

[263] See Section 4.A.2.

exist on the higher constitutional plane, when it comes to the enforcement of substantive Union policies down within the domestic criminal justice systems, the final outcome should remain the same: although defendants may benefit from better protection under the Treaties, they should not be prejudiced by an autonomous application of Union law.[264]

The point may be illustrated as follows. There undoubtedly exists a double standard in Union law's approach to situations where a member state is derogating from the Treaties as opposed to those where it is implementing its Union law obligations. In the former case, scrutiny of national sanctions is based upon the principle of proportionality alone, and thus acts in tandem with the interests of the individual. In the latter situation, Union law furthermore applies the principles of equivalence and effectiveness, which clearly act against the interests of the individual.[265] Such a discrepancy seems to reinforce the old critique that citizens perform merely an instrumental role in Union law, benefiting incidentally where they are capable of furthering the Union interest, only to be thrown to the wolves where the effectiveness of the Treaties so requires.[266] Yet that critique overlooks precisely the unifying effect of the Court's case law on judicial protection: although the substantive principles for evaluating the compatibility of national criminal law with the Treaties might differ depending on the factor of derogating from or implementing Union law, the enforcement of those substantive principles within the domestic criminal justice system is mediated through exactly the same filter, thus preventing Union law in itself from adversely affecting the defendant's criminal liabilities, even as regards situations involving member state implementation.

It is against that unifying backdrop that one should evaluate other more specific criticisms levied against the coherence of the legal framework governing criminal sanctions, and especially judicial protection, under Union law.

First, consider the accusation of another double standard at work in the case law, again depending on the context of derogating from or implementing the Treaties. In the former situation, it is argued, the Court eagerly advances the Union's own policy interests by insisting on a relatively strict application of the principle of proportionality; whereas in the latter situation, the Court is once again at pains to safeguard fulfilment of the Treaties' objectives by conducting only a cursory and light-touch proportionality assessment. But the available case law does not support any such critique. After all, the Court in 'implementation situations' usually instructs the national court to verify compliance with the principle of proportionality, within the context of their own national legal

[264] The ruling in Case C-105/03, *Pupino*, *supra* note 192 concerning the extent of the duty of consistent interpretation as regards procedural (as opposed to substantive) criminal rules stands out by way of exception.

[265] See Section 2.

[266] Consider, eg, Baker, *supra* note 90. Cf, Coppel and O'Neill, 'The European Court of Justice: Taking Rights Seriously?', 29 *Common Market Law Review* (1992) 669. Cf, de Búrca, 'The Principle of Proportionality and its Application in EC law', 13 *Yearbook of European Law* (1993) 105; Jacobs, 'Recent Developments in the Principle of Proportionality in European Community Law', in E. Ellis (ed), *The Principle of Proportionality in the Laws of Europe* (1999).

system, with specific reference to the usual benchmark that penalties should not go beyond what is strictly necessary for the (Union) objectives pursued.[267] Given the difficulties of determining whether a given obligation and its corresponding sanction constitute a derogation or an implementation,[268] it would in fact prove rather difficult to sustain in a coherent or systematic manner any such double standard in the proportionality assessment of national criminal sanctions.[269]

Secondly, consider yet another accusation of double standards by the Court, also as regards application of the principle of proportionality, but this time depending on whether the dispute involves criminal sanctions chosen by the member state or instead criminal sanctions harmonized by the Union legislature. Even if, in *Greek Maize* situations, judicial control over member state discretion were indeed accepted to be relatively strict, nevertheless, the lessons learned from analogous case law concerning the proportionality of Union 'own sanctions' in fields such as the CAP make it safe to assume that, in situations involving Union choices over the harmonization of criminal offences and/or penalties, judicial review would be limited to the test of 'manifest inappropriateness'.[270] But again, one might query whether the available case law really substantiates such a critique. Even in the field of the CAP, the Court has often been prepared to strike down specific facets of Union own sanctions as disproportionate.[271] Also in cases where such Union own sanctions are upheld, the Court usually undertakes a detailed analysis of their proportionality and provides convincing reasons for their legality.[272] Indeed, the Court has sometimes referred to its case law on the judicial review of Union own sanctions as setting the appropriate standard for judging also the proportionality of member state penalties;[273] and conversely, has occasionally cited its rulings concerning judicial review of member state penalties for the enforcement of Union law as relevant for assessing the proportionality of Union own sanctions.[274] So, even if the Court in *Environmental Crimes* or under Article 83(2) TFEU were to respect a wide margin of political discretion over the initial

[267] Eg, Case C-210/91, *Commission v Greece, supra* note 47; Case C-36/94, *Seisse*, [1995] ECR I-3573; Case C-213/99, *de Andrade*, [2000] ECR I-11083; Case C-430/05, *Pikoulas*, [2007] ECR I-5835.

[268] See Section 2.C.1.

[269] Eg, consider Case C-193/94, *Skanavi, supra* note 13; Case C-262/99, *Louloudakis, supra* note 48; Case C-156/04, *Commission v Greece, supra* note 13.

[270] Eg, Case 265/87, *Hermann Schräder HS Kraftfutter*, [1989] ECR 2237; Case C-8/89, *Zardi*, [1990] ECR I-2515; Cases C-133/93, C-300/93 and C-362/93, *Crispoltoni*, [1994] ECR I-4863; Case C-45/05, *Maatschap Schonewille-Prins*, [2007] ECR I-3997.

[271] Eg, Case 122/78, *Buitoni*, [1979] ECR 677; Case 240/78, *Atalanta Amsterdam*, [1979] ECR 2137; Case 181/84, *ex parte E D & F Man (Sugar)*, [1985] ECR 2889; Case C-118/89, *Firma Otto Lingenfelser*, [1990] ECR I-2637; Case C-319/90, *Pressler*, [1992] ECR I-203; Case C-356/97, *Molkereigenossenschaft Wiedergeltingen, supra* note 69.

[272] Eg, Case 66/82, *Fromançais*, [1983] ECR 395; Case 125/83, *Nicolas Corman*, [1985] ECR 3039; Case 288/85, *Plange Kraftfutterwerke*, supra note 72; Case C-155/89, *Philipp Brothers*, [1990] ECR I-3265; Case C-199/90, *Italtrade, supra* note 72; Case C-354/95, *R v MAFF, ex parte National Farmers Union*, [1997] ECR I-4559; Case C-94/05, *Emsland-Stärke, supra* note 69.

[273] Eg, Case C-2/93, *Exportslacterijen van Oordegem v. Belgische Dienst voor Bedrijfsleven en Landbouw and Generale Bank*, [1994] ECR I-2283.

[274] Eg, Case C-210/00, *Käserei Champignon Hofmeister, supra* note 69.

decision about whether criminal sanctions are actually 'necessary'/'essential' for the enforcement of a given Union policy, one could still expect a more rigorous judicial scrutiny of compliance with the principle of proportionality when it comes to the more detailed definition of offences and the level of penalties.[275] In any case, one should recall that the principle of proportionality applies not just at the level of judicially reviewing Union legislation in the abstract, but also at the point where the national authorities and courts come to determine individual liability and sentencing.[276] Abstract review by the Court as regards the general outlines of Union criminal law remains without prejudice to the obligation of national courts, when applying that legislation to particular circumstances, to enforce the proportionality principle—and indeed, all the other general principles of Union law, including respect for fundamental rights—in a much more detailed and rigorous manner.[277]

The third critique worth further consideration concerned the Third Pillar; in its day, this was surely the most convincing. There was no doubt that the particular constitutional regime which governed ex-Title VI TEU created problems of coherence in the system of judicial protection as regards criminal sanctions, serious enough to undermine the otherwise persuasive unifying force of the Court's own case law. For example: the lack of direct effect for framework decisions suggested that, while Union law could not directly prejudice the rights of the accused, nor could it improve his/her position either, even where the relevant legislation might have offered better safeguards than existing domestic law.[278] Or again, the lack of preliminary references where the relevant member state had failed voluntarily to accept the Court's jurisdiction as regards ex-Title VI TEU raised fundamental problems about the consistent application of Union law and, in cases involving the alleged invalidity of Third Pillar measures, grave concerns over the Union's compliance with the right of access to judicial process under Article 6 ECHR.[279] Even if such unfortunate problems will linger on for some time yet, thanks to the miserly provisions of the protocol on transitional provisions,[280] nevertheless, the new regime governing the AFSJ as created under the Lisbon Treaty has taken the sting from the tail even of this once damning critique.[281]

All of this is not to deny that real problems exist in the system of judicial protection as regards criminal sanctions for the enforcement of substantive Union poli-

[275] See Section 3.D.1.

[276] Cf, Dougan, 'The Constitutional Dimension to the Case Law on Union Citizenship', 31 *European Law Review* (2006) 613.

[277] Eg, Case C-101/01, *Lindqvist, supra* note 50; Case C-421/07, *Damgaard, supra* note 217.

[278] Unless the general principle of Union law requiring the retroactive application of the most lenient criminal law (as recognized in Joined Cases C-387/02, C-391/02 and C-403/02, *Berlusconi, supra* note 211) was itself capable of having direct effect before the national courts, and operating so as to render applicable to the defendant any more favourable rules envisaged by the relevant framework decision, even though the latter was incapable of having any direct effect of its own—surely a controversial proposition.

[279] Cf, the proposals of AG Mengozzi in Case C-355/04, *Segi*, [2007] ECR I-1657. See further, eg, Davies, *supra* note 108.

[280] Protocol No 36 on transitional provisions, OJ 2008 C 115/322.

[281] Eg, Dougan, *supra* note 160.

cies. Many doctrinal uncertainties still need to be resolved: for example, concerning how far the duty of consistent interpretation should differ depending on the character of the relevant Union legal instrument;[282] and whether the general principle requiring retroactive application of the most lenient criminal rules applies even where the relevant domestic legislation fails to meet the standards required by Union law in situations involving a directly effective regulation or Treaty provision.[283] There are also broader issues worth addressing: for example, whether the Court is institutionally equipped—in terms of its procedures and judicial expertise—for assessing criminal law issues;[284] and, pending the Union's formal accession to the ECHR as envisaged by the Lisbon Treaty,[285] concerns about the lack of external scrutiny over the Court's interpretation of Union criminal law, other than indirectly through the doctrine of equivalent protection recognized by the ECtHR in its rulings in *Matthews* and *Bosphorous*.[286]

But overall, the issues of constitutional competence are now much more settled than in previous years; for its part, the system of judicial protection is less problematic than often seems to be assumed. The real questions for the future will surely concern how far the Union should delve into the harmonization of penal sanctions at all, including whether the counsel of restraint from the German Federal Constitutional Court in its ruling on the Lisbon Treaty, and/or the power of national parliaments to deliver a 'yellow card' on subsidiarity grounds, will prompt a more cautious approach in practice from the Union legislature; as well as the need to critically assess the actual substance of the legislation enacted by the political institutions, so as to evaluate whether Union criminal law reflects the sorts of social and cultural values, and meets the accepted legal standards, we are entitled to expect of our increasingly common system of criminal justice.

[282] See Section 4.A. [283] See Section 4.B.

[284] Cf, Weyembergh, *supra* note 80. [285] Art 6(2) TEU.

[286] *Matthews v United Kingdom*, ECHR (1999); *Bosphorous v Ireland*, ECHR (2005).

5

The Role of National Constitutional Courts in Issues of Compliance

Darinka Piqani

1. Introduction

Full application and effectiveness of EU law are essential to the successful functioning of the European Union. Under the principle of sincere cooperation,[1] member states have the responsibility to fulfil their obligations and to refrain from measures which would impair the attainment of the Union's objectives. In a simplified way, the enforcement system in place provides that compliance with EU law at the EU level is monitored by the Commission or other member states[2] and judicially by the European Court of Justice. At the national level, the effectiveness of Union law as well as redress for individual rights have been 'secured' by the Court of Justice since the beginning of European integration through the introduction of the principles of direct effect, supremacy, and state liability. Member state authorities were not only put under the positive obligation to fully and correctly implement and apply EU law,[3] but also had the duty to set aside any national legislation which conflicted with EU law.[4] State liability eventually arises in 'any case in which a Member State breaches EU law, whatever is the organ of the State whose act or omission was responsible for the breach',[5] extending it also to courts of last instance.[6] Thus, the centralized model, according to which compliance is monitored at the EU level and a failure to comply is sanctioned *ex post factum*, goes hand in hand with the decentralized model, which takes place at the national level. Among all state organs national courts carry a significant burden in giving full effect to EU law and in their daily judicial practice they embrace the

[1] Art 4(3) of the Treaty on European Union (TEU), OJ 2010 C 83/13.

[2] See Arts 258–260 of the Treaty on the Functioning of the European Union (TFEU), OJ 2010 C 83/47.

[3] Case 26/62, *Van Gend en Loos v Nederlands Administratie der Belastingen*, [1963] ECR 1.

[4] Case 6/64, *Costa v ENEL*, [1964] ECR 585.

[5] Joined Cases C-46/93 and C-48/93, *Brasserie du Pêcheur v Germany and R v Secretary of State for Transport, ex parte Factortame*, [1996] ECR I-1029.

[6] Case C-224/01, *Köbler v Austria*, [2003] ECR I-239 and Case C-173/03, *Traghetti del Mediterraneo v Italy*, [2006] ECR I-5177.

Union mandate and act as Union courts[7] by applying EU law (direct effect) and giving precedence to EU law in the event that it conflicts with national law (supremacy). The mandate conferred by the Union upon national courts to fully and correctly apply EU law and set aside national law when it conflicts with EU law is one of the many pre-emptive tools for avoiding non-compliance by member states.[8]

This mandate to apply and enforce EU law applies also towards national constitutions and national constitutional courts. One of the strongest characteristics of EU law supremacy vis-à-vis national constitutional orders is its unconditional nature as claimed by the Court of Justice since the very beginning of the Community. The ideal of national constitutions as the highest law was profoundly shaken in *Internationale Handelsgesellschaft*, where the Court of Justice ruled that '[t]he validity of a Community measure or *its effect within a Member State* cannot be affected by allegations that it runs counter to either fundamental rights as formulated by the constitution of that State or the principles of a national constitutional structure'.[9] Thus, national constitutional courts 'are asked to refrain from enforcing the constitutional provisions that they have a sworn duty to uphold and protect, in favour of any act of Community law, whatever its rank or content'.[10] From a compliance perspective this means that constitutional courts cannot obstruct the full application of EU law provisions even on grounds that a tension between EU law and constitutional provisions exists.

This chapter looks at the role of constitutional courts from a compliance perspective.[11] The focus of the analysis will be on how constitutional courts deal with challenges of unconstitutionality in the course of application of EU law in the member states. First, we start with a short overview of the European mandate for national courts. Then we shift to the core of this chapter, namely the discussion of how constitutional courts in particular may hinder or facilitate compliance with EU law. The argument will be that, despite their firm position of upholding the constitution vis-à-vis EU law and some cases of restricting the full effects of EU law, constitutional courts in several ways may act as facilitators of compliance for member states. They do so, for instance, by finding the least harmful solution for the full application of EU law whilst constructing constitutional reservations; by instructing other political branches on how to introduce constitutional or legislative amendments in order to ensure full compliance; and in the pre-accession setting, by putting forward the obligation to interpret national law in conformity with EU law within the ambit of the obligation of approximation.

[7] See for more M. Claes, *The National Courts' Mandate in the European Constitution* (2006).

[8] See more recently Case C-154/08, *Commission v Spain*, [2009] ECR I-187 (summ.pub), where the Court of Justice, for the first time, held a member state responsible for a breach of EU law as a result of a decision of its Supreme Court.

[9] Case 11/70, *Internationale Handelsgesellschaft v Einfuhrund Vorratsstelle Getreide*, [1970] ECR 1125 (emphasis added).

[10] Claes, *supra* note 7, at 387.

[11] The term 'constitutional courts' is used broadly and it refers to highest jurisdictions exercising final constitutional review.

2. The European Mandate of National Courts

Through the not entirely uncontroversial move to emphasize the 'novelty' of the Community legal order in international law and its ability to confer rights to individuals, the Court of Justice in *Van Gend en Loos*[12] legitimized and opened the door to private enforcement through direct effect, complementary to public enforcement by the Commission and member states under Article 226 TEC (now Article 258 TFEU).[13] The positive obligation of national courts to apply national law was soon to be complemented with the obligation to set aside any national law which conflicts with EU law. In *Costa v ENEL*, the Court of Justice relied on a functionalist argument to hold that,

> [t]he executive force of Community law cannot vary from one state to another in deference to subsequent domestic laws, without jeopardizing the attainment of the objectives of the treaty set out in Article 5(2) and giving rise to the discrimination prohibited by Article 7.[14]

If EU law were to be really effective and not lose its force, it had to be applied in a uniform and equal manner across the whole Union (Community at the time), notwithstanding national law.

After putting forward the unconditional supremacy of EU law in *Internationale Handelsgesellschaft*,[15] the Court in *Simmenthal* ruled that a national court,

> ...is under a duty to give full effect to those [EU law] provisions, if necessary refusing of its own motion to apply any conflicting provision of national legislation, even if adopted subsequently, and it is not necessary for the court to request or await the prior setting aside of such provision by legislative or other constitutional means.[16]

Setting aside conflicting national law had to be immediate and, if needed, national procedural rules such as those regulating the annulment of national legislation on constitutional grounds had to be set aside if they rendered the application of EU law impossible. The orthodoxy of national legal orders was transgressed and the Court of Justice empowered national judges to set aside any conflicting national law on their own motion without waiting for the repeal of said national act by national parliaments or for national constitutional courts to declare the respective law unconstitutional. National courts were transformed into courts of judicial review independently of domestic institutional choices. As Claes puts it,

> [a]ll courts, including those which under their national mandate are precluded from reviewing primary legislation, are obliged to give precedence to Community law and consequently set aside or disapply conflicting measures of national law, including primary

[12] Case 26/62, *Van Gend en Loos*, *supra* note 3.
[13] P. Craig and G. De Burca, *EU Law, Text, Cases and Materials* (2008), at 269–74.
[14] Case 6/64, *Costa v ENEL*, *supra* note 4.
[15] Case 11/70, *Internationale Handelsgesellschaft*, *supra* note 9.
[16] Case 106/77, *Amministrazione delle Finanze dello Stato v Simmenthal SpA*, [1978] ECR 629, Rec 24.

legislation. Constitutional obstacles which may restrain the courts from exercising this mandate must be set aside.[17]

In terms of remedies, in *IN.CO.GE*, the Court of Justice clarified that the disapplied national law remains in force, and that the setting aside is only the minimum requirement.[18] National courts have thus the discretion of choosing other remedies available under national law in order to give effect to the EU law norm. Such assertion is complemented by the *Rewe* and *Comet* cases, which formulated the principle of equivalence; this means that:

> In the absence of community rules on this subject, it is for the domestic legal order of each Member State to designate the courts having jurisdiction and to determine the procedural conditions governing actions at law intended to ensure the protection of the rights which citizens have from the direct effect of community law, it being understood that such conditions cannot be less favourable than those relating to similar actions of a domestic nature.[19]

Thus, if a national court has the jurisdiction to annul a national measure (administrative decision, legal regulation, law, etc.) for non-compliance with a higher national norm, then it is under the obligation, as elaborated in *Rewe* and *Comet*, to apply the same national remedies and its jurisdiction in cases where such national provision does not conform to EU law. In terms of how the *Simmenthal* mandate operates, the principle of national procedural autonomy is the rule and it is qualified by the requirements of effectiveness and equivalence. Consequently, the principle of effective judicial protection does not require the national legal order of a member state to provide for a 'self-standing procedure' to review the compatibility between national law and EU law, 'provided that other effective legal remedies, which are no less favourable than those governing similar domestic actions, make it possible for such a question of compatibility to be determined as a preliminary issue, which is a matter for the national court to establish'.[20]

In principle, the *Simmenthal*[21] mandate of enforcing EU law applies to any court within its respective jurisdiction. It was not qualified in any way, meaning that any court acting within its jurisdiction had the obligation of setting aside conflicting national law. Hence, there would be no reason why constitutional courts should be exempted from this obligation.[22] This would be the situation when, for example, an individual in Germany in a constitutional complaint challenged the constitutionality of a law for breaching the constitution as well as EU law. If constitutional courts saw themselves as bearers of the *Simmenthal* mandate it would be a valid claim to provide for an annulment of the conflicting law on grounds of the principle

[17] Claes, *supra* note 7, at 102.

[18] Joined Cases C-10/97–C-22/97, *Ministero delle Finanze v IN.CO.GE'90 Srl,* [1998] ECR I-6307.

[19] Case C-33/76, *Rewe-Zentralfinanz eG et Rewe-Zentral AG v Landwirtschaftskammer für das Saarland*, [1976] ECR I-01989. The Court reaffirmed the principle of equivalence in the case C-45/76, *Comet BV v Produktschap voor Siergewassen*, [1976] ECR I-02043.

[20] Case C-432/05, *Unibet,* [2007] ECR I-2271.

[21] Case 106/77, *Amministrazione delle Finanze dello Stato v Simmenthal SpA, supra* note 16.

[22] See for a discussion Claes, *supra* note 7, at 452–64.

of equivalence and effectiveness as discussed above. This would enhance legal certainty and give an incentive to the legislator to fill in the gap, bringing an end to a situation of incompatibility between EU law and national law. In short, it would lead to better compliance.

Yet the self-perception of constitutional courts is often not in line with this broad reading of *Simmenthal* and a number of courts have been very careful since the mandate was announced to distinguish clearly between constitutional review (for which they are fully competent) and review of compatibility with EU law. Constitutional courts do not seem to accept the mandate of reviewing the compatibility of national law with EU law. For them this does not amount to a constitutional issue. For instance, in *Lütticke*, the German Constitutional Court derived from the constitutional framework of transfer of powers the obligation of German courts to apply Community provisions which 'stem from an autonomous non-State sovereign authority and which, on the basis of their interpretation by the European Court, have direct effect at the municipal level and superimpose themselves upon and displace conflicting national law'.[23] The *Bundesverfassungsgericht* excluded its own competence in the daily enforcement of EU law. Other constitutional courts have also expressed themselves on this issue.

In terms of its competence to review the compatibility of statutes with international law, the Hungarian Constitutional Court has not defined the founding treaties and subsequently Community law as international law. Hence, it cannot review the compatibility between national law and EU law.[24] In the *Excise Duty* case, the Polish Constitutional Tribunal put forward a strict competence division concerning the application, review, and interpretation of EU law by ordinary courts, the Tribunal, and the Court of Justice.[25] The Tribunal asserted that:

> The issue of solving conflicts in relation to domestic statutes falls outside the scope of jurisdiction of the Constitutional Tribunal, since the decisions of whether a statute remains in conflict with Community law, shall be delivered by the Supreme Court, administrative courts and common courts, while the interpretation of Community law norms shall be provided by the ECJ by way of a preliminary ruling.[26]

[23] *Alphons Lütticke GmbH*, German Constitutional Court, Case No 2 BvR 225/69 (1971) in A. Oppenheimer, *The Relationship between European Community Law and National Law: The Cases Vol 1* (1994), at 418.

[24] *On Call Duty Case*, Hungarian Constitutional Court, Decision 72/2006(XII.15.)AB (2006), at <http://www.mkab.hu/admin/data/file/721_72_2006.pdf> last accessed 23 October 2011.

[25] *Excise Duty Case*, Polish Constitutional Tribunal, Decision No 176/11/A/2006 Ref No P 37/05 (2006), at <http://www.trybunal.gov.pl/eng/summaries/documents/P_37_05_GB.pdf> last accessed 23 October 2011. Yet note that while arguing that its involvement in issues of compliance between statutes and EU law would probably amount to a double line of adjudication, and provoke a collision between its decisions and those of the Court of Justice, the Tribunal concluded that, by virtue of Art 8 of the Polish Constitution which puts the Constitution in the apex of the legal order, in fundamental issues related to the constitutional system, it shall retain the status of 'the last-word court'. See part II of the decision. For a comment see also Lazowski, 'Constitutional Tribunal on the Preliminary Ruling Procedure and the Division of Competences between National Courts and the Court of Justice', 4 *European Constitutional Law Review* (2008).

[26] Ibid, para 4.2.

Similarly, the French Constitutional Council has taken every opportunity to spell out the difference between 'the review of statutes for the purpose of verifying their conformity with the Constitution, which is incumbent upon [it], and the review of their compatibility with the international and European commitments of France, which is incumbent upon the Courts of law and Administrative courts'.[27] Not only that, but the Council was very careful to clarify that the priority preliminary ruling procedure (Article 61(1) of the French Constitution), which allows the Council to rule on incidental references in the course of a case when a law infringes constitutional rights, does not deprive a judge,

> ... asked to rule in litigation in which the argument of incompatibility with European Union law is raised, from doing, at any time, *all and everything necessary to prevent the application in the case in hand of statutory provisions impeding the full effectiveness of the norms and standards of the European Union*.[28]

Similarly, in *Granital* the Italian Constitutional Court asserted that conflicting national law was not to be taken into consideration for the solution of a case at hand. Instead, Community law was to be applied *directly* by national courts, thus excluding a question of constitutionality from the Constitutional Court.[29] However, more recently, the Italian Constitutional Court has ruled that in the case of a direct review of a piece of legislation, as occurred with the regional law of Sardegna which was challenged for an alleged incompatibility with the EU Treaties,[30] EU law provisions could serve as standards of constitutional review and in the event of incompatibility with national law, the latter would be annulled as unconstitutional.[31]

What transpires from these cases is a concern on the part of constitutional courts to define clearly the borderline between constitutionality review, which falls within their original jurisdiction, and compatibility review, which according to the *Simmenthal* mandate is left to ordinary courts. 'Europe clauses', which provide for the participation of member states in the EU including the transfer of powers to the EU, are not interpreted as giving to constitutional courts the mandate of ensuring the compatibility between national law and EU law, and thus the enforcement of the latter. This duty is left for ordinary courts. Even in the event that they reserve for themselves a constitutional review competence in a conflict between EU and national law, as the Italian case shows, this is done restrictively and in cooperation with the Court of Justice through the preliminary

[27] *Loi relative a l'ouverture a la concurrence et a la regulation du secteur des jeux d'argent et de hazard en ligne*, French Constitutional Council, Decision No 2010-605 DC (2010), at <http://www.conseil-constitutionnel.fr> last accessed 23 October 2011.

[28] Ibid., para 14 of the English version (emphasis added). For a detailed comment see Mehdi, 'French Supreme Courts and European Union Law: Between Historical Compromise and Accepted Loyalty', 48 *Common Market Law Review* (2011) 2.

[29] *SpA Granital v Amministrazione delle Finanze dello Stato*, Italian Constitutional Court, Case No 170/84 (1984) in Oppenheimer, *supra* note 23, at 643.

[30] *Case Regional Law of Sardinia*, Italian Constitutional Court, Decision No 102 (2008), at <http://www.cortecostituzionale.it/actionPronuncia.do> last accessed 23 October 2011. See for a comment Fontanelli and Martinico, 'Between Procedural Impermeability and Constitutional Openness: The Italian Constitutional Court and Preliminary References to the European Court of Justice', 16 *European Law Journal* (2010) 3.

[31] Ibid, para 8.2.8.1.

reference procedure.[32] By not making the incompatibility between national law and EU law a constitutional matter, constitutional courts also adhere to the spirit of the *Simmenthal* mandate and therefore contribute to the immediate application of EU law. The incompatibility between a national provision and EU law is dealt with by ordinary courts, either by interpreting the former in line with the latter, or by setting aside the conflicting national law and applying EU law, if this remedy is desirable given the case at hand. In this sense, *Simmenthal* brought an end to the exclusivity of judicial review of laws by constitutional courts and the European mandate has been part of the external pressure toward the decentralization of the European system of constitutional review.[33]

However, whereas the judicial review of laws seems ultimately to be shared with ordinary courts, albeit for different purposes and with different outcomes, constitutional review of limits to EU integration became the stronghold of constitutional courts from which they challenged the full application of EU law when the latter conflicted with fundamental rights, fundamental constitutional principles, or when it transgressed the conferred powers. The following parts of this chapter will focus on this aspect.

3. Constitutional Reservations as a Potential Threat to Compliance

Following the introduction of the supremacy doctrine by the Court of Justice, several constitutional courts were not prepared to relinquish their role as ultimate guardians of the constitution. They took the position that they could set aside EU law on constitutional grounds.[34] The resistance shown by these courts challenges the version of supremacy espoused by the ECJ. It does so by subjecting the full application of EU law in those member states to its compatibility with fundamental constitutional principles. It is interesting to study these constitutional reservations from a supremacy perspective. However, they are also intriguing from a compliance point of view because, in the end, they are conditions attached to the supremacy of EU law and can be translated into conditions for the full application of EU law in a member state.

Such review of secondary EU law in the light of national constitutional law, especially a possible annulment of implementing laws, does not fit well, however, with the supremacy of EU law. It does not do justice to the principle of loyalty and sincere cooperation which requires member states to ensure that their obligations under EU law are fulfilled. Yet it has been precisely in the ambit of this review that national constitutional courts, although generally finding national implementing measures in conformity with the constitution and thus refraining from striking

[32] Note that the Italian Constitutional Court in decision 102/2008 decided for the first time to ask a question to the ECJ within the preliminary reference procedure.

[33] Ferreres Comella, 'The European Model of Constitutional Review of Legislation: Toward Decentralization?', 2 *International Journal of Constitutional Law* (2004) 3, at 477 *et seq.*

[34] Kumm, 'The Jurisprudence of Constitutional Conflict: Constitutional Supremacy in Europe before and after the Constitutional Treaty', 11 *European Law Journal* (2005) 3, at 263–4.

down EU policies, have developed a sophisticated set of constitutional reservations regarding the application of EU law within the domestic legal order. It is well known that in *Frontini* the Italian Constitutional Court interpreted Article 11 of the Italian Constitution as allowing for a limitation of sovereignty, but only to the extent that fundamental principles of the Italian constitutional order, in conjunction with inalienable human rights as guaranteed by the Italian Constitution, are not violated.[35] These limits to the unconditional supremacy of EU law were coupled with a self-asserted jurisdiction of the Italian Court to control the compatibility between the EC treaty and those fundamental principles. In *Fragd*,[36] the same Court affirmed that it had a legitimate competence to scrutinize the constitutionality law implementing the treaty, in case a treaty provision, as interpreted and applied by Community institutions, went against fundamental constitutional provisions. The Court then added that in a context of possible infringement of fundamental human rights, *concerns of uniform application of Community law and legal certainty did not have any overriding force*.[37] This rhetoric was confirmed in several recent judgments,[38] in which the Court based direct effect of Community law on Article 11 of the Italian Constitution which, as mentioned, also allows for the limitation of national sovereignty, the only limitation being the inviolability of fundamental rights and principles.[39] Notwithstanding the strong rhetoric of the *controlimiti* doctrine, the Italian Constitutional Court has never transferred this *obiter dictum* into a judgment with direct consequences for the full application of EU law. Somehow, *controlimiti* has remained a blank letter, although it has continually been invoked by the Court in its jurisprudence.[40]

Whereas the Italian approach of constitutional limits to the supremacy of EU law seems rather stable, the German case law on constitutional reservations has undergone constant change and refinement, including fundamental rights review, *ultra vires* review, and constitutional identity review. In *Solange I*,[41] the *Bundesverfassungsgericht* ruled that due to the absence of a democratically elected parliament and the lack of a codified catalogue of human rights comparable to the standard of protection

[35] *Frontini v Ministero delle Finanze*, Italian Constitutional Court, Case No 183/73 (1973), in Oppenheimer, *supra* note 23, at 629.

[36] *Fragd v Amministrazione Delle Finanze Dello Stato*, Italian Constitutional Court, Case No 232/1989 (1989), in A. Oppenheimer, *The Relationship between European Community Law and National Law: The Cases Vol 2* (2003), at 653–62.

[37] Ibid, at 659 (emphasis added).

[38] Italian Constitutional Court, Decision No 348 and No 349 (2007), at <http://www.cortecostituzionale.it/actionPronuncia.do> last accessed 23 October 2011.

[39] Ibid, Decision No 348, para 3.3.

[40] In Decisions No 168 (1991), No 117 (1994), No 509 (1995), No 126 (1996), and No 93 (1997), the Italian Constitutional Court has repeatedly emphasized the impossibility for Community law to derogate from fundamental principles of the Italian constitutional legal order, as well as its duty to safeguard these principles. For more, see the report from Celotto and Groppi, 'Diritto UE e Diritto Nazionale: Primaute vs Controlimiti', 14 *Rivista Italiana di Diritto Pubblico Comparato* (2004), at 1347, as well as Rossi, 'Recent Pro-European Trends of the Italian Constitutional Court', 46 *Common Market Law Review* (2009). See also Adinolfi, 'The Judicial Application of Community Law in Italy', 35 *Common Market Law Review* (1998).

[41] *Internationale Handelsgesellschaft mbh v Einfuhr-und Vorratsstelle fur Getreide und Futtermittel (Solange I)*, German Federal Constitutional Court, Case No 2 BvL 52/71 (1974), in Oppenheimer, *supra* note 23, at 447.

offered by the German Constitution, the application of Community law in Germany would be subject to the obligation to observe the basic structure of the German Constitution, including fundamental rights. In practice, *Solange I* implied that the German Court found itself competent to review Community measures, as interpreted by Community institutions, against the criteria of the German Constitution, and, if necessary, to declare its inapplicability within the German legal order. After relinquishing its review powers in *Solange II*,[42] the German Constitutional Court finally confirmed in the bananas litigation[43] that any constitutional complaint by individual citizens, or reference by lower courts challenging the application of EU law in Germany, would be a priori inadmissible, unless it could be demonstrated that the minimum protection of fundamental rights, as required by the Basic Law in general, was not ensured within the Community.

In the *Maastricht Urteil*, the *Solange* precedent on a hypothetical non-application of Community law in cases of infringement of basic rights was extended by the Court to cases in which EU law was not enacted within the limits of competence provided for by the Treaty and consented to by Germany.[44] In its *Lisbon* judgment the Court introduced another form of constitutional review, namely *identity review*.[45] Accordingly, the Court would review,

> whether the inviolable core content of the constitutional identity of the Basic Law pursuant to Article 23.1 third sentence in conjunction with Article 79.3 of the Basic Law is respected... The identity review makes it possible to examine whether due to the action of European institutions, the principles under Article 1 and Article 20 of the Basic Law, declared inviolable in Article 79.3 of the Basic Law, have been violated... The *ultra vires* review as well as the identity review may result in Community law or, in future, Union law being declared inapplicable in Germany.[46]

It is interesting to note that in the view of the Court, the identity review should observe the principle of openness towards EU law and thus it does not represent a breach of the principle of loyal cooperation. Moreover, this type of review was substantiated by the Court as necessary to safeguard the national identities inherent in the constitutional structures of the member states as provided for in Article 4(3) of the TEU.[47]

Recently in *Honeywell*,[48] a case concerning the review of a presumed *ultra vires* ruling of the Court of Justice in *Mangold*,[49] the German Constitutional Court

[42] *Wunsche Handelsgesellschaft (Solange II)*, German Federal Constitutional Court, Case No 2 BvR 197/83 (1986), in Oppenheimer, *supra* note 23, at 462.

[43] *Banana Market Organization Constitutionality Case*, German Federal Constitutional Court, Case No 2 BvL 1/97 (2000), in Oppenheimer, *Vol 2*, *supra* note 36, at 270.

[44] *Maastricht Treaty 1992 Constitutionality Case*, German Constitutional Court, Case No 2 BvR 2134 and 2159/92 (1993), in Oppenheimer, *supra note* 23.

[45] *Lisbon Treaty Decision*, German Federal Constitutional Court, Case 2 BvE 2/08, 5/08, 2 BvR 1010/08, 1022/08, 1259/08, 182/09 (2009) at <http://www.bundesverfassungsgericht.de/en/decisions/es20090630_2bve000208en.html> last accessed 23 October 2011.

[46] Ibid, paras 240–1. [47] Ibid.

[48] *Honeywell*, German Constitutional Court, Case No 2 BvR 2661/06 (2010), at <http://www.bundesverfassungsgericht.de> last accessed 23 October 2011.

[49] Case C-144/04, *Mangold*, [2005] ECR I-9981.

further refined its mandate concerning constitutional review of *ultra vires* acts of Union bodies. In principle, the German Constitutional Court would be obliged to review acts of EU bodies and declare their inapplicability within Germany in the event that these acts are adopted in manifest transgression of competences or on the basis of competences in areas of constitutional identity which are not transferable.[50] However, *ultra vires* review may be considered only if the Court of Justice has been given the opportunity to rule on validity and interpretation of EU law and in cases where the transgression of competences is obvious and leads to a structural shift in the allocation of competences.[51] In a nutshell, the German Constitutional Court has limited its review powers to a high degree by undertaking identity reviews in relation to inviolable provisions of the Basic Law and *ultra vires* reviews in cases of obvious transgressions by EU institutions and after the ECJ has had the possibility to rule on the validity of the measures. These qualifications point to a significant reduction in the risk that the Court will decide on the inapplicability of EU acts.[52]

Another set of cases through which constitutional courts elaborated constitutional reservations relates to the constitutional review of domestic measures implementing the European Arrest Warrant (EAW).[53] The Czech Constitutional Court managed to reconcile the constitutional prohibition of forcing a person to leave his or her homeland with the EU obligation of surrendering one's citizens to another member state.[54] The Polish Constitutional Tribunal declared the Code of Penal Procedure article which implemented the EAW to be incompatible with Article 55(1) of the Polish Constitution, which provided for a clear prohibition of extradition.[55] However, the Tribunal decided that national provisions implementing the EAW would apply for a period of 18 months during which the legislature would take appropriate amending steps in order to prevent any infringement, and resulting political and legal consequences, in terms of EU law.[56] In fact, in 2006 the Polish Constitution was amended to allow for extradition in specific cases provided for by international treaties.[57] The solution of the Tribunal indeed provisionally reconciled constitutional obligations with obligations deriving from EU law, or, in the words of Lazowski,

> [t]his was an optimal way of marrying the supremacy of the Polish Constitution with the obligation to comply with EU law. Judges made it clear that Polish courts during this transitional period had to surrender Polish nationals if no grounds for refusal existed.[58]

[50] *Honeywell*, *supra* note 48, para 55.

[51] Ibid, paras 60 and 61.

[52] See for a comment Payandeh, 'Constitutional Review of EU Law after Honeywell: Contextualizing the Relationship between the German Constitutional Court and the EU Court of Justice', 48 *Common Market Law Review* (2011).

[53] Council Framework Decision 2002/584 of 13 June 2002 on the European Arrest Warrant and the Surrender Procedures between Member States, OJ 2002 L 190/1.

[54] *Judgment on the European Arrest Warrant*, Czech Constitutional Court, Pl. US 66/04 (2006), at <http://www.concourt.cz> last accessed 23 October 2011.

[55] *Application of the European Arrest Warrant to Polish Citizens*, Polish Constitutional Tribunal, P 1/05 (2005), at <http://www.trybunal.gov.pl> last accessed 23 October 2011.

[56] Ibid, para 5.8.

[57] Art 55 of the Polish Constitution (2006).

[58] Lazowski, 'Half Full and Half Empty Glass: The Application of EU Law in Poland (2004–2010)', 48 *Common Market Law Review* (2011), at 514.

Besides constitutional solutions by Poland and the Czech Republic which avoided non-compliance, the *obiter dicta* of these judgments contained constitutional reservations to the full application of EU law if fundamental constitutional principles were at stake. Although the Czech Constitutional Court managed to reconcile the wording of the Constitutional Charter with the EAW decision, it emphasized that conforming interpretation of national law to EU obligations could not go against the inalienable principle of a democratic and law-based state. Similarly, the Polish Constitutional Tribunal articulated that,

> [t]he obligation to implement the Framework Decisions is a constitutional requirement stemming from Article 9 of the Constitution, but its enactment does not assure automatically and in every case the material conformity of the provisions of derivative EU law and of legislative acts implementing them to national law with the norms of the Constitution.[59]

Moreover, the Tribunal designed its own mandate in this context, stating that,

> [t]he basic function of the Constitutional Tribunal in the political system consists of reviewing the conformity of normative acts with the Constitution, and the same task applies also to situations, where the claim of unconstitutionality concerns that part of the scope regulated by a legislative act, which serves the purposes of implementation of EU law.[60]

The universal value upheld by the Tribunal was and remains the supremacy of the Polish Constitution and the existing possibility of reviewing domestic acts implementing EU law for their compatibility with the Constitution.[61] There are also elements of constitutional identity as a limit to European integration present in the Polish *Lisbon* judgment. The Tribunal asserted that the scope of transfer of certain competences is determined by constitutional identity, which on its side excludes from the transfer of powers those issues which ' "are fundamental to the basis of the political system of a given state" . . . , the conferral of which would not be possible pursuant to Article 90 of the Constitution'.[62]

Lastly, the transposition of directives in France constitutes a constitutional obligation under Article 88-I of the French Constitution,[63] and as such may be hindered only in the exceptional situation that there is a contrary express constitutional provision, meaning a constitutional provision which is specific to the

59 *Application of the European Arrest Warrant to Polish citizens, supra* note 55, para 2.4.

60 Ibid.

61 *Judgment on the Constitutionality of the Lisbon Treaty*, Polish Constitutional Tribunal, K32/09 (2010), at <http://www.trybunal.gov.pl/eng/summaries/documents/K_32_09_EN.pdf> last accessed 23 October 2011.

62 Ibid, para 2.1.

63 *Loi pour la confiance dans l'economie numerique*, French Constitutional Council, Decision No 2004-496 DC (2004), at <http://www.conseil-constitutionnel.fr> last accessed 23 October 2011. This was confirmed recently in *Loi relative a l'ouverture a la concurrence et a la regulation du secteur des jeux d'argent et de hazard en ligne, supra* note 27. Basing the duty to transpose directives on the French Constitution is quite puzzling, considering that ex-Art 249 EC Treaty stipulated a clear obligation of member states to implement directives. It could be, as Dutheil de la Rochere has suggested, that this was done in order to justify the *Conseil*'s jurisdiction, albeit conditional and restricted, regarding the review of constitutionality of transposing laws, see Dutheil de la Rochere, Case note on *Decision no. 2004-496 DC Loi pour la confiance dans l'economie numerique 10 June 2004*, 42 *Common Market Law Review* (2005), at 863.

French legal order, and which has no equivalent within the EU legal order.[64] In a more recent decision,[65] the *Conseil* ruled that the constitutional obligation of transposing directives could find its (substantive) limit in a rule or a principle inherent in the French constitutional identity.[66] The French Constitution is recognized as the foundation for the constitutional obligation of transposing secondary EU law into the French legal order, and as the basis for the constitutional immunity of the transposing law. At the same time, principles inherent in the French constitutional identity constitute the source of constitutional reservations to this immunity,[67] and to full application of EU law in France. Yet if one takes, for instance, the *Electronic Commerce* case, it is interesting to note that the Council seemed to be very cautious with its decision and the impact of the decision on the application of the EU directive. As often happens, only very specific parts of the implementing law were declared unconstitutional. Moreover, those provisions of the implementing law which reproduced the exact wording of the directive were not declared in breach of the Constitution as long as they were interpreted or applied in accordance with the interpretation (*interpretation sous réserve*) given by the Council.[68]

The examples given in this section form a representative account of typologies of constitutional reservations elaborated by constitutional courts. Although the emphasis might differ from fundamental rights to constitutional identity, from *ultra vires* review to principles inherent in constitutional identities, the common denominator is a constant warning of a possible non-application of EU law in cases where constitutional principles are breached and need to be protected by the national constitutional courts. Yet there is a discrepancy between what courts say and what they in fact do. Does this language of threats and potential non-application of EU law in the absence of action turn these courts into paper tigers? No, because rather than a display of strengths or weaknesses, these reservations should be seen as part of a useful dialogue with the Court of Justice through which national constitutional concerns are exposed. If, as a result, more care was taken to accommodate these fundamental constitutional principles greater compliance would eventually follow.

[64] More clarity was provided on 'express constitutional provisions' in the case concerning the law on bioethics, see the case *Loi relative a la bioethique*, French Constitutional Council, Decision No 2004-498 DC (2004), at <http://www.conseil-constitutionnel.fr> last accessed 23 October 2011. See also commentaries in Dutheil de la Rochere, *supra* note 63; Granger, 'France is "Already" back in Europe: the Europeanization of French Courts and the Influence of France in the EU', 14 *European Public Law* (2008) 3.

[65] *Loi relative au droit d'auteur et aux droits voisins dans la societe de l'information,* French Constitutional Council, Decision No 2006-540 (2006) at <http://www.conseil-constitutionnel.fr> last accessed 23 October 2011.

[66] In French this reservation reads 'La transposition d'une directive ne saurait aller a l'encontre d'une regle ou d'un principe inherent a l'identite constitutionnel de la France, sauf que le constituant y ait consenti', para 19 of the above judgment. This has been recently confirmed in the *Gambling* Decision of May 2010, *supra* note 63.

[67] Kovar, 'Commentaire des decisions du Conseil constitutionnel du 10 juin et du 1er juillet 2004; rapport entre le droit communautaire et le droit national', 3 *Revue trimestrielle de droit européen* (2004), at 595.

[68] Decision No 2004-496 DC (2004), *supra* note 63, para 9.

4. Going beyond the Threat of Non-application of EU Law: Cases of Unconstitutionality of National Implementing Measures

The annulment of the German Law implementing the Council Decision on the EAW by the German Constitutional Court on grounds that it infringed freedom of extradition and the guarantee of recourse to a court is an exception to the above line of German jurisprudence[69] and the toothless tiger model.[70] According to the German Court, the implementing law infringed freedom from extradition in a disproportionate manner and the German legislator had not used the margin given by the EAW Decision in order to frame national extradition procedures with due respect for fundamental rights and interests of German citizens. The *Bundesverfassungsgericht* emphasized that '[t]he legislature was obliged in any case to use the latitude as concerns incorporation into national law that the Framework Decision leaves the Member States in a manner that is considerate with the fundamental rights'.[71] In terms of application of EU law and execution of arrest warrants, the judgment did not pass unnoticed.[72] The Court's approach has been criticized for not taking into account consequences at the EU level by paying tribute to national supremacy.[73] The Court did not consider the possibility of conforming interpretation, although in *Pupino*[74] the Court of Justice had extended this obligation to framework decisions.[75] The Court could have taken note of this ruling and could have tried to interpret national law in conformity with the framework decision as far as possible. The outcome of the judgment, ie the full annulment of the implementing law and as a consequence Germany's situation of non-compliance with EU law, has also been subject to criticism.[76]

[69] Similarly, the Cypriot Supreme Court declared the law transposing the EAW unconstitutional, for a summary see <http://www.supremecourt.gov.cy> last accessed 23 October 2011. The Court ruled that the reasons for the arrest of persons are exhaustively provided by the Constitution and they cannot be interpreted as allowing the arrest and surrender of Cypriot nationals. Therefore, the Court ruled out the possibility to interpret national law, here it included the Constitution, in conformity with EU law. Furthermore, the court ruled out the possibility that framework decisions transposed into national law through legislation which conflicts with the Constitution could be considered as prevailing over the latter.

[70] Expression used by Kaiser, 'German Data Retention Provisions Unconstitutional in Their Present Form; Decision of 2 March 2010', 6 *European Constitutional Law Review* (2010), at 504.

[71] *European Arrest Warrant Case*, German Federal Constitutional Court, 2 BvR 2236/04 (2005), at <http://www.bundesverfassungsgericht.de> last accessed 23 October 2011, para 95 of the Decision.

[72] For instance, according to the 30th Report of Session 2005–2006 of the European Union Committee of the House of Lords, 'In response to the German Constitutional Court's ruling, the Spanish authorities rejected several EAW requests from Germany because under Spanish Constitutional law extradition is permitted only on the basis of reciprocity', para 30 of the report, at <http://www.publications.parliament.uk/pa/ld200506/ldselect/ldeucom/ldeucom.htm> last accessed 23 October 2011.

[73] Van Sliedregt, 'The European Arrest Warrant: Extradition in Transition', 3 *European Constitutional Law Review* (2007), at 246.

[74] Case C-105/03, *Pupino*, [2005] ECR I-5285.

[75] See for a comment and alternative ways of interpretation Hinarejos Parga, 'Case note on German European Arrest Warrant Ruling', 43 *Common Law Market Review* (2006).

[76] C. Tomuschat, 'Inconsistencies—The German Federal Constitutional Court on the European Arrest Warrant', 2 *European Constitutional Law Review* (2006). For possible ways of interpretation see the dissenting opinion of Judge Lübbe Wolff, *supra* note 71, para 182.

Judge Lübbe Wolff opined that the Court could have restricted the effects of nullity and that 'by declaring a law void that could be applied in a constitutionally unobjectionable manner in many cases, the Senate forces the Federal Republic of Germany to infringe European Union Law, which could have been avoided without infringing the constitution'.[77]

A more recent example of turmoil caused by measures with an impact on personal liberties is the EU Data Retention Directive.[78] It was adopted as an internal market measure with the purpose of harmonizing member states' measures related to the obligations of service providers of electronic communications or public communications networks to retain certain data generated or processed by them, in order to investigate, detect, or prosecute serious crimes as defined in national law.[79] After the entry into force of the directive in May 2006, its transposition in the member states was not without problems: the Commission started proceedings before the ECJ for failure to comply with obligations deriving from the directive against Ireland, Greece, Sweden, and Austria.[80] Furthermore, the legality of the directive itself was challenged by Ireland[81] on the ground that it was adopted on a wrong legal basis. A parallel 'act' was being played at the national level, with complaints before high courts in Bulgaria, Romania, Germany, Cyprus, and the Czech Republic.[82] In addition, a complaint was filed with the Polish Constitutional Tribunal in January 2011 by members of the Polish Parliament. Similarly, the Hungarian Civil Liberties Union filed a constitutional complaint with the Hungarian Constitutional Court in June 2008.[83] The common feature in the way these courts dealt with the issues before them is that they were not happy with the national implementation of Directive 2006/24. In the courts' view, national legislators did not make use of the implementation discretion in a responsible way for such a sensitive matter as data protection, which for the German Constitutional Court is a matter of constitutional identity.[84]

[77] Ibid, para 183.

[78] Directive 2006/24/EC of the European Parliament and of the Council of 15 March 2006, OJ 2006 L 105/54.

[79] Art 1(1) of the Directive.

[80] Case C-202/09, *Commission v Ireland,* [2009] ECR I-203; Case C-211/09, *Commission v Greece,* [2009] ECR I-204; Case C-185/09, *Commission v Sweden,* [2010] ECR I-00014; Case C-189/09, *Commission v Austria*, judgment of 29 July 2010, not yet published.

[81] Case C-301/06, *Ireland v European Parliament and Council,* [2009] ECR I-00593.

[82] *Data Retention Decision,* Bulgarian Supreme Administrative Court (2008), in Bulgarian at <http://blog.veni.com/wp-content/uploads/2008/12/reshenievas-naredba40.pdf> last accessed 23 October 2011; *Data Retention Decision*, Romanian Constitutional Court, Decision No 1258 (2009), at <http://www.legi-internet.ro/english/jurisprudenta-it-romania/decizii-it/romanian-constitutional-court-decision-regarding-data-retention.html> last accessed 23 October 2011; *Data Retention Decision*, German Constitutional Court, Decision 1 BvR 256/08, 1 BvR 263/08, 1 BvR 586/08 (2009); Decision of the Supreme Court of Cyprus (2011), not available in English, for information see <http://www.edri.org/edrigram/number9.3/data-retention-un-lawful-cyprus> last accessed 23 October 2011; *Decision on Data Retention in Telecommunications Services,* Czech Constitutional Court, Pl. US 24/10 (2011) at <http://www.concourt.cz/view/pl-24-10> last accessed 1 November 2011.

[83] For more see <http://tasz.hu/en/data-protection/constitutional-complaint-filed-hclu-against-hungarian-telecom-data-retention-regulat>, last accessed 23 October 2011.

[84] German Decision on Data Retention, *supra* note 82, part 3 of the English summary.

Another example, albeit from another field of EU legislation, comes from Hungary. In the *Agricultural Surplus Stock* case,[85] the Hungarian Constitutional Court declared the Hungarian bill implementing European Commission regulations aimed at the prevention of accumulation of agricultural stocks before Hungary's accession to the EU unconstitutional on the grounds of legal certainty. The Surplus Act failed to comply with the constitutional requirement of non-retroactivity and the possibility for concerned subjects to become familiar with and adapt to new rules. This was so because the existence of the speculative stock and its quantity was to be determined by referring to criteria before the entrance into force of the Act (as of 1 May 2004), and the adoption of the Act did not reserve enough time for the interested subjects to familiarize themselves with the new rules and implications thereof.

Similarly to the German EAW case, the constitutional issue at hand was considered by the Hungarian Court as entirely domestic, although the challenged Hungarian Act was a reproduction of the Commission's regulations. In the view of the Court, the transitional measures and the Hungarian implementing Act corresponded to a pre-accession situation and, as such, the review was exclusively related to a domestic Act. The fact is that the Court failed to see the EU dimension of the case and decided to review the constitutionality of the Act of Parliament in the light of the constitutional principle of legal certainty, as interpreted in its own jurisprudence.[86]

The late adoption of the implementing measures, which brought about the defect in law, was caused by the lack of quorum in the Hungarian Parliament.[87] This shifts the focus to the issue of conscious and responsible participation of all political bodies in law-making, in such a way that such defects in law can be avoided and, ultimately, compliance with EU law is not hampered. Without discharging the Court for its unwillingness to see the EU dimension in the case at hand, the judgment could also be seen as,

> sending a strong message to the political branches on the need of bringing law-making to the new requirements of European membership. This message indicated that law-making should be fully responsive to the new requirements of European membership and European law should be moved out of ordinary politics.[88]

The annulment of domestic implementing measures as unconstitutional by courts is often only the tip of the iceberg, as the above episodes show. The role of courts in not hindering compliance with EU law can often be facilitated by a more responsible participation in decision-making of other political branches, such as the parliament.

[85] *Judgment 17/2004 (V.25) AB*, Hungarian Constitutional Court (2004), at <http://www.mkab.hu> last accessed 23 October 2010.

[86] See for comments Sadurski, '"Solange, Chapter 3": Constitutional Courts in Central Europe-Democracy-European Union', 14 *European Law Journal* (2008) 1; Uitz, 'EU law and the Hungarian Constitutional Court: Lessons from the First Post-accession Encounter', in W. Sadurski, J. Ziller and A. Zurek (eds), *Apres Enlargement, Legal and Political Responses in Central and Eastern Europe* (2005); Sajo, 'Learning Co-operative Constitutionalism the Hard Way: the Hungarian Constitutional Court Shying Away from EU Supremacy', 2 *Zeitschrift fur Staats- und Europawissenschaften* (2004).

[87] On the legislative history of the Act see, Sajo, *supra* note 86, at 356.

[88] Ibid, at 369.

5. Constitutional Courts Give Guidance to Political Branches on Constitutional and Legislative Amendments: Towards Better Compliance?

Alongside the rhetoric, threatening to declare EU law not applicable, constitutional courts often facilitate better compliance with EU law by placing on the agenda of political bodies the necessary legislative and constitutional amendments which would guarantee, in a constitutional manner, full application of EU law. This has taken place either in the form of a priori review of the constitutionality of EU treaties or in relation to cases of unconstitutional measures implementing EU law.

Constitutional review of treaty amendments generally takes place before their ratification and as such is followed by appropriate amendments of the constitution. The advantage of this type of review is that compatibility between treaty obligations and the constitution is checked a priori, and incompatibilities are corrected by amending the constitution. In effect, this process of indicating incompatibilities between EU law and national constitutions and accordingly amending the latter ensures that compliance with EU treaty obligations is pledged by the guardian of the constitution itself.

Thus, the French Constitutional Council has developed an abundant case law on the review of treaty constitutionality. At its centre one finds the formulation that 'international commitments of France which contradict constitutional provisions by violating constitutional rights or infringing essential conditions for the exercise of sovereignty, cannot have effect until a revision of the constitution'.[89] In this line, the French Constitutional Council, in its *Maastricht* decision,[90] ruled that the changes introduced by the Maastricht Treaty concerning the right of EU citizens to vote and to stand as candidates for municipal elections, procedures related to the establishment of a single currency, and measures concerning the entry and circulation of third-country nationals, would affect the exercise by member states of powers based on essential conditions of sovereignty. Following this ruling, the French National Assembly and Senate amended the French Constitution by introducing Article 88-I, which provides for France's participation in the European Communities and the European Union, the transfer of powers necessary for the establishment of an economic and monetary union, as well as for the determination of rules concerning the crossing of external borders of the member states. In this way, France's participation in these policies and, as a consequence, the full application of EU obligations deriving thereof, would not in principle be hindered by constitutional concerns as the Constitution itself authorizes these actions.

A more recent example comes from Germany. The German Constitutional Court in the *Lisbon* decision found no incompatibility between the Treaty and the

[89] *Traite modifiant le traite sur l'Union europeenne et le traite instituant la Communaute europeenne*, French Constitutional Council, Decision No 2007-560 (2007), at <http://www.conseil-constitutionnel.fr> last accessed 23 October 2011.

[90] *Maastricht Treaty I*, French Constitutional Council, Decision No 92-308 DC (1992), at <http://www.conseil-constitutionnel.fr> last accessed 23 October 2011.

Basic Law, while it ruled that the Act Extending and Strengthening the Rights of the *Bundestag* and *Bundesrat* in EU matters did not comply with German constitutional requirements.[91] The declaration of unconstitutionality of the Extending Act turned the focus of attention to the *Bundestag* and the *Bundesrat*, which were paradoxically admonished by the German Constitutional Court for not having sufficiently elaborated their rights of participation in EU decision-making as provided for by the Lisbon Treaty. The *Bundesverfassungsgericht* brought to the attention of the *Bundestag* and *Bundesrat* that 'they must exercise their responsibility for integration in numerous cases of dynamic development of the treaties'[92] by adopting an approving law on the basis of Article 23(1) of the Basic Law[93] in each of the following situations: the simplified treaty revision procedure,[94] the general and the special bridging clauses,[95] the flexibility clause,[96] the 'emergency brake',[97] or the use of Article 83(1)(3) in the area of judicial cooperation in criminal matters. The amendment of the Extending Act in accordance with the provisos given by the German Constitutional Court in principle would minimize the chances for constitutional challenges on the grounds that EU bodies have acted *ultra vires*, because they would presumably act under the authorization of the German Constitution given by the German Parliament. On the other hand, it could be hazardous and premature to argue that the German Constitutional Court will not review, for instance, an EU act adopted under the flexibility clause on grounds of *ultra vires* law-making in a case in which the German *Bundestag* authorized, through an approving law, the vote of the German representative in the Council for the use of this clause. What is certain is that after the 'German *Mangold*', the German Constitutional Court has considerably restricted its *ultra vires* review and chances for Germany's non-compliance with EU law on grounds of annulments by the Constitutional Court have significantly decreased.

Another typical case of constitutional courts favouring compliance is the EAW ruling of the Polish Constitutional Tribunal. As discussed above, the Tribunal declared the provision of the Code of Penal Procedure incompatible with Article 55(1) of the Polish Constitution, but the execution of surrender procedures would take place in Poland until the Constitution was revised. The Tribunal gave precedence to Poland's EU obligations and the EU legal order, asserting that:

> Given the obligations implied by membership of Poland in the European Union, it is indispensable to change the law in force in such manner, as to enable not only full implementation of the Council Framework Decision 2002/584/JHA, but also such as to assure its conformity with the Constitution. In order to enable the accomplishment of this task, therefore, *one cannot rule out the appropriate amendment of Article 55 paragraph 1 of the*

[91] *Lisbon Treaty Decision*, *supra* note 45.

[92] Ibid, para 411.

[93] A part of Art 23(1) of the German Basic Law reads 'With a view to establishing a United Europe, the Federal Republic of Germany shall participate in the development of the European Union that is committed to democratic, social and federal principles, to the rule of law, and to the principle of subsidiarity, and that guarantees a level of protection of basic rights essentially comparable to that afforded by this Basic Law. To this end the Federation may transfer sovereign powers by a law with the consent of the Bundesrat'.

[94] Art 48(6) TEU.

[95] Art 48(7)(3) TEU and Art 81(3)(3) TFEU.

[96] Art 352 TFEU.

[97] Arts 48(2), 82(3), 83(3) TFEU.

Constitution, so as to provide that this provision would foresee the exception from the prohibition of extradition of Polish citizens.[98]

Indeed, the outcome of the Tribunal's decision was not so troublesome in terms of compliance with EU law if compared to the German EAW decision: the German law implementing the Council Decision was declared unconstitutional in its entirety, even though the wording of the Basic Law gave more room to the German Constitutional Court than the Polish Constitution gave to its Polish counterpart to find a reconciling reading of the national constitution, the implementing law, and the framework decision. However, the judgment must have been bothersome for the Polish Tribunal itself, which found itself between a rock and a hard place, with 'hands thus tied by the constraints of EU membership'.[99] A pre-accession amendment of the Polish Constitution would have, in this case, avoided several problems: first of all, it would have spared the Polish Constitutional Tribunal the embarrassment of having to find ways of reconciling a clear constitutional prohibition of extradition of its own nationals with an EU obligation. Secondly, the Tribunal would not have been put in a position for which constitutional courts are often criticized, namely that of dictating to other political branches what constitutes a constitutional political choice, ie amending the Constitution with a view to allowing the extradition of Polish citizens according to the procedures provided for in the Framework Decision. This is also noted by Albi who argues that an 'inadequate constitutional framework may place an excessive burden upon constitutional courts...and shift their framework of reference from the legal and constitutional requirements to considerations of political and European/international expediency'.[100]

6. Constitutional Courts and Compliance with Pre-accession Obligations

The common element of the case law analysed above is that EU law is binding in its entirety and constitutional courts act in the capacity of courts of member states. However, constitutional courts can have and do have an important role in issues of approximation of national law with EU law before EU membership is acquired.

One of the peculiarities of the pre-accession process is that the candidate country is not *de jure* bound by EU law, but bears the ongoing obligation to approximate national law to EU law. This was a clear legal obligation deriving from the Europe Agreements with candidate countries from Central and Eastern Europe (CEE), which expressly provided that one of the preconditions for CEE countries'

[98] *Application of the European Arrest Warrant to Polish citizens, supra* note 55, para 5 (emphasis added).

[99] Albi, 'Selected EU Judgments by CEE Constitutional Courts: Lessons on How (Not) to amend Constitutions', 3 *Croation Yearbook of European Law and Policy* (2007), at 56.

[100] Albi, 'Constitutions in the Face of Europeanizing Governance: Falling behind times?', in C. Closa (ed), *The Lisbon Treaty and National Constitutions, Europeanization and Democratic Implication Arena Report No. 3/09, Recon Report No. 9* (2009), at 130.

economic integration was the approximation of their existing and future legislation to that of the Community.[101] Approximation clauses in Stabilization and Association Agreements (SAA) with the Western Balkans entail the obligation of the individual countries 'to ensure that its existing laws and future legislation shall be gradually made compatible with the Community *acquis*'.[102]

According to Petrov, approximation clauses together with harmonization commitments represent the mechanisms for exporting the *acquis* into the legal order of third countries.[103] Another mechanism for exporting the *acquis* and making it applicable within the legal order of the associated country is the direct reference within the SAA to TEU and TFEU articles, for example on competition and state aid. For instance, according to Article 70(2) of the SAA Croatia, any anti-competitive practice or state aid distorting or threatening to distort competition, and which might affect trade between parties, 'shall be assessed on the basis of criteria arising from the application of the competition rules applicable in the Community, in particular from Articles 81, 82, 86 and 87 of the Treaty establishing the European Community and interpretative instruments adopted by the Community institutions'.

In the pre-accession stage approximation entails, among other things, an obligation of 'judicial harmonization'. This means that the judiciary takes into account EU law and interpretation thereof by the Court of Justice when applying national law.[104] In contrast with the situation of member states, uniformity in interpretation and application of standards of EU law is more difficult to guarantee due to the lack of procedures or competences to ensure it. There is no possibility for national courts of associated countries to refer a question to the Court of Justice on the interpretation of EU law. While referring to the situation of state aid control, Cremona defines this as 'an uneasy combination: seeking to establish a common standard for the compatibility of State aid with the Agreement, but without any mechanism for ensuring this, via equivalent procedures and competences'.[105] What is more, there is no enforcement procedure equivalent to Articles 258–260 TFEU which would ensure that candidate countries comply with pre-accession obligations. A possible failure on the side of candidate countries to ensure harmonization would amount to a breach of international law—in this case, of the association agreements. Compliance with obligations deriving from association, including the obligation to approximate national legislation with Union law, is in fact monitored at several levels, including by the Association and Stabilization Council,[106] through progress reports drafted by the Commission, as well as in the

[101] See, eg, Art 68 of the Europe Agreement with Poland, OJ 1993 L 348. Europe Agreements with other candidate countries provided for the same obligation.

[102] See, eg, Art 69 of the Stabilization and Association Agreement with Croatia, OJ 2005 L 26 or Art 70 of the Stabilization and Association Agreement with Albania, OJ 2009 L 107.

[103] Petrov, 'Exporting the *Acquis Communautaire* into the Legal Systems of Third Countries', *European Foreign Affairs Review* (2008) 13.

[104] On this see also A. Albi, *EU Enlargement and the Constitutions of the Central and Eastern Europe* (2005), at 52.

[105] Cremona, 'State Aid Control: Substance and Procedure in the Europe Agreements and the Stabilization and Association Agreements', 9 *European Law Journal* (2003) 3, at 271.

[106] Eg, see Art 110 of SAA Croatia.

course of negotiations when enforcement through conditionality and political dialogue acquires great importance.

The pre-accession adaptation of national legal orders has gone so far as to include the constitution. In principle, there is no explicit requirement, stemming from EU law, for pre-accession constitutional adaptation, even though such an 'exercise' is often deemed necessary after screening the level of alignment of national legislation with the *acquis*.[107] There is a tendency emerging for the European Commission to identify from screening reports any potential discrepancies between the constitution and specific parts of the *acquis* before accession to the EU. Thus, the scope of approximation is expanding, including not only legislation but also constitutional provisions.

Coming back to the role of constitutional courts in 'judicial harmonization' in the pre-accession stage, one notices that judgments rendered by constitutional courts in CEE countries had a general tendency to refer to the *acquis* as the standard for interpretation and application of national law, as well as pointing to the importance of approximation of legal theory and thinking.[108] In the view of the Polish Constitutional Tribunal during the accession phase '. . . of course, EU Law has no binding force in Poland'.[109] However, the Tribunal emphasized that '[t]he obligation to ensure compatibility of legislation (borne, above all, by the parliament and government) results also in the obligation to interpret the existing legislation in such a way as to ensure the greatest possible degree of such compatibility'.[110] According to the Tribunal, although EU law could not be deemed as binding in Poland, Polish institutions—including courts and the Constitutional Tribunal itself—were under the Europe Agreement obligation to provide for the maximum compatibility between EU and domestic law.

In the *Bio-Components* case, the Tribunal emphasized the constitutional basis (Article 91.1 of the Constitution) of the principle of interpreting national law in an EU-friendly manner.[111] This new approach introduced by the Polish Constitutional Tribunal emphasized the need to reconstruct the pattern of constitutional review.[112] According to the Tribunal, the fact that EU law should serve as a source of inspiration when interpreting laws implies that it serves to reconstruct

[107] Eg, see Screening Report Croatia, Free Movement of Capital, 4 July 2006; Screening Report Croatia, Economic and Monetary Policy, 19 July 2006; Screening Report Croatia, Justice Freedom and Security, 2 June 2006; Screening Report Croatia, Financial Control, 28 September 2006, at <http://ec.europa.eu/enlargement> last accessed 23 October 2011.

[108] Albi, *supra* note 104, at 54–5.

[109] Judgment K15/97, Polish Constitutional Tribunal (1997), as reported by Kuhn, 'The Application of European Union Law in the New Member States', 6 *German Law Journal* (2005) 3, at 566. On conforming interpretation see also the case *Differentiation of the Situation of Employees at Retirement Age on the Grounds of their Gender,* Polish Constitutional Tribunal, Judgment K35/99 (2000), para 3 and 4 of the summary, at <http://www.trybunal.gov.pl> last accessed 23 October 2010. On the constitutional principle of sympathetic predisposition towards the process of European integration see *Referendum on Poland's Accession to the European Union,* Polish Constitutional Tribunal, Judgment K11/03 (2003), at <http://www.trybunal.gov.pl> last accessed 23 October 2011.

[110] Ibid.

[111] *Bio-Components Case,* Polish Constitutional Tribunal, Judgment K33/03 (2004), at <http://www.trybunal.gov.pl> last accessed 23 October 2011.

[112] For this see Biernat, 'European rulings of Polish Courts Prior to Accession to the European Union', 5 *The Polish Foreign Affairs Digest* (2005) 1(14), at 137.

the framework of constitutional review, meaning that the Constitution as the traditional standard of review would be complemented by principles of EU law.[113] However, the Tribunal suggested that it was possible to apply a Europe-friendly interpretation only when Polish law does not point to another interpretation, or when such interpretation is possible among several interpretations.[114]

In a similar tone, the Czech Constitutional Court in its pre-accession case law has stated that 'primary Community law is not foreign law for the Constitutional Court, but to a wide degree it penetrates—particularly in the form of general legal principles of European law—in its own decision making. To that extent it is also relevant to the Constitutional Court's decision-making'.[115] The Czech Constitutional Court incorporated the European Community's experience on agriculture regulation in a judgment, and directly referred to the case law of the Court of Justice, namely *Hauer*,[116] which dealt with certain limitations to the fundamental right of property, due to restrictions deriving from the community agriculture policy. In another case, reported by Zemanek, the Czech Constitutional Court found several provisions of the amendment Act on the Czech National Bank unconstitutional, not only on the basis of constitutional provisions dealing with the independent status of the Czech National Bank, but also on the basis of Article 130 TFEU (ex-Article 108 TEC), guaranteeing the independence of the European Central Bank and national banks in the member states.[117]

In a 1998 case on the constitutionality of a government regulation providing that Estonian sailors could sail on all ships, while stateless persons or aliens could only sail on ships flying the Estonian flag, Chief Justice Maruste based the unconstitutionality of the Estonian regulation *inter alia* on European law grounds. He reasoned that the principle of equal treatment in EU law is one of the 'legal-political landmarks that Estonia has to be guided by in further legal regulation of movement of labour force, including seafarers'.[118] For the Chief Justice, with the ratification of the Association Agreement, Estonia undertook 'a political, including legal-political, obligation to harmonise domestic law with EU law and its principles. Pursuant to Article 68 of the Agreement Estonia has an obligation to approximate positive law with that of European Community'.[119] What emerges from these cases is that compliance with pre-accession obligations implied not only a clear technical duty of approximation of national laws with the *acquis,* but also a redefinition of the constitutional framework for review which in turn would include not only national constitutional principles but also principles of EU law, within the possible limits of interpretation.

[113] Ibid. [114] *Bio-Components Case, supra* note 111.

[115] *Production quotas on Milk*, Czech Constitutional Court, Judgment Pl. US 5/2001 (2001), at <http://www.concourt.cz> last accessed 23 October 2011.

[116] Case 44/79, *Hauer v Land-Rheinland-Pfalz* [1979] ECR 3727.

[117] Zemanek, 'National Report on the Czech Republic', in A.E. Kellermann et al (eds), *The Impact of EU Accession on the Legal Orders of New EU Member States and (Pre-) Candidate Countries—Hopes and Fears* (2006), at 324–5.

[118] Judgment 3-4-1-4-98, Constitutional Review Chamber of the Estonian Supreme Court (1998), reported also by A. Albi, 'Central and Eastern European Constitutions and EU Integration: In a decade from "souverainism" to "federalism"?' (Doctoral Thesis European University Institute, Florence, 2003), at 66. [119] Ibid.

Yet it was not easy to completely ignore the pragmatic and formalistic view that in fact EU law was foreign law for the candidate countries. For example, the Hungarian Constitutional Court declared the implementation of an Association Council Decision partially unconstitutional while ruling that EU law could not be applied directly in Hungary when accession was still pending.[120] The petitioner challenged the constitutionality of Article 62(2) of the Europe Agreement according to which any anti-competitive practices in Hungary should be assessed in the light of respective criteria deriving from Community law (ex-Articles 85, 86, 92 TEC). According to the Court, those criteria could not be applied directly in Hungary due to the fact that Hungary was not a member of the EU and EU law as such was considered foreign law. In the view of the Court, norms of another public order, on the creation of which Hungary had no influence, could not generate an obligation of applicability in the Hungarian legal order. This, according to the Court, would require an express constitutional authorization.[121]

According to the Court, EU law criteria, although not directly applicable in the Hungarian legal order, ought to be taken into account by Hungarian authorities, due to the constitutional obligation of harmony that the obligations assumed under international and domestic law. Nevertheless,

> [a]ny provision ordering the direct applicability of internal public law norms of the Community in the Hungarian legal system, and in legal relations of a public law nature between the Hungarian state and the subjects of law under its sovereignty, violates Article 2 paras (1) and (2) of the Constitution. It is a constitutional requirement based on the principles of popular sovereignty and the democratic rule of law that in the Hungarian Republic, public authority may only be exercised on the basis of democratic legitimacy.[122]

In a similar context, the Croatian Constitutional Court dealt with a challenge on the direct applicability of EU criteria, standards, and interpretative instruments regarding anti-competitive practices as provided for in the Stabilization and Association Agreement (SAA) with Croatia.[123] The applicant in a 2006 case of the Administrative Court[124] argued that although the Association Agreement could be applied, the criteria, standards, and interpretative instruments on competition law of the EU institutions, not being included directly in the text, could not be considered as a source of law. As regards this claim, the Croatian Constitutional Court found that those '[c]riteria, standards and interpretative instruments of the European Communities are not applied as the primary source of law, but only as an auxiliary instrument of interpretation'.[125] Then, the Court went on, arguing that,

> [t]he provisions of Article 70/2 SSP and Article 35/2 of the Interim Agreement should be seen in the context of the obligation of the Republic of Croatia to harmonise its

[120] *Europe Agreement Decision*, Hungarian Constitutional Court, Decision 30/1998 (VI 25) AB (1998), at <http://www.mkab.hu> last accessed 23 October 2011. However, the Court decided to suspend the annulment of those provisions until December 1999.

[121] Ibid, part V-4.

[122] Ibid, part VII-1(4).

[123] U-III/1410/2007, Croatian Constitutional Court (2008), at <http://www.usud.hr> last accessed 23 October 2011.

[124] Decision Us-5438/2003, Croatian Administrative Court (2006).

[125] Decision U-III/1410/2007, *supra* note 123.

legislation, also that related to market competition, with the *acquis communitaire* of the European Union. When applying such harmonised legislation, government institutions are obliged to apply it in the same way as the European Communities, that is in the sense and spirit of the legislation pursuant to which the harmonisation was carried out.[126]

According to the Court, the said article of the SAA, which provides for the application of EU competition standards and criteria, does not formally introduce EU law into the Croatian legal system, but provides that Croatian competition regulations be applied by taking EU rules into account. Thus, the application of EU law criteria was upheld by the Court as an application of auxiliary instruments in order to fill the gaps in national law, and without going against the spirit of national law.[127] As to the merits of the case, the Croatian Constitutional Court rejected the constitutional complaint. Notwithstanding the formal obstacle of applying EU law *directly* before accession, constitutional courts seem to understand the importance of widening the categories and sources of law which national authorities should take into account in the daily application of domestic law. With the political decision of future membership, candidate countries' obligation of approximation requires not only bringing national laws in line with EU law, but also when applying them taking into account EU regulations.

In conclusion, a certain pattern can be identified in the attitude of constitutional courts regarding the application of EU law if one compares pre-accession case law with the case law of constitutional courts after accession: Constitutional courts which showed a high level of sensitivity towards the obligation of approximation of laws and practices in the pre-accession stage (and thus ensured higher compatibility between national law and pre-accession EU law obligations), seem to have most successfully managed to accommodate full application of EU law after accession to the European Union. Constitutional courts which, during the pre-accession stage, inferred a constitutional principle of friendly predisposition towards EU law from their national constitution and the Europe Agreements positioned themselves as courts willing and able to find constitutional solutions without hindering the effectiveness of EU law and reconciling in the best possible way their constitution with EU law obligations after accession.

The Polish Constitutional Tribunal, for instance, following its pre-accession Europe-friendly jurisprudence did not hinder the full application of EU law after accession and, as analysed above in the EAW case, managed to put forward a constitutional remedy which did not obstruct Poland's compliance with Union law. Similarly, the Czech Constitutional Court, in the light of the constitutional principle of interpreting national law in conformity with EU law, managed to find a reconciling reading of the Czech Charter of Fundamental Rights, the implementing law, and the EAW framework decision. Lastly, the Constitutional Review Chamber of the Estonian Supreme Court, in an opinion on the interpretation of the Estonian Constitution, gave one of the most favourable interpretations of

[126] Ibid. [127] Ibid.

national constitutions concerning their relation to Union law and the full application of the latter.[128] The Court ruled that,

> (t)he effect of those provisions of the Constitution that are not compatible with the European Union law and thus inapplicable, is suspended. This means that within the spheres, which are within the exclusive competence of the European Union or where there is a shared competence with the European Union, the European Union law shall apply in the case of a conflict between Estonian legislation, including the Constitution, with the European Union law.[129]

The argument also holds with regard to the jurisprudence of the Hungarian Constitutional Court. The highly dualistic stance of the Hungarian Court in the *Agricultural Surplus Stock* case can be considered as following on from the dualistic stance taken by the same Court in the *Europe Agreement* decision. In this latter case, in contrast to the Polish and Czech Constitutional Courts, concerns regarding the direct application of EU law criteria and standards regarding anti-competitive behaviours before accession were voiced in a more dramatic way.

7. Conclusions

The enforcement of EU law is an obligation incumbent upon all national bodies, including courts. This chapter has built on the European mandate of courts according to which direct effect and supremacy were translated into the obligation of courts to fully apply EU law and to set aside, if necessary, conflicting measures of national law. This mandate, deriving from the famous *Simmenthal* case, empowered ordinary courts and transformed them into review courts. At the same time, it positioned regular courts as direct competitors to constitutional courts. Furthermore, the unconditional nature of supremacy of EU law and the necessity of its uniform and effective application, notwithstanding constitutional requirements, seemed to weaken the status of national constitutional courts as guardians of their constitution. Additionally, the enforcement of EU law by courts was ensured by the Court of Justice through the *Köbler* and *Traghetti* doctrines, and for the first time through an infringement procedure brought against a member state for failure of its Supreme Court to comply with EU obligations.[130]

Yet the question is: What role is left for constitutional courts in the framework set up for the enforcement of EU law and compliance of member states with EU norms? It has been shown that, whereas their position in accepting the *Simmenthal* mandate is rather heterogeneous, with a tendency towards reserving it for ordinary courts, constitutional courts find themselves comfortable with subjecting full application of EU law to constitutional reservations based on concerns of fundamental rights protection, *ultra vires* action of EU institutions, and respect for

[128] *Opinion on the Interpretation of the Estonian Constitution*, Constitutional Review Chamber of the Estonian Supreme Court, Case No 3-4-1-3-06 (2006), at <http://www.nc.ee> last accessed 23 October 2011.

[129] Ibid, part II para 16.

[130] Case C-154/08, *Commission v Spain*, *supra* note 8.

constitutional identities. These are articulated as warnings according to which full application of EU law could be limited in case EU measures go against fundamental constitutional principles. This type of reservation has usually remained in the level of *obiter dicta* and therefore has not materialized in a concrete failure to apply EU law in the concerned member state, yet. Next to an institutional 'arrogance' of having the last word on the application of EU law, one should be able to see the constructive side of constitutional reservations. They contributed, for instance, to improving the situation of human rights protection in Europe. Furthermore, constitutional courts' objections to unconstitutional implementation of EU measures should also be taken seriously in order to ensure full application of EU law within the limits of European constitutionalism. This message is valid not only for national legislators. By formulating their reservations, constitutional courts engage in dialogues with EU institutions on the borderlines of EU competence and regulation. For instance, it seems that the Commission is willing to take on board the reservations put forward by several constitutional courts concerning the implementation of the data retention directive by considering national case law in its future proposal on revising the data retention framework.[131]

Certainly, constitutional courts could make use in a more constructive way of the institutional instruments in place in order to further the dialogue with the Court of Justice. It is precisely in the preliminary reference procedure where one could find an effective way of addressing constitutional concerns to the Court of Justice without at the same time endangering the uniform application of EU law. On its side, the Court of Justice would be under the obligation of responding to the concerns of constitutional courts not only within the spirit of EU law but also bearing in mind the obligation of respect for national identities inherent in constitutional structures. The Court of Justice, in recent cases, has shown a willingness to take such considerations on board, when necessary.

As argued throughout the chapter, constitutional courts act as facilitators for compliance. They do so when calling the attention of other political branches to necessary constitutional or legislative amendments which aim at pre-empting or rectifying unconstitutional situations. Constitutional courts often give instructions or even admonish their governments or legislatures with regard to better fulfilment of EU obligations. However, it is the responsibility of the national constituent powers or legislators to avoid such situations which force constitutional courts to point to incompatibilities in the first place. Last but not least, constitutional courts played a constructive role in the pre-accession stage where they took the lead and articulated the principle of interpreting national law in accordance with EU law before accession. This became an important part of the 'judicial approximation' necessary for smooth accession and pre-empted problems with compliance after asserting EU membership.

[131] Evaluation Report from the Commission to the Council and the European Parliament on the Data Retention Directive, COM (2011) 225 final, at <http://ec.europa.eu/commission_2010-2014/malmstrom/archive/20110418_data_retention_evaluation_en.pdf> last accessed 23 October 2011.

6

The Role of National Courts in Inducing Compliance with International and European Law—A Comparison

*André Nollkaemper**

1. Introduction

This chapter assesses how national courts can induce compliance with international and European law, and compares the relative strengths of national courts in this regard under, respectively, international and European law.

The chapter is based on the assumption that while national courts are obviously not the primary or only cause of compliance,[1] they can, in particular circumstances and under particular conditions, ensure that states comply with their obligations under international and/or European law, both in individual cases and at a more structural level. In this context it is to be recalled that independent courts are a critical element of the rule of law.[2] This is most obviously so under national law, and it is indeed in that context that the common understanding of independent courts as core elements of the rule of law finds it basis. But given the support for the rule of law at European[3] and international level,[4] and given the intertwining between European, international, and national law,[5] it is a compelling argument that (national) courts

* I thank Anna Gilsbach, Christopher Hopwood, Isabelle Swerissen, and Camilla Wright for research assistance.

[1] Other and probably more important mechanisms to secure compliance include self-interest and reputation: J.L. Goldsmith and E.A. Posner, *The Limits of International Law* (2005); A.T. Guzman, *How International Law Works* (2007). Of course, there is good evidence that accountability processes can help to spur compliance; see Koh, 'Transnational Legal Process', 75 *Nebraska Law Review* (1996) 181, at 194–206.

[2] B.Z. Tamanaha, *On the Rule of Law: History, Politics, Theory* (2004), at 124; Raz, 'The Rule of Law and its Virtue', 83 *The Law Quarterly Review* (1977) 195, at 200.

[3] Art 2 of the Treaty on the European Union, OJ 2010 C 83/13.

[4] See 2005 World Summit Outcome, UNGA Res 60/1, 24 October 2005, para 134; UNGA Res 63/128, 15 January 2009; UNSC Presidential Statement, S/PRST/2006/28, 22 June 2006.

[5] See generally on the intertwining of international and domestic law Ferrari Bravo, 'International and Municipal Law: The Complementarity of Legal Systems', in R. St. J. Macdonald and D.M. Johnston (eds), *The Structure and Process of International Law: Essays in Legal Philosophy, Doctrine and Theory* (1986) 715, at 738; H. Keller, *Rezeption des Völkerrechts* (2003), at 6; Thürer, 'Völkerrecht und Landesrecht.

likewise should play a key role in the protection of the rule of law at European and international level. They will not guarantee effective compliance. But the rule of law is not only and certainly not primarily concerned with guaranteeing or causing general patterns of rule-conforming behaviour; it is also concerned with ensuring compliance in those cases where public powers choose not to comply with their obligations.

Comparing the role of national courts in inducing compliance with European and international law may not be to some observers an obvious approach, given the structural differences between the international and the national legal order. However, both the common roots and the shared ideals justify a comparative perspective.

As to the common roots, for some time subsequent to the introduction of Community law, in the late 1950s, there was little difference in the way in which national courts handled arguments involving public international law, on the one hand, and E(E)C law, on the other. The courts' reception of *all* rules of international law, including E(E)C law, was governed by disparate constitutional provisions and the undeveloped doctrine on the invocability of treaties in national courts set forth by the Permanent Court of International Justice (PCIJ) in the *Danzig Case*.[6] According to the common wisdom of modern international legal scholarship, all this changed with the judgments of the European Court of Justice (ECJ) in *Van Gend en Loos*[7] and *Costa/ENEL*.[8] The Court's finding that E(E)C law was different from ordinary international treaties was on the whole accepted by member states; it transformed EC law from being purely inter-state law to include rights and responsibilities of private parties, and brought national courts to centre stage in the enforcement of EC law. In cooperation with the ECJ, national courts proceeded to develop subtle and intricate doctrines pertaining to the rights and liabilities of private parties in regard to EC law. When we contrast this development with the common understanding of public international law in general, which in all major textbooks is still depicted as a system of law whose enforcement is primarily in the hands of *states*,[9] public international law looks 'ordinary' indeed.

As to the shared ideals, EU law is one particularly successful form of deep integration—it has parted ways with general international law. But it is not principally different and it constitutes a model that may be followed in other regions and perhaps in functional regimes. Charles Leben wrote:

> Community law is 'successful international law', and...is thus a possible horizon of international law, indicating the route that international law must follow if it is to move forward.[10]

Thesen zu einer theoretischen Problemumschreibung', 9 *Schweizerische Zeitschrift für internationales und europäisches Recht* (1999) 217; Weiler, 'The Geology of International Law: Governance, Democracy and Legitimacy', 64 *Heidelberg Journal of International Law* (2004) 547; Kumm, 'The Legitimacy of International Law: A Constitutionalist Framework of Analysis', 15 *European Journal of International Law* (2004) 907.

[6] *Jurisdiction of the Courts of Danzig (Advisory Opinion)*, 1928 PCIJ Rep Series B, No 15, at 17–18.

[7] Case 26/62, *Van Gend en Loos*, [1963] ECR 1.

[8] Case 6/64, *Costa v ENEL*, [1964] ECR 585.

[9] P. Malanczuk, *Akehurst's Modern Introduction to International Law* (1997), at 3–5.

[10] Leben, 'Hans Kelsen and the Advancement of International Law', 9 *European Journal of International Law* (1998), at 298.

Indeed, the differences in how courts treat public international law, on the one hand, and EC law, on the other, are less black and white than is often assumed. The distinctive features of the operation of Community law 'almost all exist but in a far less developed and efficient state in the international legal order'.[11] In certain legal contexts, the reception of public international law has moved beyond the purely inter-state model, and shares some features of EC law.

There is another aspect to the relationship between international and European law that makes it relevant to consider international and European law in a comprehensive manner. International law has increasingly become part of the legal order of the EU.[12] In practical terms, the ECJ case law 'absorbs' international agreements—both mixed and non-mixed[13]—to which the Community is a party[14] and also, to a degree, decisions of international organizations and customary international law, into the Community legal system. As far as international agreements are concerned, this case law is based on what is now Article 216(2) TFEU, according to which international agreements concluded under the procedure laid down in that article 'shall be binding on the institutions of the Community and on Member States'.[15]

To the extent that international law indeed becomes part of the European legal order, the application of 'Europeanized' rules of international law is no longer only a function of the combination of weak principles of international law and constitutional law, but becomes a matter of EU law proper, notably with a view to its uniform application and interpretation.[16] Rules of international law become a part of the legal order of the EU and can 'profit' from the principles and procedures governing the role of national courts, such as direct effect, consistent interpretation, and liability.

The chapter first discusses the relative role of courts as agents of compliance (Section 2) and the key condition of independence of courts (Section 3). It then examines four key principles that govern the practice of national courts in terms of their compliance-effects: supremacy, direct effect, consistent interpretation, and liability (Section 4). Section 5 explores the interaction between international and

[11] Ibid, at 295.

[12] See generally J. Wouters, P.A. Nollkaemper and E. de Wet (eds), *The Europeanization of International Law* (2008).

[13] See Case 12/86, *Demirel v Stadt Schwaebisch Gmuend,* [1987] ECR 3719, Rec 9 and Case C-13/00, *Commission v Ireland,* [2002] ECR I-2943, Rec 14: 'mixed agreements concluded by the Community, its Member States and non-member countries have the same status in the Community legal order as purely Community agreements, as these are provisions coming within the scope of Community competence'.

[14] See already Case 181/73, *Haegemann v Belgian State,* [1974] ECR 449, Rec 5, where it is held that the provisions of an international agreement concluded by the Community 'from the coming into force thereof, form an integral part of Community law'.

[15] See Case 104/81, *Kupferberg,* [1982] ECR 3641, Rec 13, where it is derived from this provision that '... [i]n ensuring respect for commitments arising from an agreement concluded by the Community institutions the Member States fulfill an obligation not only in relation to the non-member country concerned but also and above all in relation to the Community which has assumed responsibility for the due performance of the agreement'. See also Case 12/86, *Demirel, supra* note 13, Rec 11; Case C-13/00, *Commission v Ireland, supra* note 13, Rec 15.

[16] Case 104/81, *Kupferberg, supra* note 15, Rec 15.

European law in so far as they relate to the practice of national courts. Finally, Section 6 draws some conclusions.

2. Courts as Agents of Compliance

A. The Concept of Compliance

The concept of compliance is used here to refer to the conformity of behaviour of states with a specified legal rule.[17] The concept of compliance does not necessarily entail a cause–effect relationship between a rule and behaviour: it is 'agnostic about causality'.[18] The only question is whether behaviour conforms to a rule.[19]

In the concept of compliance as used here, the law is external to behaviour. It assumes that what the law is can be objectively defined with reference to its source, and in principle is not dependent on compliant or non-compliant behaviour. Approaches that make law more dependent on actual behaviour[20] make the concept of compliance largely irrelevant. Even though it is recognized that non-compliant behaviour can lead to changes in the law, particularly as a matter of customary law,[21] the core of the problem of compliance as it presents itself in respect to both European law and international law is not so much states seeking to develop new rules, as it is a problem of states simply failing to comply with their obligation without any intention to effect a change in the law.

The concept of compliance is distinguished from implementation. This latter term refers to the process of putting obligations into practice, whether at international level or (in the context of this chapter) at national level.[22] Implementation is

[17] Raustiala and Slaughter, 'International Law, International Relations and Compliance', in W. Carlnaes, T. Risse and B. Simmons (eds), *The Handbook of International Relations* (2002), at 539; Simmons, 'Money and the Law: Why Comply with the Public International Law of Money', 25 *Yale Journal of International Law* (2000) 323, at 333, referencing O. Young, *Compliance and Public Authority* (1979), at 2; Kingsbury, 'The Concept of Compliance as a Function of Competing Conceptions of International Law', 19 *Michigan Journal of International Law* (2000) 345. Kingsbury also notes that 'the concept of "compliance" with law does not have, and cannot have, any meaning except as a function of prior theories of the nature and operation of the law to which it pertains. "Compliance" is thus not a free-standing concept, but derives meaning and utility from theories, so that different theories lead to significantly different notions of what is meant by "compliance". Thus as a research concept, "compliance" cannot stand on its own, but must depend on a stipulated and shared theory of law.' Ibid, at 346.

[18] Raustiala and Slaughter, *supra* note 17. But see Ho, 'Compliance and international Soft Law: Why do Countries Implement the Basle Accord?', 5 *Journal of International Economic Law* (2002) 647, at 649 (defining 'compliance as state behavior that conforms to and arises out of an obligation of international law'). Also Koh, 'Review Essay: Why Do Nations Obey International Law?', 106 *Yale Law Journal* (1997) 2599, discusses compliance in terms of obedience, suggesting some form of causation.

[19] That of course does not preclude that the question is examined, as is done in this article, how a particular agent or factor, such as courts, may or may not contribute to conformity.

[20] For approaches that make the concept of law itself more dependent on behaviour, see eg, A.T. Guzman, *How International Law Works* (2007); J. Alvarez, *International Organizations as Law-makers* (2006).

[21] *Military and Paramilitary Activities in and Against Nicaragua, Nicaragua v United States, Merits, Judgment* (1986), ICJ Reports (1986) 14, para 186.

[22] Raustiala and Slaughter, *supra* note 17, at 539 (defining implementation as 'the process of putting international commitments into practice: the passage of legislation, creating of institutions (both domestic and international) and enforcement of rules').

often important for compliance, but it is neither a necessary[23] nor sufficient condition.[24] In particular, through the mechanisms of direct effect, courts may secure compliance without implementing measures.[25]

The term 'compliance' is also to be distinguished from the effectiveness of a particular rule. The term 'effectiveness' refers to the degree to which a rule contributes to achieving the goals of that rule.[26] Compliance generally helps effectiveness, but there may be effectiveness without compliance or compliance without effectiveness.[27] A regime can be effective with little compliance if it induces changes in behaviour that are not required by the rule, yet helps to achieve the objectives. On the other hand, a regime can have high compliance and still be ineffective.[28]

Finally, compliance needs to be distinguished from 'enforcement'. This term refers to processes of mechanisms 'by which the law is made effective'[29] and by which actors are compelled to comply with the law.[30] As a legal concept, it includes legal sanctions that can be applied to the violator with a view to compelling compliance.[31] The role of national courts can be a part of the process of enforcement, at least as far as their role in individual cases is concerned, since they can compel the political branches of the state into compliance with the law.

In short, this chapter is concerned with the role of courts in ensuring conformity between the acts of the legislature and political branches, on the one hand, and a predetermined rule of European and international law, on the other. It is not really dependent on implementation by these branches, and rather can be seen as a correction when such implementation is not forthcoming. The role of national courts may in specific cases be construed as enforcement, but that

[23] Ibid (noting that compliance can also happen without implementation through continuing practice that already happens to comply with international rules, or other events that happen to cause compliance with international rules).

[24] Simmons, *supra* note 17, at 333 (noting that implementation is 'the adoption of domestic rules or regulations meant to facilitate, but which themselves do not constitute, compliance with international agreements').

[25] See this chapter Section 4. C.

[26] Raustiala and Slaughter, *supra* note 17, at 539 (defining effectiveness as 'the degree to which a rule induces changes in behavior that furthers the rule's goals; improves the state of the underlying problem; or achieves its policy objectives'); O. Young (ed), *The Effectiveness of International Environmental Regimes: Causal Connections and Behavioral Mechanisms* (1999), at 1 (defining effectiveness as a 'regime that channels behavior in such a way as to eliminate or substantially ameliorate the problem that led to its creation'); Young, 'The Effectiveness of International Institutions: Hard Cases and Critical Variables', in J.N. Rosenau and E.-O. Czempiel (eds), *Governance Without Government: Order and Change in World Politics* (1992) 161 (stating that effectiveness 'impels actors to behave differently than they would if the institution did not exist or if some other institutional arrangement were put in place').

[27] Raustiala and Slaughter, *supra* note 17. This is also stated by Simmons, *supra* note 17, at 333.

[28] Raustiala and Slaughter, *supra* note 17. But see A. and A.H. Chayes, 'On Compliance', 47 *International Organization* (1993) 176, at footnote 3 (noting that 'compliance may be a fair first approximation surrogate for effectiveness').

[29] Smiley, 'Taking the Force out of Enforcement: Giving Effect to International Human Rights Law Using Domestic Immigration Law', 28 *California Western International Law Journal* (1998) 339, at 341–2 quoting *Black's Law Dictionary 528* (1990, 6th edn). See for a narrower definition Hayashi, 'Soviet Policy on International Regulation of High Seas Fisheries', 5 *Cornell International Law Journal* (1972) 131, at 133 (referring to 'the process of putting rules of law into execution through actual use or threat of legitimate physical force').

[30] Ouma, 'Optimal Enforcement of Music Copyright in Sub-Saharan Africa: Reality or a Myth?', 9 *Journal of World Intellectual Property* (2006) 592.

[31] Ibid, at 592.

depends on the nature of the case, and is not a useful concept for the diversity of ways in which national courts can consider and apply rules of international law.

B. Courts as Agents of Compliance

For the EU, the role of courts, both the ECJ and national courts, in inducing conformity of national law and policy with EU law is generally recognized.[32] The ECJ has established and obtained acceptance of the broad principle of direct integration of Community law into the national legal orders of the member states and of the supremacy of Community law.[33] By co-opting domestic courts, the legal order of the EU has helped to ensure compliance with EU law (however imperfect that may remain).[34] National courts also have remedied the lack of enforcement power of the ECJ. It has become impossible for governments to ignore EU law, without countering their own courts.[35] In the rule of law systems that characterize the legal systems of most member states, that will not be possible in a systemic form. The cooperation between national courts and the Court has produced what Weiler has called an 'all-or-nothing effect' requiring a state to either leave the Community or basically comply completely.[36]

At first sight, the situation in international law is entirely different. In most compliance theories, the role of courts is relatively marginal. In realist theory, courts obviously are not assigned any particular role as agents that have to secure compliance.[37] Also in rational choice theory, courts are considered as irrelevant. If it is accepted that states 'do not comply with norms of [customary international law] because of a sense of moral or legal obligation; rather, their compliance and the norms themselves emerge from the states' pursuit of self-interested policies on the international stage',[38] courts will not play any relevant role. Goldsmith and Posner note that even domestic courts change their opinion of what customary international law is to suit their best interests.[39] Guzman attaches critical weight to such factors as reputation, reciprocity, and retaliation[40]—in none of them are (national) courts of much significance.

[32] Raustiala and Slaughter, *supra* note 17, at 541.

[33] Stein, 'Lawyers, Judges, and the Making of a Transnational Constitution', 75 *American Journal of International Law* (1981) 1.

[34] Raustiala and Slaughter, *supra* note 17, at 541; Mattli and Slaughter, 'Law and Politics in the European Union: A Reply to Garrett', 49 *International Organization* (1995) 183; Burley and Mattli, 'Europe before the Court: A Political Theory of Legal Integration', 47 *International Organization* (1993), at 41–76.

[35] Raustiala and Slaughter, *supra* note 17, at 541.

[36] Weiler, 'Community, Member States, and European Integration: Is the Law Relevant?', 21 *Journal of Common Market Studies* (1982) 39, at 55.

[37] D'Amato, 'The Concept of Human Rights in International Law', 82 *Columbia Law Review* (1982) 1110.

[38] J.L. Goldsmith and E.A. Posner, *A Theory of Customary International Law* (University of Chicago Law School, John M. Olin Law and Economics Working Paper, No 63, 1998), at 3.

[39] Ibid, at 10.

[40] A.T. Guzman, *How International Law Works: A Rational Choice Theory* (2007).

Legitimacy theories likewise do not accord any particular role to national courts. For none of the four elements that Franck thought relevant as indicators of a rule's legitimacy—determinacy, symbolic validation, coherence, and adherence to a normative hierarchy—are national courts of any relevance.[41] Franck did recognize that *international* courts may play a relevant role. In respect of determinacy (or 'the ability of a text to confer a clear meaning'), courts have a role in clarifying international legal provisions.[42] In respect of symbolic validation, 'a new rule may be taken more seriously if it arrives on the scene under the aegis of a particularly venerable sponsor such as a widely ratified multilateral convention, or a virtually unanimous decision of the International Court of Justice.'[43] Franck also pointed to the International Court of Justice, various regional courts, and arbitral tribunals to show that the international legal system does have some measure of adherence to a normative hierarchy.[44] However, in none of this did he appear to assign any particular role to national courts.

The situation is not very different in regime theory. Though regime theorists focus on the role of institutions, they do not appear to accord any significant role to (national) courts. They theorize that states establish regimes when it is in their long-term interest to cooperate,[45] and regimes can tip the cost-benefit analysis towards compliance. In principle this may allow for a role of courts, as one form of institution, in explaining behaviour and thus compliance. However, it is significant that in Keohane's *After Hegemony*, the entire section of the book devoted to addressing the question of why states comply with international laws makes no mention at all of courts.[46]

Also in managerial theory, courts play a negligible role. Chayes and Chayes write that 'when nations enter into an international agreement of this kind, they alter their behavior, their relationships, and their expectations of one another over time in accordance with its terms'.[47] They credit a state's propensity to comply with international commitments to the fact that, first, the legal rules are largely endogenous and 'an assumption of rational behavior predicts that states have an interest in compliance with rules', and secondly, 'compliance is efficient from an internal, decisional perspective. Extant norms induce a sense of obligation in states to comply with legal undertakings.'[48] Courts play little to no role in their view of why states comply with international law. Even though Chayes and Chayes see ambiguity and indeterminacy of treaty provisions as one of the primary reasons for non-compliance,[49] due to the fact that compulsory adjudication is so rare and most interpretation issues do not arise in a two-party context that is easily amenable to a court setting, they do not see the role of courts as important for the interpretation or clarification of international law.[50]

[41] Franck 'Legitimacy in the International System', 82 *American Journal of International Law* (1988) 706.

[42] Ibid, at 724.

[43] Ibid, at 727.

[44] Ibid, at 752.

[45] Raustiala and Slaughter, *supra* note 17, at 540.

[46] R. Keohane, *After Hegemony: Cooperation and Discord in the Word Political Economy* (1984), at 98–107.

[47] A. and A.H. Chayes, *supra* note 28, at 176.

[48] Raustiala and Slaughter, *supra* note 17, at 542.

[49] Downs, 'Enforcement and the Evolution of Cooperation', 19 *Michigan Journal of International Law* (1998) 328.

[50] A. and A.H. Chayes, *supra* note 28, at 190.

Beyerlin and Marauhn, in an analysis that shares many features with managerial scholarship, note that the best way to attain compliance with international environmental law is through a flexible approach, including reporting, monitoring, fact-finding, consultation, education, training, and technology transfers, rather than traditional, repressive means of law enforcement.[51] Courts, again, are not attributed any particular relevance.

Other theories, however, do accord a role to national courts as agents of compliance.[52] In his *How Nations Behave,* Henkin views courts as one of the factors aiding compliance. While he argues that states comply with international law because of forces such as reciprocity, dislike of criticism, and desire for friendly relations,[53] he recognizes that the extent to which national institutions, including domestic courts, accept international law is a relevant factor.[54] Hathaway too recognizes that compliance in part is a matter of 'legal enforcement of the terms of the treaty', in addition to 'collateral consequences for state interests'.[55] Legal enforcement happens not only at the transnational level (where international bodies or other states that are party to the treaty respond to violations in ways provided for in the treaty), but also at a domestic level, where 'domestic actors use the country's own legal system to enforce the terms of international legal agreements'.[56]

The role of national courts as agents of compliance is best developed in the so-called transnational legal process theory, which in its explanation of compliance attributes considerable weight to the extent to which international law is incorporated in domestic legislation and given effect in the domestic courts.[57] Koh critiques the managerial theories of Chayes and Chayes and the legitimacy theories of Franck, as they overlook the 'process of interaction, interpretation, and internalization of international norms into domestic legal systems' which 'is pivotal to understanding why nations "obey" international law, rather than merely conform their behavior to it when convenient'.[58] He states that the most effective form of law enforcement 'is not the imposition of external sanction, but the inculcation of internal obedience'.[59] Courts, including domestic, regional, and international courts, have a role in the interpretation of international norms into the domestic legal system.[60] For Koh, '[j]udicial internalization occurs when

[51] U. Beyerlin and T. Marauhn, *Law-Making and Law-Enforcement in International Environmental Law After the 1992 Rio Conference* (1997).

[52] See also Ginsburg and Adams, 'Adjudicating in Anarchy: An Expressive Theory of International Dispute Resolution', 45 *William and Mary Law Review* (2004) 1229, at 1232 (arguing that pronouncements of third-party legal adjudicators can influence the behaviour of states towards compliance); Downs, *supra* note 49, at 328 discussing adjudication as mode of enforcement with international agreements, in particular in relation to regulatory agreements and that as multilateral organizations such as the EU or WTO increase their level of cooperation they also increase their level of enforcement).

[53] L. Henkin, *How Nations Behave* (1979), at 50–3, 60–8. [54] Ibid, at 60–8.

[55] Hathaway, 'Between Power and Principle: An Integrated Theory of International Law', 71 *University of Chicago Law Review* (2005) 469, at 473. [56] Ibid.

[57] Koh, *supra* note 18, at 2602. See also R. Fisher, *Improving Compliance with International Law* (1981).

[58] Koh, *supra* note 18, at 2603.

[59] Koh, 'How Is International Human Rights Law Enforced?', 74 *Indiana Law Journal* (1998–1999) 1401.

[60] Koh, *supra* note 18, at 2640.

litigation in domestic courts provokes judicial incorporation of international law norms into domestic law, statutes, or constitutional norms.'[61]

From a different angle, Slaughter and Helfer also underscore the role of national courts as possible agents of compliance.[62] Examining the causes of compliance with judgments of international courts, Slaughter and Helfer note that such compliance is determined by three categories of factors: factors within the control of states establishing a court (composition, functional capacity, binding nature of decisions); factors within the control of courts (awareness of audience, partnership with domestic courts, autonomy from politics, incrementalism, deference, quality of reasoning, dialogues); and factors beyond the control of states or judges (nature of the violations, autonomous domestic institutions, relative homogeneity of states).[63] Depending on one's perspective on the independence of courts (see Section 3 below), national courts can qualify in each of these three categories. Either way, the degree of interaction between the international and national levels, with consequences for the role of national courts, is one of the variables relevant to compliance.[64]

It is quite obvious that none of the above theoretical approaches holds a compelling claim to an exhaustive account of compliance. They provide alternative perspectives, which in part operate at different levels of analysis, but together combine to enhance our understanding.[65] Cassell notes:

> As each theory stems from a different theory about law and society, it would be insufficient to limit oneself to one theory and thereby construe the meta-rule of identification on a too narrow concept of society. To the contrary, it is more probable that each theory reveals a particular aspect of the truth.[66]

The relative strength of the theories that accord a strong role to national courts depends in large part on the internal focus of the rules of international law in question, that is, on the degree to which international law does not so much share the features of the historical purely intra-state model, but has in its substance and procedural aspects significant domestic effects.[67] Apart from EU law, that internal focus is particularly present in regard to human rights law. Also in that area, national courts are far from being the only or even the dominant cause, but their role seems inextricably interwoven with other factors. Cassel argues that domestic legal institutions deserve some credit for the improvement in human rights, as part of a 'complex interweaving of mutually reinforcing processes'. He argues that 'what pulls human rights forward is not a series of separate, parallel cords, but a "rope" of multiple, interwoven strands. Remove one strand, and the entire rope is weakened. International human

[61] Koh, *supra* note 59, at 1413.

[62] Helfer and Slaughter, 'Toward a Theory of Effective Supranational Adjudication', 107 *Yale Law Journal* (1997) 273.

[63] Ibid.

[64] See also Tan, 'Upholding Human Rights in the Hemisphere: Casting Down Impunity Through the Inter-American Court of Human Rights', 43 *Texas International Law Journal* (2008) 276, at 283–4.

[65] See also Nollkaemper, 'On the Effectiveness of International Rules', 27 *Acta Politica* (1992) 49.

[66] Goldmann, 'Inside Relative Normality: From Sources to Standard Instruments for the Exercise of Public International Authority', in A. von Bogdandy et al (eds), *The Exercise of Public Authority by International Institutions: Advancing International Institutional Law* (2010) 661, at 683.

[67] Slaughter and Burke-White, 'The Future of International Law is Domestic', in P.A. Nolkaemper and J. Nijman, *New Perspectives on the Divide between International and National Law* (2007), at 111–12.

rights law is a strand woven throughout the length of the rope.' The fact that national courts increasingly look to human rights treaties is one part of that rope.[68]

The role of national courts in other areas of international law, such as humanitarian law, international trade law, and international environmental law remains much weaker.[69] In such areas, other compliance theories may have a stronger claim to accuracy. Much depends on bottom-up processes, rather than on what is expected from international obligations themselves.[70] But there is little doubt that we are bound to see a differentiation in international law between different areas, and between states, where the power of national courts to induce compliance may vary.

3. Independence

A preliminary problem for considering national courts as an institutional force that can help to secure compliance is the fact that these courts are organs of the very entities that they are to control.[71] Apart from the formal status of courts as organs of the state, and the resulting tension with the assumption against self-judging, several factors undermine the independent role of national courts. These include the courts' perception of the need to speak with one voice, their association with the national interests of the state, and the power of political branches over the courts. Such factors make any assumption that national courts can be expected and trusted to properly hold their state to the requirements of international law shaky.[72]

In EU law these problems seem comparatively modest. Although it is easy to underestimate the problems caused by a national rather than European orientation of national courts, it is inherent in the partnership between the ECJ and national courts that national courts are to adjudicate the application of EU law independently from the political branches.

In international law, the problems, and resulting barriers against considering national courts as agents of compliance, are to some extent mitigated by the principle of independence of the judiciary. The principle requires that courts are independent from the executive branch[73] and the legislative branch,[74] as well as from

[68] Cassel, 'Does International Human Rights Law Make a Difference?', 2 *Chicago Journal of International Law* (2001) 121.

[69] O'Connell, 'Enforcement and the Success of International Environmental Law', 3 *Indiana Journal of Global Legal Studies (*1995) 47.

[70] Slaughter and Burke-White, *supra* note 67, at 113.

[71] Cf., Bell, 'Judicial Cultures and Judicial Independence', 4 *Cambridge Yearbook of European Legal Studies* (2001) 47, at 50 (referring to independence in general, not confined to the international domain).

[72] W. Friedmann, *The Changing Structure of International Law* (1964), at 146–7.

[73] *Ringeisen v Austria*, ECHR (1971) Series A, No. 13, 95; see also *Van de Hurk v Netherlands*, ECHR (1994) Series A, No. 288, 54 (holding that the power of the Crown of the Netherlands, part of the government, to deprive the judgments of the Industrial Appeal Tribunal, an administrative tribunal, of their effect to the detriment of an individual party, was incompatible with the principle of independence). See also, *Oló Bahamonde v Equatorial Guinea*, Human Rights Committee, Communication No. 468/1991 (20 October 1993) UN Doc CCPR/C/49/D/468/1991 (considering that 'a situation where the functions and competences of the judiciary and the executive are not clearly distinguishable or where the latter is able to control or direct the former is incompatible with the notion of an independent and impartial tribunal within the meaning of Art 14, paragraph 1, of the Covenant').

[74] *Assanidze v Georgia*, App no 71503/01 (ECtHR, 8 April 2004), 129 (holding that 'the rule of law and the notion of fair trial enshrined in Art 6 of the Convention preclude any interference by the legislature with the administration of justice designed to influence the judicial determination of the dispute').

the parties to the dispute: in the type of compliance problem cases with which we are concerned, this is the forum state.[75]

Where it exists, the principle of independence is quite powerful and allows us to consider courts as compliance-inducing agents. In human rights law, the principle of independence has two bases. The first is the obligation to provide effective remedies. The right to a fair trial by an independent court with respect to civil and criminal cases, or 'suits at law', requires that the courts adjudicating such claims are independent. And under Article 13 of the ECHR and comparable articles in other human rights treaties, remedies are only effective if the courts are independent.[76]

However, these requirements hardly extend beyond human rights law. There is some support for a broader principle of independence to extend to international law as such. For instance, the *Institut de Droit international* (IDI) recommended that national courts should be allowed to decide on international claims independently from the government.[77] Such a broader principle of independence, beyond human rights law, may be based on the concept of the international rule of law as such. At least to the extent that international law intertwines with domestic law, the performance of international obligations—not necessarily limited to human rights law—should be subject to similar rule of law principles as apply to national law.[78] It may also be said that the independence of the judiciary is a general principle of law as all major legal systems, and perhaps all states, appear to formally embrace the principle.[79]

Even leaving aside the very imperfect application of the principle of independence as such in practice,[80] it seems most doubtful that this would apply in full to the domestic judicial application of *international* law. General international law has traditionally not opposed the wide variety of doctrines that limit the independent power of courts—on the contrary, it has protected them. Indeed, it would be surprising if it were to have been otherwise: traditional (European) international law was founded precisely by the same executive powers that, at the domestic level, profited from those principles that limit the power of courts. In these areas, states have intentionally allowed the rule of law to give way and to allow the executive

[75] *Ringeisen v Austria*, *supra* note 73, 95.

[76] *Leander v Sweden*, ECHR (1987) Series A, No 116, 9, 433, 80–1; *Al-Nashif v Bulgaria*, App no 50963/99 (ECtHR, 20 June 2002), 136; *Muminov v Russia*, App no 42502/06 (ECtHR, 11 December 2008), 101 (discussing Art 13 of the Convention for the Protection of Human Rights and Fundamental Freedoms and its Protocols, hereinafter the 'European Convention on Human Rights', as amended).

[77] Art 1(1) of the 1993 Resolution of the Institute of International Law on the Activities of National Judges and the International Relations of their State. See for an overview of international principles Olbourne, 'Independence and Impartiality: International Standards for National Judges and Courts', 2 *The Law and Practice of International Courts and Tribunals* (2003) 97.

[78] Crawford, 'International Law and the Rule of Law', 24 *Adelaide Law Review* (2004) 3, at 12.

[79] *Supreme Court of the Republic of Serbia v People's Assembly of the Republic of Serbia*, Constitutional Court of the Republic of Serbia, Case No 17/2003, in Oxford Reports on International Law in Domestic Courts (hereinafter 'ILDC') 31 (CSXX 2003), 9 (holding that the provisions of a domestic statute that lowered the achieved level of autonomy and independence of the courts and judges 'is in violation of the generally accepted principle of international law proclaimed in the European Charter on the Statute for Judges adopted in Strasbourg between 8 and 10 July 1998'); see for a comparative overview P.H. Russell and D.M. O'Brien (eds), *Judicial Independence in the Age of Democracy: Critical Perspectives from around the World* (2001).

[80] Paulsson, 'Enclaves of Justice', 4 *Transnational Dispute Management* (2007) 1.

power to perform acts that are not conceivable in a domestic, rule-of-law-based society.[81]

The freedoms left by international law for the internal organization of a state and the domestic separation of powers to be arranged are thus mutually supportive. In many areas, most notably the law of armed conflict, the application of international law retains its 'high politics' nature, and courts may be inclined to step back and leave the matter to the executive. Indeed, it is precisely in these areas, where the one-voice argument prevails, that the unity of the state at the international level is mirrored by a unitary stance at the domestic level.[82] International law cannot neglect that practice.[83]

The weakness of international law in securing independence may in part be compensated by a bottom-up process. Many states, by accepting international law as part of national law, have granted their courts an independent role in adjudication of international claims against the state. Where international law is part of national law and in principle can be subject to regular proceedings in the courts, there may not be a need for a separate principle of independence. However, this remains a feeble basis, and there are significant differences across the world in the degree to which national courts indeed are able to play a role in securing compliance in those cases where the political branches choose otherwise.

4. The Role of National Courts in International Law and European Law Compared

A General Aspects

It is commonly thought that one of the key differences between EC law and public international law is that while in public international law the effect of a norm in the national legal order (a critical determinant of the role of national courts in inducing compliance) is determined by national law, not international law, in EC law such effect is a matter of EC law, not national law.

This was indeed the distinction the ECJ created in *Van Gend en Loos*.[84] The Court held that unlike 'normal' international conventions, the EEC Treaty is more than an agreement creating mutual obligations between the Contracting States. An independent legal order shared by the member states has been created: Community law is intended to confer rights upon individuals, independently of the legislation of member states. Moreover, the Court held that EC law, rather than national law,

[81] Allott, 'State Responsibilty and the Unmaking of International Law', 29 *Harvard International Law Journal* (1988) 3, at 15.

[82] See eg, *Campaign for Nuclear Disarmament v The Prime Minister of the United Kingdom*, EWHC 2777 (Admin) (47) (2002); ILDC 662 (UK 2002) (forthcoming), discussed in Reece Thomas, 'The Changing Status of International Law in English Domestic Law', 53 *Netherlands International Law Review* (2006) 371, at 386.

[83] See also Russell, 'Towards a General Theory of Judicial Independence', in P.H. Russell and D.M. O'Brien (eds), *Judicial Independence in the Age of Democracy. Critical Perspectives from Around the World* (2001) 1, at 12.

[84] Case 26/62, *Van Gend en Loos*, *supra* note 7.

determines the effects in the national legal order. This ruling also had institutional consequences: in order to ensure that the particular provision of EC law has the same effect throughout this new legal order, it is for the ECJ and not the national courts to rule on the effect of Community law.[85]

In contrast, public international law is thought to be silent on the validity and the effects of international law in the national legal order. Many states, in particular those in which parliamentary approval is not a precondition for the entry into force of treaty obligations, consider themselves at liberty to separate their international rights and obligations from the national legal order and disallow their organs to apply rules of international law that are not made part of national law. No international court has said that these practices as such are 'illegal' and that international law creates, out of its own force, effects in the national legal order.[86] These effects are conditional upon a prior decision of states to accept the validity of public international law. Without the unqualified acceptance of the principle of validity, international law lacks the force to empower national courts to apply international law—and to secure compliance—where national law fails.[87]

However, this fundamental distinction between EU law and international law needs to be qualified in two respects. On the one hand, EU law necessarily remains contingent and potentially limited by national (constitutional) law.[88] On the other hand, the national law of a substantial number of states has accepted the validity of international law. These include such diverse states, and from such diverse regions,

[85] This also follows from the subsequent case 6/64, *Costa v ENEL*, *supra* note 8: 'The executive force of Community law cannot vary from one State to another in deference to subsequent domestic laws, without jeopardizing the attainment of the objectives of the Treaty set out in Article 5 (2) and giving rise to the discrimination prohibited by Article 7.'

[86] While the European Court of Human Rights, which supervises a part of international law that is particularly integrated with national law, has held that while incorporation of the European Convention on Human Rights in national law would be a faithful method of applying the Convention (see *Ireland v United Kingdom*, ECHR (1978) Series A, No 25, 239), the European Convention formally is neutral as to the mode of implementation and does not require incorporation. See the case of *Swedish Engine Drivers' Union v Sweden* ECHR (1976) Series A, No 20, 50 (stating that the Convention does not lay down 'for the Contracting States any given manner for ensuring within their internal law the effective implementation of any of the provisions of the Convention'). See also Frowein, 'Incorporation of the Convention into Domestic Law', in The British Institute of International and Comparative Law and The British Institute of Human Rights, *Aspects of Incorporation of the European Convention into Domestic Law* (1993) 2–11 (noting that while arts 1 and 13 may suggest an obligation to apply the convention directly, the fact that six of the original contracting parties did not allow for incorporation makes an interpretation to that effect implausible). What matters is that the substance of the rights should in fact be enjoyed by individuals, see M.A. Janis, R. Kay and A. Bradley, *European Human Rights Law. Text and Materials* (2000), 472.

[87] See Buergenthal, 'Self-Executing and Non-Self-Executing Treaties in National and International Law', in *Recueil des Cours* (1992) IV, at 320–1, noting that 'a treaty that, as a matter of international law, is deemed to be directly applicable is not self-executing ipso facto under the domestic law of the states parties to it. All that can be said about such a treaty is that the States party thereto have an international obligation to take whatever measures are necessary under their domestic law to ensure that the specific provisions of the treaty…, not only of its substantive obligations, are accorded the status of domestic law'.

[88] Craig, 'National Courts and Community Law', in J. Hayward and A. Menon (eds), *National Courts and Community Law in Governing Europe* (2003), at chapter 2.

as Benin,[89] Cape Verde,[90] China,[91] Côte d'Ivoire,[92] the Czech Republic,[93] the Dominican Republic,[94] Egypt,[95] Ethiopia,[96] France,[97] Japan,[98] the Netherlands,[99] Portugal,[100] Senegal,[101] the Russian Federation,[102] Switzerland,[103] Turkey,[104] and the United States.[105] In this group of states, the condition of validity is fulfilled on the basis of a general (mostly constitutional) rule of reference that makes international law part of national law, and that as such empowers the courts to give effect to international law—and to insure compliance. This practice may or may not be based on a perceived obligation, but that is of little relevance for the actual consequences in terms of empowering courts as agents for ensuring compliance.

However, significant differences exist between states. A thorough search during the start-up phase of what is now the International Law in Domestic Courts module of the *Oxford Reports on International Law* has shown about 30–40 states in which courts very frequently give effect to international law, and about 40 more in which courts with some regularity give effect to international law. The list is certainly not exhaustive, but it seems certain that there are dozens of states in which courts, at best very infrequently, give effect to international law and dozens more states in which courts hardly ever give effect to it or do not do so at all. In that respect, any trend by which state practice resembles part of the practice in respect of EU law is limited to a relatively small number of states.

It can be added that both in EU law and in international law the integration of international law in national law and the recognition of the principle of supremacy can in part be based on and explained by the principle of effectiveness.[106] As to the

[89] Art 147 of the Constitution of the Republic of Benin (1990).

[90] Art 11 of the Constitution of the Republic of Cape Verde (1980).

[91] B. Ahl, *Die Anwendung völkerrechtlichter Verträge in China.* Beiträge zum ausländischen öffentlichen Recht und Völkerrecht, Band 207 (2009), at chapter 8; Guo, 'Implementation of Human Rights Treaties by Chinese Courts: Problems and Prospects', 8 *Chinese Journal of International Law* (2009) 161, at 165.

[92] Art 87 of the Constitution of the Republic of Côte d'Ivoire (2000).

[93] Art 10 of the Constitution of the Czech Republic (1992).

[94] Art 3 of the Constitution of the Dominican Republic (1994).

[95] Art 151 of the Constitution of the Arab Republic of Egypt (1971).

[96] Art 9(4) of the Constitution of the Federal Democratic Republic of Ethiopia (1994).

[97] Art 55 of the Constitution of the French Republic (1958).

[98] Iwasawa, 'The Relationship Between International and National Law: Japanese Experiences', 64 *BYIL* (1993) 343, at 345.

[99] Nollkaemper, 'The Netherlands', in D. Sloss et al (eds), *The Role of Domestic Courts in Treaty Enforcement: A Comparative Study* (2009), at 326.

[100] Eg, Art 8(2) of the Constitution of Portugal; see eg, *A and B v Portugese State,* Supreme Administrative Court of Portugal, Case No 0308/07; ILDC 1441 (PT 2007).

[101] Art 91 of the Constitution of the Republic of Senegal (2001).

[102] Art 15(4) of the Constitution of the Russian Federation (1993); V.I. Kuznetsov and B.R. Tuzmukhamedow (eds), *International Law—A Russian Introduction* (2009), at 188.

[103] *A and B v Government of the Canton of Zurich*, Federal Supreme Court of Switzerland, BGE 126 I 242; ILDC 350 (CH 2000) [2b].

[104] Art 90(5) of the Constitution of Turkey; see also *Ray Sigorta AS v Nunner Lojistik Ticaret Limited Sti*, Court of Cassation of Turkey, E 2007/2970, K 2008/4599; ILDC 1034 (TR 2008).

[105] Art VI of the Constitution of the United States.

[106] See generally, Accetto and Zleptnig, 'The Principle of Effectiveness: Rethinking its Role in Community Law', 11 *European Public Law* (2005) 375; Becker, 'Application of Community Law by

former, the ECJ said that 'any recognition that national legislative measures which encroach upon the field within which the Community exercises its legislative power or which are otherwise incompatible with the provisions of Community law had any legal effect would amount to *a corresponding denial of the effectiveness of obligations* undertaken unconditionally and irrevocably by member states pursuant to the treaty and would thus imperil the very foundations of the Community'.[107] As to the latter, acceptance of the principle of supremacy of international law is in line with the principle of effective treaty performance.[108] The basis, scope, and effect of the principle of effectiveness as it operates in both legal systems differ.

B. Supremacy

The principle of supremacy (or 'precedence') is key to the compliance-inducing potential of national courts. Where the principle is fully recognized, it allows courts to set aside a law adopted by the political branches, in particular the legislature, and thereby to ensure conformity of the policy and law of the state with its international or European obligations. Apart from its application in individual cases, the mere power of courts to apply the principle can be expected to exert a systematic incentive for compliance since political branches will know that contraventions of international legal obligation may not survive judicial scrutiny.

In *Costa v ENEL*, the Court said:

> The integration into the laws of each member state of provisions which derive from the Community, and more generally the terms and the spirit of the Treaty, make it impossible for the states, as a corollary, to accord precedence to a unilateral and subsequent measure over a legal system accepted by them on a basis of reciprocity. Such a measure cannot therefore be inconsistent with that legal system.[109]

And in *Simmenthal* it added that directly applicable provisions of EU law not only by their entry into force render automatically inapplicable any conflicting provision of current national law but—in so far as they are an integral part of, and take

Member States' Public Authorities: Between Autonomy and Effectiveness', 44 *Common Market Law Review* (2007) 1035, at 1043.

[107] Judgment of the Court of 9 March 1978 for *Amministrazione delle Finanze dello Stato v Simmenthal SpA*, reference for a preliminary ruling: Pretura di Susa, Italy. Discarding by the national court of a law contrary to Community law. Case 106/77, para 18.

[108] *Exchange of Greek and Turkish Populations,* (Advisory Opinion), 1925 PCIJ Series B, No 10, 51; see also *Greco-Bulgarian 'Communities',* (Advisory Opinion), 1930 PCIJ Series B, No 17, 84. See in this context also Art 33 proposed by Special Rapporteur Fitzmaurice in his 'Fourth Report on the Law of Treaties', II *Yearbook of the International Law Commission* (hereinafter the 'YB ILC') (1959), at 49 (providing that 'where a treaty provides for rights, interests or benefits to be enjoyed by private parties, or where the treaty otherwise rebounds to their advantage, it is the duty of the contracting States to place no obstacle in the way of enjoyment of these rights, interests, benefits or advantages by the individuals or juristic entities concerned, and to take all such steps as may be necessary to make them effective on the internal plane'). Special Rapporteur Waldock thought that this provision was superfluous as it was inherent in the principle *pacta sunt servanda*, II *YB ILC* (1964), UN Doc A/CN4/167, 47. Also: G. Schwarzenberger, *International Law* (1976), at 68–9. See also Zimmermann, 'Is it Really All about Commitment and Diffusion? Why Do States Incorporate International Law in Their Domestic Constitutions?', 1 *Illinois Law Review* (2008) 253.

[109] Case 6/64, *Costa v ENEL*, *supra* note 8.

precedence in, the legal order applicable in the territory of each of the member states—also preclude the valid adoption of new national legislative measures to the extent to which they would be incompatible with Community provisions.[110]

This includes primacy over their national constitutional law. From the perspective of EU law, this principle is independent from the system laid down in national constitutions.

In international law all this is very different. It is true that the supremacy of international law prioritizes international law over national law. Gerald Fitzmaurice wrote that the principle of supremacy is 'one of the great principles of international law, informing the whole system and applying to every branch of it'.[111] In general terms, the principle of supremacy of international law seeks to subordinate the sovereignty of states to international law.[112] One of its manifestations is that international law is supreme over—and takes precedence in the international legal order over—national law.[113] In the event of a conflict between international law and domestic law, international law will have to prevail in the international legal order, domestic law being considered a fact from the standpoint of international law. This aspect is at the heart of the law of treaties[114] and the law of international responsibility.[115] The principle of supremacy of international law is central to the international rule of law, which, if anything, requires that states exercise their powers in accordance with international law, not domestic law.[116] There cannot be any rule of law without the precedence of some principles over others deemed to be of lesser importance.[117]

However, none of this extends to the domestic level. The general understanding is that international law cannot itself realize supremacy at the domestic level and indeed does not contain the normative ambition to realize such domestic

[110] Case C-106/77, *Simmenthal II*, [1978] ECR 629.

[111] Fitzmaurice, 'The General Principles of International Law Considered from the Standpoint of the Rule of Law', in *Recueil des Cours* (1957) 92, at 85 *et seq.*

[112] Ibid, at 6.

[113] See for a comprehensive treatment of this aspect of the principle of supremacy D. Carreau, *Droit International* (2004), at 43 *et seq.*; Fitzmaurice, *supra* note 111, at 68 *et seq.* See also C. Santuli, *Le Status International de L'Ordre Juridique Étatique* (2001), at 427.

[114] Arts 27 and 46 of the Vienna Convention on the Law of Treaties (hereinafter the 'VCLT'), adopted 23 March 1969, entered into force 29 January 1980, 1155 UNTS 331.

[115] Arts 3 and 32 of the Articles on the Responsibility of States for Internationally Wrongful Acts (hereinafter the 'Articles on State Responsibility'). The Articles on State Responsibility are contained in the Annex of UNGA Res 56/83, 28 January 2002 and reproduced in J. Crawford, *The International Law Commission's Articles on State Responsibility: Introduction, Text and Commentaries* (2002). A comparable principle is contained in Art 35 of the Draft Articles of the International Law Commission (hereinafter the 'ILC') on the Responsibility of International Organizations, UN Doc A/CN.4/L.270 (2007). The Draft Articles of the ILC on the Responsibility of International Organizations do not contain an article comparable to Art 3 of the Articles on State Responsibility, see discussion in ILC Report on the work of its 55th Session (2003), UN Doc A/58/10, Suppl 10, paras 9–10 of the Commentary to draft Art 3.

[116] I. Brownlie, *The Rule of Law in International Affairs, International Law at the Fiftieth Anniversary of the United Nations* (1988), at 213 *et seq.* See also G. Fitzmaurice, *The Law and Procedure of the International Court of Justice Vol II* (1986), at 587 (noting that the principle is generally accepted as 'a *sine qua non* of the efficacy and reality of international obligation').

[117] Fitzmaurice, *supra* note 111, at 69 (equating the principle that the sovereignty of states is subordinated to the supremacy of international law with the rule of law in the international field). See also (more critically) Watts, 'The International Rule of Law', 36 *German Yearbook of International Law* (1993) 15.

supremacy. This is true even for a relatively integrated treaty such as the EEA Agreement, of which the EFTA Court said that its scope and objective goes beyond what is usual for an agreement under international law.[118] The Court concluded from the fact that the EEA Agreement does not entail transfer of legislative powers that individuals cannot rely directly on non-implemented EEA rules and that this entails that EEA law does not require that non-implemented EEA rules take precedence over conflicting national rules that fail to transpose the relevant EEA rules correctly into national law.[119] Only in the case of a transfer of powers would the conditions under which international law could mandate supremacy be fulfilled; this is the case in integrated regional systems such as the EU.[120]

However, again the difference between EU law and international law is somewhat less absolute than it may appear. On the one hand, ultimately the scope and operation of the principle of supremacy in EU law remains conditional on national constitutional law—notwithstanding the case law of the ECJ. Several national constitutional courts have great difficulty in accepting this view of the ECJ on absolute primacy of Community law.[121] On the other hand, a not insignificant number of states have given effect to the monist ambition of the principle and allow for legal restitution by 'disapplying' the Act or statute of national law that conflicts with international law.[122] There is a large practice of states and courts that has placed international law at the level of constitutional law, and thus accepted domestic supremacy of all or some (notably human rights) rules of international law, whether domesticated or not, impliedly recognizing the hierarchically higher status of international law.[123] In effect, this locks international law into the constitution and provides a barrier against (easy) deviation through legislation.[124] This, for instance, is the case in Cape Verde,[125] the Czech Republic,[126] Japan,[127] the Netherlands,[128] and for human rights in Bulgaria,[129]

[118] Case E-1/07, *Request for an Advisory Opinion from the EFTA Court by Fürstliches Landgericht by decision of that court of 31 January 2007 in the criminal proceedings against Sedin Poric*, [2007], Rec 37.

[119] Ibid, Rec 40.

[120] Case 6/64, *Costa v ENEL*, *supra* note 8; T.C. Hartley, *The Foundations of European Community Law* (1994), at 234.

[121] Craig, *supra* note 88.

[122] Eg, *Re Víctor Raúl Pinto*, Supreme Court of Chile, Case No 3125-04; ILDC 1093 (CL 2007), 23 (holding that the international obligation binding upon Chile to prosecute crimes against humanity made an amnesty law inapplicable in the case at hand); *Chile v Arancibia Clavel*, Supreme Court of Justice of Argentina, Case No 259, A 533 XXXVIII; ILDC 1082 (AR 2004), 28 (holding that customary international law of *ius cogens* nature stipulated the non-applicability of statutory limitations to war crimes and crimes against humanity); *Mazzeo (Riveros v Office of the Public Prosecutor)*, Supreme Court of Justice of Argentina, M 2333 XLII; ILDC 1084 (AR 2007), 28.

[123] Cassese, 'Modern Constitutions and International Law', in *Recueil des Cours* (1985) 192, 331, at 402.

[124] Ginsburg, 'Locking in Democracy: Constitutions, Commitment and International Law', 38 *New York University Journal of International Law and Politics* (2006) 707.

[125] Art 11(4) of the Constitution of the Republic of Cape Verde (1980).

[126] Art 10 of the Constitution of the Czech Republic (1992).

[127] Iwasawa, *supra* note 98, at 372.

[128] Art 94 of the Constitution of the Kingdom of the Netherlands (1983).

[129] *Al-Nashif v National Police Directorate at the Ministry of the Interior*, Supreme Administrative Court of Bulgaria, Administrative Case No 11004/2002; ILDC 608 (BG 2003) [H11] (holding

Norway,[130] and Portugal.[131] Some states have even done so in express recognition of the international principle of supremacy—requiring that international law, once duly introduced in domestic law, also prevails over domestic law in the *domestic* legal order. Courts in Argentina,[132] Belgium,[133] Chile,[134] Indonesia,[135] Latvia,[136] and Peru[137] have set aside domestic law that conflicted with international law, expressly referring to Article 27 of the Vienna Convention on the Law of Treaties. There are also cases where courts have suggested that domestic conflict rules, which grant precedence to international law, were appropriate since they respect the supremacy claimed by international law, or by particular international treaties or courts, such as the ECtHR.[138] In Nigeria, Justice Uwaifo said in *Abacha*:

> [T]he African Charter is a special genus of law in the Nigerian legal and political system; the Charter has some international flavor and in that sense it cannot be amended or watered down or sidetracked by any Nigerian law;... But like the experience under the

that '... [t]he provision of Article 6(1) of the ECHR proclaiming the right to a fair trial was a directly applicable norm and took priority over the provision of Article 46(2) of the Law for Foreigners, which contradicted it').

[130] Under the Human Rights Act 1999, the European Convention on Human Rights and the International Covenant on Civil and Political Rights (hereinafter the 'ICCPR', adopted 16 December 1966, entered into force 23 March 1976, 999 UNTS 171) enjoy, under para 3, precedence over other Norwegian law. See eg, *A v The Norwegian Immigration Appeals Board,* Supreme Court of Norway, HR-2008-681-A, Norwegian Supreme Court Gazette (Rt, Retstidende) 2008, 513; ILDC 1326 (NO 2008) (forthcoming), 35–6.

[131] *A and B v Portuguese State,* Supreme Administrative Court of Portugal, Case No 0308/07; ILDC 1441 (PT 2007).

[132] *Ekmekdjian, Miguel A v Sofovich and Gerardo,* Supreme Court of Justice of Argentina, Codices No E.64.XXIII, ARG-1995-3-002, (1992), Fallos de la Corte Suprema de Justicia de la Nación (Official Digest), Vol 1492, *Revista Jurídica La Ley,* Vol 1992-C, 540; Buergenthal, 'International Tribunals and Courts: the Internationalization of Domestic Adjudication', in U. Beyerlin et al (eds), *Recht Zwischen Umbruch und Bewahrung. Festschrift für Rudolf Bernhardt* (1995) 687, at 698.

[133] *ING België v B I,* Court of Cassation of Belgium, Case No C.05.0154.N; ILDC 1025 (BE 2007) (forthcoming). This builds on the Belgian Court of Cassation's judgment in the case *Minister for Economic Affairs v Franco-Suisse 'Le Ski',* Court of Cassation of Belgium, *Common Market Law Reports* (1972) 330; *Journal des Tribunaux,* 460 (1971) 93 ILR 203, in which it was established case law that a directly effective treaty provision had primacy over a conflicting legislative act.

[134] *Perú v Chile,* Supreme Court of Chile, Rol No 2242-06; ILDC 1443 (CL 2007) (forthcoming).

[135] *Sianturi v Indonesia,* Constitutional Court of Indonesia, Nos 2-3/PUU-V/2007; ILDC 1041 (ID 2007).

[136] *Linija v Latvia,* Constitutional Court of Latvia; ILDC 189 (LV 2004). The court had to consider whether the Latvian Code of Administrative Penalties was compatible with the International Convention on Facilitation of International Maritime Traffic, which provides that states shall not impose any penalty upon ship owners if their passengers possess inadequate control documents. The Court derived from the obligations of Latvia under the VCLT, in particular the obligation to perform treaties in good faith that in a case of contradiction between rules of international law and national legislation, the provisions of international law must be applied. Hence, the court set aside the domestic law.

[137] *Martin Rivas v Constitutional and Social Chamber of the Supreme Court,* Constitutional Court of Peru, 679-2005-PA/TC; ILDC 960 (PE 2007), 49 (accepting that a party could not invoke the provisions of its internal law as justification for its failure to perform a treaty and, partially on that basis, deciding that amnesty laws that violated the American Convention on Human Rights, adopted 22 November 1969, entered into force 18 July 1978, 1144 UNTS 123, lacked legal effect.

[138] *Al-Nashif v National Police Directorate at the Ministry of the Interior, supra* note 129, at 10–11.

European Communities Act, 1972 in regard to the policy towards the European Economic Communities Treaty, by comparison, the African Charter cannot also be submitted, as I hope I have shown, to the sheer vagaries of any other municipal or domestic law.[139]

The parallel between EU law and international law has one other dimension. Both in regard to EU law and international law, states have retained the right as a matter of national law (though not necessarily as a matter of EU law and international law), to protect fundamental constitutional values.[140] That reservation may collide with the requirements of EU law and international law. However, it is also an inevitable consequence of the incomplete political system of, respectively, the EU and the international legal order. That reservation of ultimate authority is critical for explaining the pluralistic relation of legal orders. In incidental cases it may preclude compliance with international (or even EU) demands that may collide with national constitutional law. However, questions of ultimate authority are not decisive for explaining general patterns of compliance or non-compliance when no such collisions occur.

C. Direct Effect

Like supremacy, direct effect has a significant compliance-inducing potential. A court that gives 'direct effect' to an obligation, is not dependent on an intervening legislative step. More precisely: it can then give effect to an international obligation also when the political branches fail to give effect, and thereby secure compliance.[141] This compliance-inducing potential can be caught in the notion of direct effect as a 'sword': the power of the court to give direct effect to an international obligation allows enforcement of international law in the national legal order where this, without direct effect, would not be possible.

The power-controlling potential of direct effect was well reflected in *Foster v Neilson*, perhaps the earliest pronouncement of the concept of self-executingness—a notion that is conceptually closely related to the notion of direct effect. Chief Justice Marshall first described the normal effect of treaties in international law and in other states: 'A treaty is in the nature of a contract between two nations, not a legislative act. It does not generally effect, of itself, the object to be accomplished...but is carried into execution by the sovereign power of the respective parties to the instrument.'[142] He added that in the United States a different principle is established: 'Our constitution declares a treaty to be the law of the land. It is, consequently, to be regarded in courts of justice as equivalent to an

[139] *Abacha v Fawehinmi*, Supreme Court of Nigeria, SC 45/1997; ILDC 21 (NG 2000) (discussing the African Charter on Human and People's Rights, adopted 27 June 1981, entered into force 21 October 1986 1520 UNTS 217).

[140] Von Bogdandy, 'Pluralism, Direct Effect, and the Ultimate Say: On the Relationship between International and Domestic Constitutional Law', 6 *International Journal of Constitutional Law* (2008) 397.

[141] Skouris, 'Effet Utile versus Direct Effect: The Case-law of the Court of Justice on the Direct Effect of Directives', 17 *European Business Law Review* (2006) 241, at 242.

[142] *Foster v Neilson*, US Supreme Court, 2 Pet. 253, 314 (1829); J.J. Paust, *International Law as Law of the United States* (2003), at 71–3.

act of the legislature, whenever it operates of itself without the aid of any legislative provision.'[143] This clearly expresses a principally different choice—a system in which international law is regularly part of the law to be applied by the courts also when political branches do not act.[144]

The choice for such a different principle can only be understood as a will to control executive power, and reflects the conviction that an open constitution is better able to achieve that purpose. Indeed, this choice has commonly been made in post-revolutionary constitutional developments.[145] While provisions for domestic legal effect had no place in states with autocratic or dictatorial leadership, the trend towards opening constitutions towards international law so as to allow for control of the previously unassailable government could be seen in the Constitution of the Weimar Republic, the German Constitution of 1949, the 1946 Constitution of Japan,[146] the Spanish Constitution of 1978, and a range of Eastern European constitutions set in place after the fall of the Berlin Wall in 1989.[147]

The concept of direct effect plays a key role in the doctrinal understanding of the application of EC law by national courts and takes centre stage in the textbooks on EU law. Even though the original treaty did not provide a hint that EU law would deviate from general international law,[148] since its *Van Gend en Loos* judgment, and (for directives) *Van Duyn*,[149] the ECJ routinely holds that private individuals can rely on provisions of EC law before the national courts of the member states, if the Community law provision invoked is 'sufficiently clear and precise, and unconditional'.[150] This is regardless of the system laid down in national constitutions with respect to the relationship between international law and domestic law.

The leading textbooks on public international law do not consider direct effect to be a matter of much interest and relegate the topic to national law.[151] International

143 Ibid.

144 Vazquez, 'Treaties as Law of the Land: the Supremacy Clause and Presumption of Self-Execution', 122 *Harvard Law Review* (2009) 599, at 622.

145 Stein, 'International Law in Internal Law: Towards Internationalization of Central-Eastern Constitutions', 88 *American Journal of International Law* (1994) 427, at 428; Cassese, *supra* note 123, at 351.

146 Iwasawa, *supra* note 98, at 375.

147 Vereschetin, 'New Constitutions and the Old Problem of the Relationship between International Law and National Law', 7 *European Journal of International Law* (1996) 29.

148 Becker and Campbell, 'The Direct Effect of European Directives: Towards the Final Act', 13 *Columbia Journal of European Law* (2006–2007) 401.

149 Case 41/74, *Van Duyn v Home Office,* [1974] ECR 1337.

150 See also Case C-194/08, *Susanne Grassmayr v Bundesminister für Wissenschaft und Forschung,* judgment of 1 July 2010, not yet published. (Rec 44: 'According to settled case law, whenever the provisions of a directive appear, so far as their subject-matter is concerned, to be unconditional and sufficiently precise, they may be relied on before the national courts by individuals against the State where the latter has failed to implement the directive in domestic law by the end of the period prescribed or where it has failed to implement the directive correctly.')

151 See eg, I. Brownlie, *Principles of Public International Law* (2008, 7th edn), at 53–4. Also M. Shaw, *International Law* (1997), at chapter 4, confines himself to a discussion of how various states proceed. A similar approach is taken in M. Sorensen, *Manual of Public International Law* (1968), at 166. More appreciative of the significance of international law for the question of direct effect is the treatment in A. Cassese, *International Law* (2001), at 173–4, 166–81.

law generally respects the right of states to determine for themselves whether or not they allow their courts to give direct effect to an international obligation. International obligations are generally formulated as obligations of result, stopping 'short at the outer boundaries of the State machinery'.[152] The holding of the ICJ in its Request for Interpretation of the Judgment of 31 March 2004 in the *Case concerning Avena and Other Mexican Nationals*[153] reflects the situation in general international law. The Court said:

> The *Avena* Judgment nowhere lays down or implies that the courts in the United States are required to give direct effect to paragraph 153(9). The obligation laid down in that paragraph is indeed an obligation of result which clearly must be performed unconditionally; non-performance of it constitutes internationally wrongful conduct. However, the Judgment leaves it to the United States to choose the means of implementation, not excluding the introduction within a reasonable time of appropriate legislation, if deemed necessary under domestic constitutional law.[154]

The neutrality of customary international law in this respect reflects the continuing significant differences in the practice of states as regards the way in which they give effect to their international obligations.[155] Given these differences, international law could indeed hardly do otherwise than express a liberty. States are at liberty to determine, according to their own national legal systems, whether direct effect is possible at all and, if so, what conditions[156] and consequences[157] apply. All this excludes what Iwasawa called the 'given-theory': the idea that international law would determine whether or not a particular rule of international law has direct effect.[158] The European Free Trade Association (EFTA) Court opined that direct effect would only be mandatory in the case of a transfer of powers as had been given in EU law, and would not extend to the European Economic Area

[152] ILC, 'Report of the Commission to the General Assembly on the work of its twenty-ninth session, 9 May–29 July 1977', Commentary to Art 21 of the draft Articles on State Responsibility 'Breach of an international obligation requiring the achievement of a special result adopted on first reading', (1977) II *YB ILC* (Part Two), 19(1).

[153] *Request for Interpretation of the Judgment of 31 March 2004 in the Case concerning Avena and Other Mexican Nationals (Mexico v United States of America) (2008),* ICJ Reports (2008) 13, at 44.

[154] Ibid.

[155] Sørensen, 'Die Verplichttungen eines Staates im Bereich seiner nationalen Rechtsordnuung auf Grund eines Staatsvertrages', *Menschenrechte im Staatsrecht und im Völkerrecht* (1967) 15, at 21.

[156] This of course also holds for the procedural conditions governing the actions of interested parties that seek to protect their legal interests under a treaty; also here the liberty left by EU law is magnified (see Case C-228/98, *Kharalambos Dounias v Minister for Finance,* [2000] ECR I-577, at 58).

[157] For instance, this holds for the question of whether international law can be applied directly in a horizontal sphere; in public international law there is not even the beginning of the relative uniformity that exists on this point in EU law. This applies also to the European Convention on Human Rights; P. van Dijk, F. van Hoof and A. van Rijn (eds), *Theory and Practice of the European Convention on Human Rights* (2004), at 22–6.

[158] Iwasawa, 'The Doctrine of Self-Executing Treaties in the United States: A Critical Analysis', 26 *Virginia Journal of International Law* (1986) 627, at 650. For a somewhat curious example of a case where a national court found an international obligation to give direct effect in Art 48(2) of the Charter of the United Nations (adopted 26 June 1954, entered into force 24 October 1945) 1 UNTS 16, see *Kadi v Prime Ministry and Ministry of Foreign Affairs of Turkey,* Council of State of Turkey, E 2006/2824, K 2007/115; ILDC 311 (TK 2007) (forthcoming).

(EEA) Agreement, even though that is an integrated treaty regime, with a scope and objective that goes beyond what is usual for an agreement under international law:[159]

It follows from Article 7 EEA and Protocol 35 to the EEA Agreement that EEA law does not entail a transfer of legislative powers. Therefore, EEA law does not require that individuals and economic operators can rely directly on non-implemented EEA rules before national courts.[160]

It is only in the EU, which has acquired a further degree of integration, with a corresponding transfer of powers, that a binding requirement of direct effect is expressed—one that is generally recognized by the member states.[161]

The fact that general international law does not require states to allow their courts to apply international law directly is perhaps the single greatest limitation of the role of national courts as a systemic force in the protection of the international rule of law. The position of national courts is thus totally different from that of international courts, where by their very nature international law is part of the applicable law and can be applied as such.[162] In the absence of any rules that require direct effect, the decision whether to allow courts to give direct effect to international law—as well as the decision of courts whether to grant direct effect—is primarily a political and normative choice, both for states and their courts.[163]

But again, considering direct effect as a matter that is of no interest for international law fails to recognize the diversity between states and indeed within international law. Direct effect is possible in a great many states, including such diverse states as Belgium,[164] Bulgaria,[165] the Czech Republic,[166] the Dominican

[159] Case E-1/07, Rec 37, *supra* note 118, discussing the European Economic Area Agreement, (hereinafter the 'EEA Agreement'), OJ 1994 L 1/3, and Protocol 35 adjusting the EEA Agreement, OJ 1994 L 1/572.

[160] Case E-4/01, *Karl K Karlsson hf v The Icelandic State, Request for an Advisory Opinion to the EFTA Court by Héraðsdómur Reykjavíkur (Reykjavík District Court)*, [2002], Rec 28.

[161] The Constitutional Court of Italy said that Art 11 of the Constitution—stipulating that Italy 'agrees, on equal footing with other states, to limitations of sovereignty where they are necessary to a legal system which ensures peace and justice amongst nations; it promotes and encourages international organizations furthering such ends'—provided the basis for the constitutional rank of EU law, see *EP v Municipality of Avellino*, Case No 349/2007 in *Rivista di diritto internazionale* (2008) 1, at 230; ILDC 301 (IT 2007) [6.1].

[162] Verhoeven, 'Article 21 of the Rome Statute and the Ambiguities of Applicable Law', 33 *Netherlands Yearbook of International Law* (2002) 3, at 15.

[163] See generally on the political nature of judicial decisions D. Kennedy, *A Critique of Adjudication: (Fin de Siècle)* (1997), at 40; B. de Sousa Santos, *Toward a New Common Sense: Law, Science and Politics in the Paradigmatic Transition* (1995), at 114, referring to 'the politics of definition of law'.

[164] *BM v Belgium*, Court of Cassation of Belgium, Judgment on Appeal, No P.04.0644.N (2004); ILDC 58 (BE 2004).

[165] *Council of Ministers v TSD and ors*, Supreme Court of Cassation of Bulgaria, Cassation appeal, Judgment No 1177, Civil Case no 241/2007 (2007); ILDC 972 (BG 2007).

[166] Art 10 of the Constitution of the Czech Republic (1992); see for an application eg, *Minister of Justice v Šenk*, Supreme Court of the Czech Republic, 8 Tz 38/2000; ILDC 1444 (CZ 2000) (holding that Art 6 of the European Convention on Human Rights was directly binding on the state).

Republic,[167] Egypt[168] France,[169] Latvia,[170] the Netherlands,[171] Portugal,[172] and Switzerland.[173]

For all the states that allow for direct effect, the neutrality of *general* international law is deceptive. The fact that public international law does not *oblige* states to allow for direct effect in the same manner as is done by EC law does not negate the influence of international law over direct effect. To the extent that domestic law allows its courts to give direct effect to international law, if the appropriate conditions are satisfied, international law will exert a considerable influence.[174]

The reasons why these states have allowed for direct effect may vary, but they will have in common that this practice is not driven by a perceived obligation of international law. It may be true that direct effect furthers the effectiveness of international law, but there is no obligation to do so.[175] However, this is not different to EU law, where at least initially the direct effect of directives is more based on a choice of legal policy by the Court, seeking to further the effectiveness of EU law,[176] than on a coherent legal basis.[177]

A dominant explanatory variable of direct effect is the allocation of individual rights by international law. Individual rights at the same time pierce the veil of dualism in the relationship between state and individual, and empower national courts. For instance, the Federal Supreme Court of Switzerland held that a provision of a treaty is only self-executing if it regulates the legal position of an individual, even though the question of whether that is the case is then made dependent on the substantive completeness of the norm.[178]

[167] Art 3 of the Constitution of the Dominican Republic (1994). See eg, *Gallardo Montilla v Gallardo Concepción,* Supreme Court of Justice, ILDC 1490 (DO 1997) (forthcoming) (holding that treaties, duly approved by Congress, had the authority of an Act of Congress and that tribunals must apply treaty provisions that are relevant to the resolution of a legal dispute).

[168] Art 151 of the Constitution of the Arab Republic of Egypt (1971). See eg, *Public Prosecution of Egypt v Salah Aldian Mustafa Ismail,* Supreme Court of State Security of Egypt, No 4190/86 Ozbekia (121 Koli Shamal) (1987); ILDC 1483 (EG 1987) (forthcoming) (stating that a treaty that had satisfied the constitutional requirements to be incorporated into national law thus became part of the national laws, and courts are obliged to apply its provisions).

[169] *X v Y,* Court of Cassation of France, Cassation appeal, Information Bulletin of the Court of Cassation No 626 of 1 October 2005, No 1810 (2005); ILDC 770 (FR 2005).

[170] *Re Latvian Education Law,* Constitutional Court of Latvia, Constitutional Review Case No 2004-18-0106 (2005); ILDC 190 (LV 2005).

[171] *Reinier van Arkel Foundation and ors v Minister for Transport, Public Works and Water Management,* Council of State of the Netherlands, 200401178/1 (2004); ILDC 129 (NL 2004).

[172] *Merck & Inc and Merck Sharp & Dohme Lda v Merck Genéricos–Produtos Farmacuticos Lda,* Supreme Court of Justice of Portugal, final Appeal Judgment No 4416/04 (2005); ILDC 667 (PT 2005).

[173] *A. and B. v Government of the Canton of Zurich,* Federal Supreme Court of Switzerland, Appeal Judgment, Case No 2P.273/1999 (2000); ILDC 350 (CH 2000).

[174] Buergenthal, *supra* note 87, at 319 (noting that in some states, the determination of whether a treaty is self-executing is made dependent on its international characterization).

[175] *Request for Interpretation of the Judgment of 31 March 2004 in the Case concerning Avena and Other Mexican Nationals, supra* note 153.

[176] Dashwood, 'From Van Duyn to Mangold via Marshall: Reducing Direct Effect to Absurdity?', 9 *Cambridge Yearbook of European Legal Studies* (2006–2007) 81, at 85; Skouris, *supra* note 141, at 242.

[177] Becker and Campbell, *supra* note 148, at 413.

[178] *A. and B. v Government of the Canton of Zurich,* BGE 126 I 242; ILDC 350 (CH 2000) [2b]. Similarly Belgium, see *Art Research & Contact Naamloze Vennootschap v BS,* ILDC 44 (BE 2001)

However, there is no necessary or automatic connection between individual rights and direct effect. It is to be recalled that while in EU law the direct effect of primary law was based on the recognition of subjective rights, that did not initially hold for directives, which were addressed to states, not individuals, even though individuals were always the true beneficiaries.[179] In regard to the latter, EU law has decoupled the connection between direct effect and subjective rights, and replaced it with an objective conception.[180]

The practice of states with regard to international law on this point is varied and, within states, often inconsistent. While in some states, such as in the above example Switzerland, direct effect is coupled with subjective international rights, in other states it has been recognized that the concepts of direct effect and subjective rights are best kept separate.[181] This was clear in the follow-up to the *Avena* case in the United States. While there continues to be considerable uncertainty as to whether the Vienna Convention on Consular Relations (VCCR) creates individually enforceable rights in domestic courts, there was no dispute as to the self-executing nature of the Convention.[182] What counts, both in EU law and international law, is whether a norm is part of the applicable law for the courts and whether it is sufficiently unconditional and precise so that the courts can apply it as a rule of decision.

D. Indirect Effect: Consistent Interpretation

The practice of consistent interpretation has much potential to secure compliance with European and international obligations. It allows a court to give effect to an international obligation which, though binding on the state, has not been

[29] (holding that a treaty had direct effect in regard to citizens of a state party if the provision was clear, precise, and unconditional; and if the state parties had intended to confer subjective rights and obligations to individuals).

179 Becker and Campbell, *supra* note 148, at 403; Dougan, 'When Worlds Collide! Competing Visions of the Relationship Between Direct Effect and Supremacy', 44 *Common Market Law Review* (2007) 931, at 934.

180 Becker and Campbell, *supra* note 148, at 405.

181 See for the distinction also Jackson, 'Status of Treaties in Domestic Legal Systems: A Policy Analysis', 86 *American Journal of International Law* (1992) 310, at 318. The distinction is also made, eg, in Simma et al, 'The Role of German Courts in the Enforcement of International Human Rights', in B. Conforti and F. Francioni (eds), *Enforcing International Human Rights in Domestic Courts* (1997). See also Vázquez, 'Treaty-Based Rights and Remedies of Individuals', 92 *Columbia Law Review* (1992), at 1133–41, who distinguishes between the questions of whether a treaty is self-executing and whether individuals have standing to invoke it. He rightly notes that the two issues may overlap: 'standing doctrine addresses the same issue that the courts sometimes address as a "self-execution" issue: whether the duty imposed by the treaty gives rise to a correlative primary right of the litigant such that the litigant may enforce the rule in court'.

182 *Medellin v Texas*, US Supreme Court, 552 US 491, 128 S Ct 1346 (2008); ILDC 947 (US 2008), 21 (noting on the Vienna Convention on Consular Relations 596 UNTS 261, adopted 24 April 1963 and entered into force 19 March 1967, that '... [e]ven when treaties are self-executing in the sense that they create federal law, the background presumption is that "[i]nternational agreements, even those directly benefiting private persons, generally do not create private rights or provide for a private cause of action in domestic courts"', citing the Restatement (Third) of Foreign Relations Law of the United States §907, Comment a, 395,1986); *Sanchez-Llamas (Moises) v Oregon*, US Supreme Court, 548 US 331, 126 S Ct 2669 (2006); ILDC 697 (US 2006) 8 (Judge Breyer dissenting) (noting that 'it is common ground that the Convention is "self-executing".... That is to say, the Convention "operates of itself without the aid of any legislative provision." *Foster v Neilson*, 2 Pet. 253, 314 (1829)'.)

incorporated or transformed into domestic law and as such is not part of the applicable law of that court. In this respect, seen from an integrated perspective on the rule of law, consistent interpretation is a key element of the rule of law.[183]

Its powers are particularly clear in so-called dualist states, where delays may occur between the entry into force of treaties and domestic implementation, and courts may, through a process of interpretation, ensure domestic compliance with a treaty even if the political branches are not (yet) ready for it. By construing national law in the light of international law, national courts compensate for the refusal of the legislature to give effect to a treaty and can themselves ensure that international obligations are performed. In many cases, through this process, national courts in dualist states were as powerful in securing conformity of national with international law as their counterparts in 'monist' states.[184] For instance, the Supreme Court of Bangladesh held that even though Bangladesh had not yet incorporated all the provisions of the Convention on the Rights of the Child into its domestic laws, '[i]f the domestic laws were not clear enough or there was nothing therein', the national courts should draw upon the principles incorporated in the treaty.[185] The Canadian Supreme Court held that even while international obligations pertaining to freedom of association were not incorporated and thus not part of Canadian law, they could assist courts in interpreting guarantees under the Canadian Charter of Rights and Freedoms. This led, for instance, to the court recognizing a process of collective bargaining as part of the Charter's guarantee of freedom of association.[186] The Court also said that the Charter should be presumed to provide at least as great a level of protection as that found in the international human rights documents which Canada had ratified.[187] In *Sabally v Inspector General of Police*, the Supreme Court of Gambia said that as Gambia had not legislated to implement the African Charter, it could not directly apply it, yet the principles laid down in the Charter were 'pertinent and relevant to the instant case'.[188]

[183] Drake, 'Twenty Years after Von Colson: The Impact of "Indirect Effect" on the Protection of the Individual's Community Rights', 30 *European Law Review* (2005) 329.

[184] Buergenthal, *supra* note 132, at 700–1.

[185] *State v Metropolitan Police Commissioner*, Supreme Court of Bangladesh, 60 DLR (2008) 660; ILDC 1410 (BD 2008), 28; see also *Ershad v Bangladesh,* Supreme Court of Bangladesh, 21 BLD (AD) (2001) 69; ILDC 476 (BD 2000), 3 (BB Roy Chowdhury) (discussing the Convention on the Rights of the Child (adopted 20 November 1989, entered into force 2 September 1990) 1577 UNTS 3, noting that national courts should not ignore the international obligations undertaken by a country. National courts should draw upon the principles incorporated in the international instruments if the domestic laws are ambiguous or absent.) See also *Dr Shipra Chaudhury and another v Government of Bangladesh and ors,* Supreme Court of Bangladesh, 29 BLD (HCD) (2009); ILDC 1515 (BD 2009) (forthcoming), at 28 (holding that courts could look to the ICCPR and the International Covenant on Economic, Social and Cultural Rights, 993 UNTS 3, 1966, hereinafter the 'ICESCR', as an aid to interpretation of the provisions of Part III of the Constitution, particularly to determine the rights implicit in rights such as the right to life and the right to liberty, that were not enumerated in the Constitution).

[186] *Health Services and Support—Facilities Subsector Bargaining Assn v British Columbia, The Supreme Court of Canada,* 2 SCR 391, 2007 SCC 27 (2007); ILDC 857 (CA 2007), 69 (discussing the African Charter on Human and People's Rights, 1520 UNTS 217, 27 June 1981, entered into force 21 October 1986).

[187] Ibid, at 70.

[188] *Sabally v Inspector General of Police,* Supreme Court of Gambia, Civil ref No. 2/2001; AHRLR 87 (GaSC 2001) (2002); ILDC 11 (GM 2001), 13.

The practice of consistent interpretation is not contingent on the question of whether a rule of international law can be given direct effect, and thus may allow a court to circumvent the shield that the concept of direct effect may set up. This is both true for EU law and international law.[189] While courts generally restrict direct effect to a narrow category of rules that satisfies the criterion of completeness, application of the principle of consistent interpretation is not dependent on any a priori qualities of a rule of international law. In quite a few instances, national courts, in jurisdictions where the criteria for direct effect may function as a shield against the application of international law, were able to circumvent that shield by engaging in consistent interpretation.[190]

In the EU the principle of consistent interpretation is, similarly to the principle of direct effect, governed by EU law, not national law.[191] EU law obliges the national courts to construe their domestic law in conformity with the law of the EU. In the *Von Colson* case, the ECJ held that 'all the authorities of the member states' must interpret their national law in the light of the wording and the purpose of the directive in order to achieve the result referred to in the third paragraph of Article 189 EC (now Article 288 TFEU).[192] The courts must, insofar as they are given discretion to do so according to national law, construe and apply that national law, and in particular the implementing legislation, in conformity with the requirements of Community law.[193] In *Marleasing*[194] the ECJ elaborated on this issue as follows: '[I]n applying national law, whether the provisions in question were adopted before or after the directive, the national court called upon to interpret it is required to do so, as far as possible, in the light of the wording and purpose of the directive…'.[195] The ECJ finds that this requirement for national law to be interpreted in conformity with European Union law is inherent in the system of the Treaty, since it permits the national court, within the limits of its jurisdiction, to ensure the full effectiveness of EU law when it determines the dispute before it.[196]

189 Eg, *Mathilda/RK Schoolbestuur (Mathilda v School Management)*, Supreme Court of the Netherlands, NJ 1995/259; AB 1993 (1993), 440 (stating that Art 7 ICESCR does not have direct effect, but its purpose must be taken into account).

190 Ibid; *Ziers v Gedeputeerde Staten Gelderland*, Council of State of the Netherlands, Case No AB 1995/24 (1993); Decision of South African Constitutional Court which held that the concept of sustainable development in the law of South Africa must be construed and understood in the light of developments in the international law of environment and sustainable development.

191 Dashwood, *supra* note 176, at 90.

192 Case 14/83, *Von Colson and Kamann*, [1984] ECR 1891, Rec 26; see also Case 79/83, *Harz*, [1984] ECR 1921. See discussion in Drake, *supra* note 183, at 329.

193 See *Von Colson and Kamann, supra* note 192, at para 28.

194 Case C-106/89, *Marleasing*, [1990] ECR I-4135, Rec 8.

195 See also Case C-98/09, *Francesca Sorge v Poste Italiane SpA*, judgment of 24 June 2010, not yet published, Rec 51 (holding that the national courts are bound to interpret domestic law, so far as possible, in the light of the wording and the purpose of the framework agreement in question in order to achieve the result sought by the latter and, consequently, to comply with the third paragraph of Art 288 TFEU).

196 Case C-555/07, *Seda Kücükdeveci v Swedex GmbH & Co. KG*, [2010] ECR I-00365, Rec 48; Joined Cases C-378/07 and C-380/07, *Kiriaki Angelidaki and Others v Organismos Nomarkhiaki Aftodiikisi Rethimnis and Dimos Geropotamou*, [2009] ECR I-3071, Rec 198.

It is also significant that the practice of consistent interpretation is not contingent on the question of whether a rule of international law can be given direct effect, and thus may allow a court to circumvent the shield that the concept of direct effect may set up. The obligation to interpret national law in conformity with European Union law concerns all provisions of national law, whether adopted before or after the framework agreement in question.[197]

In public international law, one cannot find a comparable authoritative formulation of the principle that as a matter of public international law courts should construe their domestic law in conformity with international law. However, there appears sufficient acceptance of the notion of international law as 'higher law' that must be given effect in the national legal order, and that courts, as state organs, are responsible for the proper application of international law within their jurisdiction,[198] to accept that the position that public international law is neutral on the matter of consistent interpretation is too narrow.[199] It has been said that state practice allows one to infer an international duty of courts to interpret, within their constitutional mandates, national law in the light of international law.[200]

The practice of courts that engage in consistent interpretation is widespread. It includes both civil law[201] and common law systems.[202] It also includes states that allow for automatic incorporation and those that require transformation. The former category includes states like Austria,[203] Ethiopia,[204] Japan,[205] Latvia,[206]

[197] Case C-98/09, *Francesca Sorge, supra* note 195, Rec 51.

[198] This notion seems also to underlie the case law of the Court of Justice, see Joined Cases C-46/93 and C-48/93 *Brasserie du Pêcheur SA v Bundesrepublik Deutschland* and *The Queen v Secretary of State for Transport, ex parte: Factortame Ltd and others,* [1996] ECR I-1029, Rec 34.

[199] There is truth in the observation of Morgenstern, 'Judicial Practice and the Supremacy of International Law', 27 *British Yearbook of International Law* (1950) 92, stating that true supremacy of public international law would be 'obscured by the fact that, owing to the absence of compulsory judicial dispute settlement in the international sphere, responsibility is not always the automatic consequence of violation of rules of law'.

[200] Ibid, at 85–6. Morgenstern states that 'The trend of judicial opinion is significant. It shows that courts have realized that international law, by its very nature, must be enforced contrary provisions of municipal law notwithstanding'.

[201] Eg, *Switzerland v A and B,* Federal Supreme Court of Switzerland, BGE 128 IV 117; ILDC 347 (CH 2002) [6d].

[202] Eg, *Minister for Immigration and Ethnic Affairs v Teoh,* High Court of Australia, 183 CLR 273; HCA 20, 128 ALR 353 (1995); ILDC 779 (AU 1995) (forthcoming) (holding that the provisions of an international convention to which Australia is a party, especially one which declares universal fundamental rights, may be used by the courts as a legitimate guide in developing the common law); *Evans v New South Wales,* Federal Court of Australia, FCAFC 130 (2008) 79; *A (FC) v Secretary of State for the Home Department, A (FC) v Secretary of State for the Home Department (joined appeals), Appellatte Committee of House of Lords,* 71[2005]; ILDC 363 (UK 2005), 33 (holding that the principles of English common law did not stand alone and regard should be had to international instruments prohibiting torture).

[203] Balthasar, '"Pacta sunt servanda. Zur innerstaatlichen Relevanz von durch Staatsvertrag" eingegangenen Verpflichtungen Osterreichs', 50 *ZOR* (1996) 161, at 169.

[204] Art 13(4) of the Constitution of the Federal Democratic Republic of Ethiopia (1995) (providing that '[t]he fundamental rights and freedoms enumerated in this Chapter shall be interpreted in a manner consistent with the Universal Declaration of Human Rights, international human rights covenants and conventions ratified by Ethiopia').

[205] Iwasawa, 'The Domestic Impact of International Human Rights Standards; The Japanese Experience', in P. Alston and J. Crawford (eds), *The Future of UN Human Rights Treaty Monitoring* (2000) 245, at 259.

[206] *Re Latvian Education Law, supra* note 170, 5.

the Netherlands,[207] Poland,[208] and the United States;[209] in the latter category are states like Australia,[210] Canada,[211] Iceland,[212] Israel,[213] Uganda,[214] South Africa,[215] Zambia,[216] and the United Kingdom.[217]

It indeed may be possible to infer from this practice, in combination with the general principle of effective treaty interpretation,[218] a general principle of interpretation such that, within the limits of their domestic powers, national courts should interpret domestic law in conformity with the international obligations of the state. It is noteworthy that the ECtHR, in considering the interpretation of the jurisdictional aspects of 'genocide' by German courts, noted that 'the German courts' interpretation of the applicable provisions and rules of public international law, *in the light of which the provisions of the Criminal Code had to be construed*, was not arbitrary'.[219] Apparently, the 'had to' refers to an obligation under international law. In this context, the decision of the EFTA court in *Karlsson* is also relevant. It stated that even though the EFTA Agreement, unlike EU law, did not require direct effect,

> it is inherent in the general objective of the EEA Agreement of establishing a dynamic and homogeneous market, in the ensuing emphasis on the judicial defence and enforcement of the rights of individuals, as well as in the public international law principle of effectiveness, that national courts will consider any relevant element of EEA law, whether implemented or not, when interpreting national law.[220]

[207] *TSM Compagnie d'Assurance Transports v Geisseler Transport AG*, Supreme Court of the Netherlands, NJ 1992/107, (1990). The Supreme Court has ruled that 'Dutch courts should, as far as is possible, interpret and apply Dutch law in such a way that the State meets its treaty obligations'.

[208] *Stanisław K v Zakład Techniczno-Budowlany P Spółka Zoo*, Supreme Court of Poland, II PK 100/05; ILDC 388 (PL 2005), 10.

[209] *Murray v The Charming Betsy 2 Cranch 64*, US Supreme Court, 6 US 64 (1804), 118. See generally R.G. Steinhardt, 'The Role of International Law as a Canon of Domestic Statutory Construction', 43 *Vanderbilt Law Review* (1990) 1103.

[210] *Minister for Immigration and Ethnic Affairs v Teoh*, *supra* note 202, 27.

[211] *United States (Minister of Justice) v Burns and Rafay*, Supreme Court of Canada, 1 SCR 283, 2001 SCC 7; (2001) 195 DLR (4th) 1; ILDC 187 (CA 2001).

[212] *State Social Security Institute v Organization of the Disabled in Iceland*, Supreme Court of Iceland, Case No. 125/2000, H 2000 4480 (2000); ILDC 68 (IS 2000).

[213] *Kurtz and Letushinsky v Kirschen*, Supreme Court of Israel sitting as a Court of Civil Appeal, 21 Piskei Din (II) 20, 47 ILR 212(1967), 214–15; *Kav La'oved Association v Israel*, Supreme Court of Israel sitting as the High Court of Justice, HCJ 4542/02; ILDC 382 (IL 2006) 37 (holding that '... [e]ither way, everyone agrees that by virtue of the "presumption of compliance" between internal law and the provisions of international law, we are required to interpret statutes—as well as powers acquired by government authorities—in a manner which complies with the provisions of international law').

[214] *Onynango-Obbo and Mwenda v Attorney-General*, Supreme Court of Uganda, Case No 2 (2002); ILDC 166 (UG 2004).

[215] *Mazibuko v City of Johannesburg*, High Court of South Africa, ZAGPHC 128 (2008); ILDC 973 (ZA 2008), 31 ('In terms of section 39(1) (b) of the Constitution, the Courts in interpreting the Bill of Rights must consider international law. In terms of section 233 of the Constitution a reasonable interpretation of any legislation which is consistent with international law, must be preferred.').

[216] *Re Order 53 of the Rules of the Supreme Court and Re Application for Leave for Judicial Review by Roy Clarke, Attorney General v Roy Clarke*, Supreme Court of Zambia, Appeal No 96A/2004; ILDC 1340 (ZM 2008).

[217] *R v Secretary of State for the Home Department, ex parte Brind, House of Lords*, 1 AC 696 (1991).

[218] Lauterpacht, 'Restrictive Interpretation and the Principle of Effectiveness in the Interpretation of Treaties', 26 *British Yearbook of International Law* (1949) 67.

[219] *Jorgic v Germany*, App no 74613/01 (ECtHR, 12 July 2007), 70 (emphasis added).

[220] Case E-4/01, *supra* note 160.

Such an interpretative principle is formulated in Principle 7 of the Bangalore Principles:

It is within the proper nature of the judicial process and well-established judicial functions for national courts to have regard to international obligations which a country undertakes—whether or not they have been incorporated into domestic law—for the purpose of removing ambiguity or uncertainty from national constitutions, legislation or common law.[221]

The principle of consistent interpretation straddles international law and national law. As such it is one of the most visible manifestations of the situation of mixity that results from the interplay of international and national law. It is both induced by the international legal requirement to perform international obligations, and by the domestic mandate to interpret national law in the light of international law.

However, it has to be taken into account that there are major differences in the concept as it applies in different states. The practice of consistent interpretation, while fairly uniform across the world, shows substantial differences in conditions under which it can be applied, as well as differences in the scope and limits of judicial powers. In some jurisdictions, it has been understood that the principle was primarily intended to limit the extra-territorial reach of legislation, resulting in a much narrower scope than if the practice were applied to the interpretative application of substantive international law that had not been made part of national law.[222] Another major cause of variation is that in some jurisdictions the practice of consistent interpretation is limited to incorporative statutes,[223] whereas in other jurisdictions it can be applied to all rules of international law. In this respect, the normative guidance of the principle is relatively limited. It does create a presumption, but it can only function under the conditions set by national law. International courts, while not irrelevant to the application of international law at the national level,[224] cannot perform the role of the ECJ in controlling uniformity. All this is in keeping with the normal process of auto-appreciation in the application of international law.[225]

[221] Conclusions of Judicial Colloquia and other meetings on the Domestic Application of International Human Rights Norms and on Government under the Law ('Bangalore Principles'), 1988–92, Principle 7. The Principles were cited in *RM and Cradle v Attorney General,* High Court of Kenya, Civil Case 1351; ILDC 699 (KE 2006), 2. See also General Comment No 9 of the UN Committee on Economic, Social and Cultural Rights on the Domestic application of the Covenant, UN Doc A/CONF.39/27, para 15: 'It is generally accepted that domestic law should be interpreted as far as possible in a way which conforms to a State's international legal obligations. Thus, when a domestic decision maker is faced with a choice between an interpretation of domestic law that would place that state in breach of the Covenant and one that would enable the State to comply with the Covenant, international *law* requires the choice of the latter' (emphasis added). See on the existence of an obligation of consistent interpretation also S. Bhuiyan, *National Law in WTO Law Effectiveness and Good Governance in the World Trading System* (2007), at 35.

[222] J.F. Coyle, 'Incorporative Statutes and the Borrowed Treaty Rule', 50 *Virginia Journal of International Law* (2010) 655, at 702.

[223] See *supra* Section 3.

[224] This is daily routine for the European Court on Human Rights. Also decisions of the ICJ can be relevant, for instance in *LaGrand Case, Germany v United States, Judgment (2001),* ICJ Reports (2001) 466.

[225] Weil, 'Le droit international en quête de son identité. Cours général de droit international public', in *Recueil des Cours* (1992) 237, at 220–3.

E. Liability

Compared to the previous three principles, the compliance-inducing potential of the principle of liability is uncertain. Liability for non-compliance with European and international law primarily serves to provide relief to individuals who have suffered damage as a result of such non-compliance.

Nonetheless, in EU law the development of the principles of liability appears based on the presumption that liability can have a compliance-inducing and preventive potential.[226] In any case, if such potential exists, it would prima facie appear to depend on a fairly consistent pattern of application of such a principle and a reasonable certainty on the side of the non-compliant state that determinations of liability will follow.

In EU law the principle of liability is now well established. If the result prescribed by a directive cannot be achieved by way of interpretation, EU law requires the member states to make good damage caused to individuals through failure to transpose that directive.[227] The Court said that the principle of state liability for loss and damage caused to individuals as a result of breaches of European Union law for which the state can be held responsible 'is inherent in the system of the treaties on which the European Union is based'.[228] According to settled case law, harmed individuals have a right to reparation where three conditions are met: the rule of European Union law infringed must be intended to confer rights on them; the breach of that rule must be sufficiently serious; and there must be a direct causal link between the breach and the loss or damage sustained by the individuals.[229]

Significantly for the scope of this chapter, liability can extend to decisions of a Member State's judiciary.[230]

In contrast to EC law, no general principle of liability for imputable breaches of international law exists that requires a state to provide compensation at national level. It is true that a state, by non-compliance with an international obligation, commits an internationally wrongful act, and on that basis is obliged to provide reparation.[231] Depending on the situation, this may imply that measures have to be taken at national level, for instance by withdrawing or annulling a law that contravenes the international obligation or by adopting a law that ensures that the result required by that international obligation is achieved. However, significantly, international law leaves states much freedom to choose the remedies required. Moreover, international law has to recognize that in some states, such as the United States, the state enjoys immunity from damage claims.[232]

[226] See eg, S. Douglas-Scott, *Constitutional Law of the European Union* (2002) 329.

[227] Joined Cases C-6/90 and C-9/90, *Francovich and Others v Italian Republic,* [1991] ECR I-5357, Rec 39; Joined Cases C-46/93 and C-48/93, *Brasserie du Pêcheur and Factortame, supra* note 198, Rec 51; Case C-5/94, *Hedley Lomas,* [1996] ECR I-2553, Rec 25; and Case C-278/05, *Robins and Others v Secretary of State for Work and Pensions,* [2007] ECR I-1053, Rec. 69; Joined Cases C-378/07 and C-380/07, *Angelidaki, supra* note 196, Rec. 202.

[228] Case C-118/08, *Transportes Urbanos y Servicios Generales SAL v Administración del Estado,* [2010] ECR I-00635, Rec 29.

[229] Ibid., Rec. 30.

[230] Case C-224/01, *Köbler v Republik Österreich,* [2003] ECR I-10239; Pfander, 'Köbler v Austria: Expositional Supremacy and Member State Liability', 17 *European Business Law Review* (2006) 275.

[231] Art 31 of the Articles on State Responsibility.

[232] Meltzer, 'Member State Liability in Europe and the United States', 4 *International Journal of Constitutional Law* (2006) 39.

It is also to be recalled that under EU law, national law inevitably plays a role. It is on the basis of the rules of national law on liability that the state must make reparation for the consequences of the loss and damage caused.[233] However, the situation is fundamentally different in EU law as compared to international law. In EU law reparation on the basis of national law is subject to the right to reparation which flows directly from EU law. More particularly, it is subject to the requirement that the conditions for reparation of loss and damage laid down by national law are not less favourable than those relating to similar domestic claims (principle of equivalence) and are not so framed as to make it, in practice, impossible or excessively difficult to obtain reparation (principle of effectiveness).[234] These conditions do not exist in general international law.

The gap between EU law and general international law is only narrowed in particular treaty regimes that provide for liability. Specific obligations grant individuals a right to reparation within the domestic legal order for the breach of an international obligation by the state. Examples are Article 14 of the Convention Against Torture (providing that 'each State Party shall ensure in its legal system that the victim of an act of torture obtains redress and has an enforceable right to fair and adequate compensation'); Article 14(6) of the ICCPR (stating that individuals who have suffered punishment as a result of miscarriage of justice, 'shall be compensated according to law'). Under the ECHR, the Court has declared, for instance, that in the case of a breach of Articles 2 and 3 of the Convention, 'compensation for the non-pecuniary damage flowing from the breach should, in principle, be available as part of the range of redress'.[235]

Particularly instructive is the situation under Article 5(5) of the ECHR, according to which '[E]veryone who has been the victim of arrest or detention in contravention of the provisions of this Article [Articles 5(1)–5(4)] shall have an enforceable right to compensation'. This right to compensation presupposes that a violation of Article 5(1)–(4) has been established—whether by the ECtHR or indeed by a domestic authority.[236] Violation of Article 5(1)–5(4) leads to two questions of compensation on 'two different levels'.[237] On the one hand, at the international level, Article 41 authorizes the Court to afford compensation to the victim if a national measure violates Article 5. On the other hand, Article 5(5) guarantees an individual a right to compensation that is to be provided at national level—and in that respect it is, as in EU law, a direct consequence of non-compliance.

Although there is some discussion about the possibility of applying Article 5(5) directly,[238] most states apply an obligation to compensate under domestic liability law. More generally, while the ECHR defines the principle of right to compensation and some modalities (for instance, the ability to claim compensation for distress), it does not prohibit Contracting States from making the award of compensation

[233] Case C-118/08, *Transportes Urbanos y Servicios Generales SAL v Administración del Estado*, *supra* note 228, Rec 31. [234] Ibid.

[235] *Bubbins v The United Kingdom*, App no 50196/99 (ECtHR, 17 March 2005), para 171.

[236] *Vachev v Bulgaria*, App no 42987/98 (ECtHR, 8 July 2004), para 78.

[237] *Neumeister v Austria*, App no 1936/63 (ECtHR, 27 June 1968).

[238] *Ciulla v Italy*, ECHR, (1989) Series A, No 148, dissenting opinion of Judge Valcitos.

dependent upon, for instance, the ability of the person concerned to show damage resulting from the breach.[239]

Compared with EU law, the scope of such principles for liability is extremely narrow, and international law otherwise leaves the matter to national law, which may or may not provide for compensation for breach of international law.[240]

5. International and European Law Connected

It appears from the above that there remain fundamental differences between EU law and international law with respect to the principles that underlie the compliance-inducing role of national courts. The principles of EU law, with regard to supremacy, direct effect, consistent interpretation, and liability are more developed, more powerful, and more embedded in national law. The distinction is mitigated in states which, through a bottom-up process, move in the direction of EU law, a practice that moreover is supported by the general principles of effective treaty performance which may, depending on the contents and nature of the international obligation, require adjustment of national law. Nonetheless, practice is very uneven and even in Europe significant differences remain.

In this context a significant additional compliance-inducing potential is provided by the connection between international law and EU law. As bits and pieces of public international law become a part of the sphere of competence of the EU, they become part of the EU legal order. In *Haegemann,* the Court said that the provisions of an international agreement concluded by the Community 'from the coming into force thereof, form an integral part of Community law'.[241] From the case law on association agreements, it can be inferred that this also applies to decisions of international organizations.[242] In *Poulsen* the Court stated that this also applies to customary international law.[243]

This is even true in instances where the EU is not as such a party to a treaty. For example, although the European Community was not a party to the GATT 1947, it effectively assumed the powers of EC member states due to its exclusive competences in the area of common commercial policy and hence became bound

[239] *Wassink v The Netherlands*, ECHR (1990) Series A, No 185-A, para 38.

[240] Note that where such liability is available, that generally will be related to the application of directly effective treaty provisions. In this regard also the conceptual basis of liability in EU law (which is separated from direct effect) is quite different. See generally on the relationship between direct effect and liability Prechal, 'Member State Liability and Direct Effect: What's the Difference After All?', 17 *European Business Law Review* (2006) 299, at 300.

[241] Case 181/73, *Haegemann, supra* note 14.

[242] Case 30/88, *Greece v Commission*, [1989] ECR 3711, Rec 13; Case C-192/89, *Sevince v Staatssecretaris van Justitie* [1990] ECR I-3461; Kuijper, 'Customary International Law, Decisions of International Organisations and Other Techniques for Ensuring Respect for International Legal Rules in European Community Law', in J. Wouters, P.A. Nollkaemper and E. de Wet (eds), *The Europeanisation of International Law* (2008) 87, at 98.

[243] Case C-286/90, *Anklagemyndigheden v Peter Michael Poulsen and Diva Navigation Corp*, [1992] ECR I-6019; Case C-308/06, *Intertanko and Others v Secretary of State for Transport,* [2008] ECR I-4057, Rec 51.

by GATT 1947.[244] At the same time, the ECJ made it clear that the question of possible invocability and direct effect of GATT was to be addressed on its own terms.[245]

The extent to which they do so ultimately depends on EU law. The EU has constituted itself as a separate legal order—separate from national law, but also separate from international law; this latter separation was recognized by the ECJ in its *Kadi* judgment.[246]

In such cases, the substance and procedure of public international law as it applies within the EU are influenced and transformed by EU law. To this extent public international law is 'Europeanized' and becomes a system that is distinguishable from general international law.

Significantly for present purposes, this development also has an impact on the status of public international law within the national legal orders of the EU's member states. Normally, the constitutional law of each state determines the implementation of international obligations and the status and effect of such obligations on the national law level. However, for EU member states, this 'classical' dual legal relationship *international law/national law* is gradually becoming replaced by a new triangular relationship *international law/EU law/national law*. The 'Europeanization' of international law means that it is EU law that determines how international law is to be applied in the EU member states. Concretely, this means that the ECJ typically determines the status and direct effect of 'Europeanized' international instruments, from treaties to decisions adopted by international organizations and bodies.[247] The Court also has jurisdiction to interpret agreements that are approved by the Community—these are acts of the Community institutions which the Court has jurisdiction to interpret in preliminary ruling proceedings.[248]

[244] See *inter alia* Joined Cases 21-24/72 *International Fruit Company NV and Others v Produktschap voor Groenten en Fruit* [1972] ECR 1219, Rec. 18, where reference is made to the fact that 'the Community has assumed the powers previously exercised by Member States in the area governed by the General Agreement'; Joined Cases 267/81, 268/81 and 269/81 *Società Petrolifera Italiana and Michelin Italiana,* [1983] ECR 801, Rec 17.

[245] It is interesting to recall the two defining considerations of the Court of Justice from the *International Fruit Company* case, *supra* note 244, Rec 7: 'Before the incompatibility of a Community measure with a provision of international law can affect the validity of that measure, the Community must first of all be bound by that provision' (this question was answered affirmatively later in the judgment); ibid, Rec 8: 'Before invalidity can be relied upon before a national court, that provision of international law must also be capable of conferring rights on citizens of the Community which they can invoke before the courts' (this question was answered negatively).

[246] Joined Cases C-402/05 P and C-415/05 P, *Kadi & Al Barakaat v Council of the European Union and EC Commission,* [2008] ECR I-6351. But see the Arbitral Award in *AES Summit Generation Limited and AES-Tisza Erőmű Kft. v Republic of Hungary,* International Centre for Settlement of Investment Disputes, Case No. ARB/07/22, para 7.6.6 (stating 'that the Community competition law regime, it has a dual nature: on the one hand, it is an international law regime, on the other hand, once introduced in the national legal orders, it is part of these legal orders', apparently not considering the option of a third way in between international and national law).

[247] See eg, decisions of the Association Council in the context of the EC–Turkey Association Agreement: Case C-192/89, *Sevince, supra* note 242.

[248] See, to this effect, Case 181/73, *Haegemann, supra* note 14, Rec 4–6; Case C-162/96, *Racke GmbH and Co v Hauptzollamt Mainz,* [1998] I-3655, Rec. 41; and Case C-301/08, *Irène Bogiatzi, Married name Ventouras v Deutscher Luftpool and Others,* [2009] ECR I-10185, para 23.

As far as status is concerned, a corollary of being part of Community law means that there will in any event be primacy over conflicting provisions of national law, irrespective of the position of these provisions in the national legal system,[249] and that even in the hierarchy of sources in the Community legal system proper there will be primacy over instruments of secondary Community law.[250] The Court based this in part on Article 216(2) TFEU, providing that Agreements concluded by the Union are binding upon the institutions of the Union and on its member states.[251]

This is particularly significant for those member states which commonly transformed international law into national law—as a result of this Europeanization, such member states become as it were 'monistic'.

In principle, it also follows that provisions of treaties and decisions of international organizations that are part of the legal order of the EU can acquire direct effect as defined by EU law, not international law. Moreover, that question is ultimately determined by the ECJ, not national law. In *Ioannis Katsivardas—Nikolaos Tsitsikas OE v Ipourgos Ikonomikon*,[252] the Court was asked whether an individual can plead before a national court the most-favoured-nation clause in Article 4 of the Cooperation Agreement concluded between the European Economic Community, on the one hand, and the Cartagena Agreement and the member countries thereof—Bolivia, Colombia, Ecuador, Peru, and Venezuela—on the other ('the Cooperation Agreement'), in order to oppose the application of a national fiscal provision. This question thus concerned the ability of that clause to give rise to direct effect for an individual.

However, treaties are not entirely equated to internal EU rules, and the principle of direct effect as it applies to treaties is not identical to the principle as it applies to internal rules. In particular, examination of the direct effect of provisions contained in an agreement concluded by the European Union with non-member countries invariably involves an analysis of the spirit, general scheme, and terms of that agreement—not only of the criteria of unconditionality and so on.[253] These conditions have in particular been developed in the Court's case law on the question whether the Court can review measures of secondary law against international agreements. In *Christian Dior*, the Court said that 'having regard to their nature and structure, the WTO Agreement and the annexes thereto are not in principle among the rules in the

[249] See Lenaerts and Corthaut, 'Of Birds and Hedges: the Role of Primacy in Invoking Norms of EU Law', 31 *European Law Review* (2006) 287, at 289–91, with interesting reflections on the relationship between primacy and direct effect. See also J. M. Prinssen, *Doorwerking van Europees recht. De verhouding tussen directe werking, conforme interpretatie en overheidsaansprakelijkheid* (2004), at 11.

[250] Case C-61/94, *Commission v Germany*, [1996] ECR I-3989, Rec 52. See Holdgaard, 'Principles of Reception of International Law in Community Law', 25 *Yearbook of European Law* (2006) 263, at 266–7. No such primacy is recognized over instruments of *primary* Community law: see, with arguments, Peters, 'The Position of International Law Within the European Community Legal Order', 40 *German Yearbook of International Law* (1997) 9, at 38–40; see also, Cheyne, 'International Agreements and the European Community Legal System', 19 *European Law Review* (1994) 581, at 586.

[251] Case C-308/06, *Intertanko and Others, supra* note 243, Rec 13.

[252] Case C-160/09, *Ioannis Katsivardas—Nikolaos Tsitsikas OE v Ipourgos Ikonomikon*, [2010] ECR I-04591.

[253] Ibid, Rec 36.

light of which the Court is to review measures of the Community institutions'.[254] In *Intertanko*, the Court said that the Court can examine the validity of Community legislation in the light of an international treaty only when, first, the treaty's provisions as regards their content are unconditional and sufficiently precise and, second, where the nature and the broad logic of the latter do not preclude this.[255]

On this basis, the Court has found that the WTO agreements, but also the UN Convention on the Law of the Sea, do not have direct effect. As to the latter, the Court found in *Intertanko* that this Convention regulates inter-state rights and obligations and states which breach the Convention are liable to other state parties; in consequence, it 'does not establish rules intended to apply directly and immediately to individuals and to confer upon them rights or freedoms capable of being relied upon against States, irrespective of the attitude of the ship's flag State'.[256] It is to be added that in such cases the result is not that member states retain their discretion in determining whether or not to accord direct effect, but rather that they are not allowed to provide direct effect.

These additional conditions do not preclude direct effect of all rules of international law, in the sense that the Court could not review compliance with the obligations of the Community. The Court said that they do not apply to the Convention on Biological Diversity, 'which, unlike the WTO agreement, is not strictly based on reciprocal and mutually advantageous arrangements'.[257] It can be noted that while the distinction between the WTO agreements and the Biodiversity agreement is relatively easily drawn, it is hard to follow the Court's distinction between the Law of the Sea Convention and the Biodiversity Convention—surely both treaties regulate the relationship between states, and if it is true that the Law of the Sea Convention does not create individual rights, that certainly is true for the Biodiversity Convention.

However, the Court did not pronounce on the question of direct effect for domestic courts. It noted that '[e]ven if, as the Council maintains, the CBD contains provisions which do not have direct effect, in the sense that they do not create rights which individuals can rely on directly before the courts, that fact does not preclude review by the courts of compliance with the obligations incumbent on the Community as a party to that agreement'.[258]

This approach also shows that the Court recognizes that the parties to an agreement can preclude that a treaty acquire effect in the EU legal order. In *Ioannis Katsivardas—Nikolaos Tsitsikas OE v Ipourgos Ikonomikon*, the Court stated, confirming earlier case law, that the question is whether 'the general scheme of the agreements and their aims show that the contracting parties intended, by the difference in drafting, to deny Article 4 of the Framework Agreement on Cooperation direct effect previously accorded to Article 4 of the Cooperation Agreement'.[259]

[254] Joined Cases C-300/98 and 392/98, *Parfums Christian Dior v Tuk Consultancy*, [2000] ECR I-11307, Rec. 43; see also Case C-149/96, *Portugal v Council*, [1999] ECR I-8395, Rec 47.

[255] Case C-308/06, *Intertanko and Others*, *supra* note 243, Rec. 45.

[256] Ibid, Rec 64.

[257] Case C-377/98, *Netherlands v Parliament and Council*, [2001] ECR I-7079, Rec 53.

[258] Ibid, Rec 54.

[259] Case C-160/09, *Ioannis Katsivardas—Nikolaos Tsitsikas OE v Ipourgos Ikonomikon*, *supra* note 252, Rec 38.

Furthermore, national courts and authorities will be under the EU law obligation to interpret provisions of national law in conformity with such international instruments or norms.[260] Apart from this obligation of consistent interpretation of national provisions in light of EC law, the ECJ has also recognized the obligation to interpret EC law itself in conformity with such international law instruments since 'the European Community must respect international law in the exercise of its powers'.[261] The obligation of consistent interpretation applies not only for treaties to which the EU is a party but also, in a somewhat modified form, for treaties to which the member states, but not the EU are a party, such as MARPOL.[262]

Finally, the non-compliance with 'Europeanized' international law—whether treaty-based or customary in nature—may imply that member state authorities can be held responsible under the ECJ's *Francovich* case law on state liability—provided of course that the conditions for such state liability as developed by the ECJ are fulfilled.[263] This potential benefit has so far been limited, however, in the context of WTO law where the restrictive approach to direct effect has been extended to liability claims.[264]

The fact that in the hierarchy of norms international instruments and norms occupy an intermediate position, ie, between primary and secondary EU law, also implies that such international instruments and norms can be used as part of the ECJ's and/or the Court of First Instance's control of the validity of EU norms. No direct effect is required for this and the international norm may be

[260] See *inter alia* C-61/94 *Commission v Germany, supra* note 250, Rec 52, where the Court of Justice holds explicitly that 'the primacy of international agreements concluded by the Community over provisions of secondary Community legislation means that such provisions must, so far as is possible, be interpreted in a manner that is consistent with those agreements'; see also Case C-53/96, *Hermès v FHT,* [1998] ECR I-3603, Rec 28. See in general terms on the obligation of consistent interpretation in Community law, Joined Cases C-397/01 to C-403/01, *Bernhard Pfeiffer and Others v Deutsches Rotes Kreuz, Kreisverband Waldshut e.V.,* [2004] ECR I-8835, Rec 115: 'The requirement for national law to be interpreted in conformity with Community law is inherent in the system of the Treaty, since it permits the national court, for the matters within its jurisdiction, to ensure the full effectiveness of Community law when it determines the dispute before it.'

[261] See Case C-286/90, *Anklagemyndigheden v Poulsen, supra* note 243, Rec 9.

[262] Case C-308/06, *Intertanko and Others, supra* note 243, Rec 52 (holding that the fact that Marpol 73/78 binds the Member States is 'liable to have consequences for the interpretation of, first, UNCLOS and, second, the provisions of secondary law which fall within the field of application of Marpol 73/78. In view of the customary principle of good faith, which forms part of general international law, and of Article 10 EC, it is incumbent upon the Court to interpret those provisions taking account of Marpol 73/78').

[263] See *inter alia,* Joined Cases C-6/90 and C-9/90, *Francovich, and* Joined Cases C-46/93 and C-48/93, *Brasserie du Pêcheur and Factortame, supra* note 198. For an interesting linkage between the international and EC doctrine of state liability, see Case C-224/01, *Köbler, supra* note 230, Rec 32: 'In international law a State which incurs liability for breach of an international commitment is viewed as a single entity, irrespective of whether the breach which gave rise to the damage is attributable to the legislature, the judiciary or the executive. That principle must apply *a fortiori* in the Community legal order since all State authorities, including the legislature, are bound in performing their tasks to comply with the rules laid down by Community law which directly govern the situation of individuals'.

[264] Joined Cases C-120/06 P and C-121/06 P, *FIAMM and Giorgo Fedon & Figli v Council and Commission,* [2008] ECR I-6513; Steinbach, 'EC Liability for Non-compliance with Decisions of the WTO DSB: The Lack of Judicial Protection Persists', 43 *Journal of World Trade* (2009) 1047; Kuijper, *supra* note 242, at 104–5.

both treaty-based[265] or custom-based.[266] Lenaerts and Corthaut rightly stress in this respect:

> As long as an obligation can be identified, as long as a behavioural norm for the Community can be derived from an international agreement, this agreement can serve as a norm for reference when the validity of EC law is at stake. As a result the ECJ can also, even in the interest of individuals, assess the validity of Community law in the light of international custom, without having to wonder whether those customary norms create rights which individuals can rely on directly before the courts.[267]

The fact that an international instrument or norm forms part of the Community legal order also means that the Commission can—at least theoretically—bring infringement proceedings against member states that are not in compliance with it.[268]

The aforementioned corollaries of 'Europeanization' have profound effects, not just in terms of the role of the ECJ in regard to public international law, but also for the reception, interpretation, and application of public international law within Europe in general, both at the EU and national level. For the member states of the EU, the distinction in the power of national courts vis-à-vis international law and vis-à-vis EU law is very limited. However, it is also true that the full potential still remains to be realized.

6. Conclusion

In the 1960s, EU law largely, but never entirely, separated itself from the system of public international law from which it originated, and started to form a separate legal order within, or to a certain extent beside, public international law. One of the many institutional consequences was that national courts, which from the perspective of international law are simply an organ of a unitary state, were engaged in the process of reviewing and ensuring compliance by the very state of which they were an organ.

This model, which proved powerful and relatively successful, has provided a model for the rest of international law. (Non-)compliance remained one of the eternal problems of the decentralized international legal order based on sovereign states. Next to many other attempts to improve records of compliance, including the establishment of more and more international courts and a variety of other international

[265] See, eg, Case C-377/98, *Netherlands v European Parliament and Council, supra* note 257, Rec 54, where the Court holds, concerning the Convention on Biological Diversity, that even if it 'contains provisions which do not have direct effect, in the sense that they do not create rights which individuals can rely on directly before the courts, that fact does not preclude review by the courts of compliance with the obligations incumbent on the Community as a party to that agreement'.

[266] Case C-162/96, *Racke, supra* note 248.

[267] Lenaerts and Corthaut, *supra* note 249, at 298.

[268] See, eg, Case C-61/94, *Commission v Germany, supra* note 250, on Germany's failure to comply with the International Dairy Arrangement; Case C-13/00, *Commission v Ireland, supra* note 13, on Ireland's failure to adhere within the prescribed period to the Berne Convention for the Protection of Literary and Artistic Works. See generally Kuijper, *supra* note 242, at 102–4.

institutional mechanisms such as non-compliance procedures, national courts have a significant potential for inducing and securing compliance. That holds both for individual cases, where the role of national courts takes the form of enforcement, for their role in norm-internalization, and for the possible 'deterrent' effect on political branches, as they know they may not get away with violations of the law.

Even though one can speak of EU law as a model in this regard, there is only limited evidence that it as such has an influence on states or that states intentionally seek that model. Rather, it seems that the transformation in the reception of international law in states, allowing for a greater role of national courts, is driven by processes that somehow are comparable to the processes that have characterized the transformation of EU law, notably the recognition of private parties as holders of subjective rights. This recognition pierces the shield of the national legal order, and empowers national courts to review (non-)compliance in respect of such rights.

It remains true, however, that compared with EU law, the normative pull of international law, beyond the general principle of effectiveness and beyond primary rules in particular treaty obligations, remains relatively weak. In this situation, much depends on bottom-up processes. Such processes may be induced by comparable factors (such as recognition of individual rights), and perhaps by a process of learning by example, but they cannot easily be framed in terms of legal obligation.

The cause and effect of the weak position of general international law is a very significant diversity in the practices of states; while there are dozens of states in which the principles of supremacy, direct effect and consistent interpretation, and, to a much lesser extent, liability can be found, there are at least as many states where such concepts are unknown. This process has significant effects for compliance and effectiveness across states, and indeed for the understanding of the role of international law in relation to national law as such.

It is quite obvious that with the increasing connection between international law and European law, the diversity in terms of reception of international law within the member states of the EU is problematical, and indeed has become a matter of concern to the EU itself. The principles that the ECJ has developed on the effects of international agreements in the legal order of the EU, and indirectly in the national legal order of the member states, go some way to ensuring to a much greater extent uniformity between the member states in terms of the status of international agreements in national law, and the resulting power of national courts.

The case law of the Court on the direct effect of international agreements, which is not only based on criteria of precision and unconditionally, but takes into account the inter-state nature of obligations and questions of reciprocity, shows that international obligations are not equated with the 'normal' rules of EU law, and that international agreements cannot profit to the full extent of the power of direct effect. It remains an open question, in particular in the light of the *Intertanko* judgment, which treaties would on that ground be disqualified for direct effect. In this respect, we can say that the integration of the EU in its relationship to international law is still at the crossroads, with a pivotal role for the ECJ.

Index

Lightning Source UK Ltd.
Milton Keynes UK
UKOW06n1232040216

267622UK00002B/26/P